Also by Robert O. Snelling, Sr.

The Opportunity Explosion

Jobs!

What They Are . . . Where They Are . . . What They Pay

by Robert O. Snelling, Sr. and Anne M. Snelling

A Fireside Book
Published by Simon and Schuster, Inc.
New York

First Fireside Edition 1986
Published by Simon & Schuster, Inc.
Simon & Schuster Building
Rockefeller Center
1230 Avenue of the Americas
New York, New York 10020

FIRESIDE and colophon are registered trademarks of Simon & Schuster, Inc.
SNELLING AND SNELLING is a registered trademark of
Snelling and Snelling, Inc.
Designed by Irving Perkins Associates
Manufactured in the United States of America

10 9 8 7 6 5 4 3 2
10 9 8 7 6 5 4 3 2   Pbk.

Library of Congress Cataloging in Publication Data

Snelling, Robert O.

  Jobs! what they are—where they are—what they pay.

  Includes index.
  1. United States—Occupations.   2. White collar workers.
I. Snelling, Anne M.   II. Title
HF5382.5.U5S55   1985   331.7'92'0973   84-23670

ISBN: 0-671-49383-2
      0-671-50246-8 Pbk.

Acknowledgments

Our gratitude to:

Our many Snelling and Snelling and Bryant Bureau owners, managers, and professional employment counselors who encouraged and helped us with duties, descriptions, and salary ranges.

Fred Hills, senior editor at Simon and Schuster, who kept us on track, thought innovatively, and inspired us continually; and his able assistant, Kate Connell, whose editing enhanced the manuscript at every point.

Kate Kelly, who researched, wrote, and worked diligently on the manuscript, adding her inimitable style through, during, and after the birth of her daughter, Elizabeth.

Irv Settel, our agent, for his faith in us and his creative ideas.

Our staff, Maxine Christie and Vicki Jackson, for dozens of rewrites.

The U.S. Government for its *Occupational Outlook Handbook,* and to the many societies, associations, and unions that gave so freely of their time and knowledge.

BECAUSE WE ARE TRYING TO MAKE THE BEST USE
OF THE "TALENTS" THAT HAVE BEEN GIVEN US,
WE DEDICATE THIS WORK TO OUR LORD.

Contents

10

14

Preface: Why We Wrote This Book

Our years of experience in counseling millions of people about their career choices have taught us three basic truths:

1. Most people, regardless of sex or age, do not know exactly what it is they would like to do with their lives.

2. Most people do not realize their true worth or potential and have placed self-imposed limits on their capabilities and opportunities.

3. Most people have a deep-seated fear of the unknown, which is aroused when they consider a career change, and therefore they do nothing.

Thus, the race goes not to the swiftest, the smartest, or the best-educated, but to those who have the will to be in the race in the first place.

Our times present job and career opportunities unparalleled in the history of our nation, and they will only get better and better. The reduced number of young people coming into the labor market for the next four or five years simply means that instead of individuals competing for the best jobs, companies will be competing for the best people available.

The jobs described in this book are designed to open your eyes, to whet your appetite, to acquaint you with the incredible variety of career choices. Do not restrict yourself to preconceived ideas of what you should do, or what your friends or family think you should do.

Our files are filled with stories of people who changed careers and in doing so changed their lives: a personnel manager for a national retail chain, married with two children, quit his job at the age of thirty-two, went back to school, and became a doctor—and a darn good one at that; a housewife decided to get in on job counseling at the age of thirty and became an outstanding success by being named number one in her company three years in a row; then there is the high school graduate who switched from selling shoes to selling nuts and bolts and now runs a $5 million company.

Our purpose is to jar your thinking, expand your universe—even disturb you a bit—so that you'll consider *all* the possibilities. This does not mean you have to kill yourself to reach the top, sacrificing your family along the way. It means you should strive to use to the fullest the many abilities you've been endowed with, so that whatever you choose to do, you will not have to look back when you are ready to retire and ask, "Why, why didn't I do more with my life?"

We have a saying at Snelling and Snelling

that he who aims at nothing is likely to hit it. So set goals and work toward them. This does not mean that at times you can't realign your goals according to your personal situation or the opportunities that are before you; but a goal will keep you from vacillating, keep you on target, and that means feeling excited and enthusiastic about your future.

Work is an important part of our lives. It should be treated as a blessing rather than a curse, something to be looked forward to and enjoyed. There is no reason to be unhappy in your work. You have many options open to you. You *can* reach out and change your job. The choice is in your hands.

—Bob and Anne Snelling

How to Use This Book

Many of the applicants at our employment offices across the nation—and we see hundreds of thousands each year—have vague or distorted conceptions of most jobs and the duties and responsibilities they involve. When it comes to careers, they have no idea what they involve, what it takes to get onto a particular career track, or where it can lead. Job titles can be misleading, and television often compounds the problem by portraying only certain aspects of jobs, or stereotyping them, in either a glamorous or a deprecating light. This book is designed to clarify what jobs are available, what they consist of, where they are located, what they pay, and what you need to do to qualify for them.

There are two ways to explore this book:

1. Read through the contents. For ease of use we have divided this book into broad industry categories. This way, as you skim through the table of contents, you can identify the basic areas that appeal to you. For instance, let's say that health care interests you, because it combines stability and growth with an element of public service. Our health services and technology sections cover a variety of jobs, from nurse and laboratory technician to hospital administrator and medical equipment technician. Start with the overviews ("Careers in Health Services" and "Careers in Health Technology"), which will give you a quick picture of the entire spectrum of jobs. Then skim through the sections and read about the jobs that interest you.

2. Consult the index. Look for actual job titles you have heard of or seen in the newspaper, and then read up on these jobs and those adjacent to them in the book. It will lead you across industry boundaries and into new areas.

As you read, keep in mind that the salary figures we've given are, at most, merely a guide. They come from a variety of sources: federal government studies, chamber of commerce studies, association studies, and our own research. They should be considered rough guidelines, subject to change. And remember to add at least 5 percent cumulatively to these wage figures for each year after 1984. For example, if the average salary is listed as $20,000 in 1984, then it becomes $21,000 in 1985, $22,050 in 1986, and so on.

Training and education requirements should also be considered guidelines, though of course you will not become a doctor without graduating from medical school, nor will you become a top-notch secretary without mastering the typewriter. As a rule, the more education you can get, the better. However, you'll benefit only if you put it to use—not if you become a professional student. Schooling does not necessarily have to be accomplished in one uninterrupted period. In fact, in some cases it helps to intersperse related work experience with education. For instance, going back for your master's degree in marketing *after* two or three years of marketing experience would allow you to gain a great deal more from the additional education.

Once you find some career areas or specific jobs that appeal to you, then go into them in greater depth. Wherever possible, we've provided names and addresses of organizations you can contact for further details. Write to them for more material, find books that describe those careers in greater detail, or ask your school counselor or college placement officer for help. Study the help wanted ads, talk to employment services, talk to people who work in those fields. Choosing or changing a career is an important decision. Put some time and effort into it!

A Word About Salaries

We all care how much money we earn; it affects our lifestyles as well as our egos. And while it should not be the only factor when we consider whether or not to take a job, it's important enough to take a few minutes to understand thoroughly.

As you know, salaries vary greatly from one job to the next, and so do additions to the base pay such as commissions, bonuses, and overtime. But even jobs that appear to be very similar may pay surprisingly different salaries. The reasons for the discrepancy in pay usually have to do with one or more of several factors.

Benefits are probably the most important consideration in evaluating what a job pays, after the actual dollar amount of your salary. Fringe benefits can add up to more than 30 percent of the base wages paid. Thus a salary of $15,000 might carry as much as $4,500 worth of benefits annually. Fringe benefits may include major medical and hospital insurance for an employee and his or her family; dental, life, and disability insurance; paid vacations and holidays; free legal or financial counseling services; discount purchasing privileges; the option of shorter hours, longer hours, overtime, part-time, and temporary work; seasonal work; summers off; and profit-sharing and pension plans. Some pension and profit-sharing programs are designed so that full participation by the employee over a lifetime yields terrific results. In some companies, for instance, a thirty-year-old employee starting at $9,000 per year and getting a 5 percent raise per year would have over $1 million in his retirement fund upon retiring at sixty-five.

Other factors have a bearing on how much you may make in a job, though not in as tangible or obvious a way as fringe benefits. Probably the first one you think of is experience. Any highly skilled and experienced employee, whether accountant, secretary, or sales representative, can run circles around a novice; and employers usually recognize this and pay accordingly. Companies that pay the same wages to all workers of a certain class or title, for whatever reason, find their good people leaving to take positions where their years of experience and commitment will be properly rewarded.

The degree of responsibility in a job also has a great deal to do with the salary it carries. The term manager denotes a position in which one directs the activities of others. However, one office manager may supervise an office with three clerks, while another supervises a staff of a hundred with a total budget responsibility in excess of a million dollars. Their salaries will reflect the difference. The same holds true for plant managers, sales managers, vice presidents, and presidents. By the same token, an airline pilot who is responsible for the lives of hundreds is paid more than the commuter pilot whose plane holds only twenty people. A purchasing agent responsible for buying $5 million worth of parts a year is paid more than the one who spends half a million. Area managers are paid more than the smaller district managers, and regional managers more than area managers. Increased responsibility, whether for more people, more money, or greater area, means a higher salary.

Supply and demand also affect salaries. Fields in which there are many more applicants than jobs available are simply not compelled to pay top dollar for their people. The same principle applies in reverse to industries experiencing rapid growth, where they need people and are willing to pay high salaries to get them. Higher salaries may also be used to attract people to parts of the country where they're needed. For instance, a few years ago the colleges supposedly poured out 180,000 more teachers than our schools could absorb and we had a "teacher glut," a case of the supply far exceeding the demand. Yet in some inner-city and rural farm areas there were schools that still could not find teachers. A higher salary is one way to fill the demand. By the same token, a physical therapist in rural Alabama may be paid up to $6,000 a year more than one in Sarasota, Florida, even though the cost of living in Florida is much higher. The

reason, again, is supply and demand. While the demand is not as great in Alabama as in Sarasota, there are even fewer physical therapists available to live and work in rural Alabama.

Some companies are more stable than others, and thus security of employment enters the job/salary equation. A bookkeeper who is constantly in danger of being laid off because he or she works for a contractor whose business fluctuates will usually be paid more than one who works for a more stable business. As a rule, the greater the security the lower the pay. This is one reason why there are such differences in pay between industrial firms, which experience layoffs, and banks, which usually do not.

In sum, weigh *all* the factors when choosing a job or making a career change. Don't just look at the dollars in your pocket at the end of the week. Put that salary into context. Look at the alternatives, study the job situation in the areas where you're considering living and working, and remember everything that comes into play: location, working conditions, ability to advance, stability of company and industry, and fringe benefits. Are the skills you will be learning transferable? Could you earn more in a different location using the same skills? Where would you rather live? Where would you rather raise a family? Don't feel you have to make a decision until you have considered these questions carefully.

The Top Seven Entry-Level Job Areas

While two equally talented beginners may eventually reach comparable levels of career success, the job seeker who starts out in a promising field is almost surely destined to move farther faster than the one who aspires to work in a field that is experiencing little or no growth. Being aware of today's trends is one sure way of choosing a field that is destined to grow.

In the post-industrial age, we have witnessed major upheavals in the workplace as traditional manufacturing is increasingly being replaced by service industries as the dominant force in our society. In fact, almost 75 percent of the 20 million new jobs in the next decade will be found in service industries—including communications, finance, medical care, insurance, and high technology. And information services are among the most prominent. Thus new white-collar job opportunities have emerged in communications and media, and the vast need for information storage and retrieval has created new jobs in computer technology.

In the new high-tech field of advanced technology, exciting careers are possible in job areas that did not exist even five or ten years ago, with great opportunities for engineers of almost every type. Similarly, the world of finance is being revolutionized by the deregulation of the banking industry, and an increasing number of people are needed to provide new, more sophisticated financial services for consumers.

Increased life expectancy has produced a larger population of people over sixty-five and has generated an enormous need for people to work in health services and preventive medicine. And finally, the areas of marketing and sales have always been, and will continue to be, the crucial vehicles that bring products and services to the consumer.

Let's take a closer look now at the seven top areas with the best entry-level jobs.

1. Computers

From the bank machine where you withdraw cash and the mainframe computer that prepares your paycheck, to the personal computer you may already have in your home, computers are becoming an important part of our everyday lives.

Large businesses and government are just beginning to maximize the use of the machines they've had available to them for years, and now with the introduction of microchips, the potential for computer use in the home and in small business is beginning to be more fully explored. We're in the midst of a computer explosion, and job growth in the field is destined to be superb. What's more, computer expertise can lead to employment in fields as diverse as health services, scientific research, retailing, and finance.

Jobs where entry-level workers can do particularly well:

Computer service technicians maintain and repair the computers. No matter how great the machines, there will always be a need for those who know how to repair them. One young man who trained for this field was whisked away by his new employer before he even got his diploma. After attending their training program he was sent into the field to supervise four Japanese technicians, and he has yet to repair his first computer! Starting salaries range from $19,500 to $23,000.

Systems analysts analyze business procedures, determine customers' needs, pinpoint specific problems, and design and test the computer programs that solve them. Wherever there are computers there will be a need for systems analysts to help utilize them most efficiently. Be aware that the rapid growth in the field has created a diversity of job titles which vary from one company to the next. Systems programmer and applications programmer are other titles to look for. A college degree with some training in computer science can launch a successful career. Starting salaries range from $22,500 to $28,500.

2. Engineering

A degree in engineering is once again a golden passport to an excellent career. The many changes occurring in industry are the reasons why. Robotics, computers, telecommunications, manufacturing, transportation, and construction are just a few of the areas experiencing growth because of the incredible pace of today's technological advances. In addition, foreign competition has encouraged American companies to increase their efforts in research and development and bring about new manufacturing processes to cut costs and boost productivity. Of course, any of this work requires the effort of qualified engineers, and the current growth in this field means that there is a constant demand for new workers.

Starting salaries range from about $22,000 to over $30,000. (The entry-level pay of all the specialties listed below falls within this range.) Job outlook is excellent for at least the next five years.

See "Careers in Engineering" for an overview of the profession. Also take a look at the following specialties where beginning workers are likely to do particularly well because of growth in these fields.

Biomedical engineers use engineering principles to solve medical and health-related problems. Advances such as pacemakers, artificial hearts, and lasers for use in surgery are due to the efforts of biomedical engineers. There is no doubt that exploration in this field will continue to grow rapidly as our need for improved methods of health care continues.

Chemical engineers design equipment and develop processes for ways to use chemicals in research, production, and manufacturing. The need for chemical solutions to environmental pollution problems, the necessity for developing more and better synthetic fuels, and the development of new chemicals used in manufacturing consumer goods will lead to growth in employment.

Electrical engineers design, develop, test, and supervise the production of electrical and electronic equipment. A growing demand for electrical products is being spurred by the computer and communications industries as well as the military. There is also great growth in the demand for electronic consumer goods, meaning more jobs for more workers.

Petroleum engineers develop and implement new ways to recover and process oil and gas and provide technical consultation during drilling operations. As economic expansion requires increasing supplies of petroleum and natural gas, employment in this field will see great growth.

3. Finance

While most people used to be content with receiving 5¼ to 5½ percent interest on their savings, the problems of inflation combined with deregulation of the banking industry have brought vast changes to the world of finance. Managing people's money has become big business. Banks and savings and loans have taken a new attitude toward selling their services; brokerage firms are benefiting from the public's new inflation-conscious awareness of the importance of wise investing; and the insurance industry is responding with new types of policies to better meet the needs of today's consumers.

All these changes mean great opportunities in the financial field. Here's a preview of some good entry-level jobs.

Junior analysts (see "Financial Analysts") assist financial analysts in studying the financial health of businesses and institutions in order to make statistical evaluations of their financial standing. In today's competitive marketplace, where this in-depth knowledge is vital, financial analysts are becoming a very important part of the business world. Starting salaries for junior analysts with M.B.A.'s range from $18,000 to $22,500.

Securities sales representatives (stockbrokers) buy and sell stocks for individuals and organizations as representatives of brokerage firms. Whether you're twenty-two or sixty-two, the opportunities here are unlimited, since success depends primarily on your willingness to learn the business and apply yourself diligently. Starting salaries range from $14,500 to $25,000.

Banking trainees (see main text entry under "Bank Officers") enter a bank training program or start out in a junior officer position (such as junior loan officer) to prepare for a career in banking. Since deregulation has permitted other types of businesses to offer financial services, those businesses have raided banks for employees, creating an even greater need for bank trainees. Starting salaries range from $18,600 to $21,400.

Claims representatives investigate insurance claims, negotiate settlements, and authorize payments. An excellent entry position to a growing field. Starting salaries range from $16,200 to $17,600.

Accountants examine, analyze, and interpret clients' financial records in order to give advice or prepare statements. While there are opportunities for those who do not have a college degree, those with a bachelor's or a master's degree are in especially great demand. One young woman with a B.S. had her choice of five positions with starting pay ranging from $17,500 to $22,500.

4. Health Services and Technology

Employment in health services and in positions in hospitals and laboratories is expected to grow quickly during the coming decade because of the expanding health care needs of a growing and aging population. The increasing availability of public and private health insurance, broader access to health care, and an increased interest in preventive medicine and rehabilitation are also leading to an increase in the number and types of jobs available. In addition, the field is relatively recession-proof, since illness and the problems of aging continue whatever the state of the economy.

It has been said that this is the decade of the technician, and this is particularly true in health-related jobs. With the increase in the numbers and types of diagnostic equipment, more and more technicians will be needed to run them. People who go into the technical area generally don't even need a college degree, and yet they are going to be well paid and have good job security as well as an excellent opportunity for advancement.

There are many promising jobs in the health services and technology area, but the following are where beginning workers are particularly needed:

Nurses are responsible for the day-to-day care of the physically or mentally ill or the infirm. Government statistics forecast 240,000 job openings every year in nursing and nursing-related jobs, making this an area greatly in need of workers. Starting salaries range from $15,600 to $18,900.

Physical therapists plan and administer

physical therapy programs to restore bodily functions, relieve pain, or help prevent permanent disability following a disabling injury or disease. There are currently 34,000 physical therapists, and by 1990 these jobs are expected to increase by 90 percent! Starting salaries range from $16,700 to $22,300.

Electrocardiograph technicians administer the EKG, a diagnostic test that records heart activity. Basic training can be received in about six weeks, and the job is an excellent way of entering the field of cardiovascular technology. Starting salaries range from $12,600 to $14,800.

Emergency medical technicians are part of an emergency medical team. They administer first-aid treatment to sick and injured people and transport them to a medical facility. A U.S. Department of Transportation course can prepare candidates for entry-level jobs where salaries range from $12,000 to $17,000.

Radiologic (X-ray) technologists use X-ray technology for diagnostic purposes and for radiation therapy. Both two- and four-year training programs are available for a growing field with a future. Starting salaries range from $15,000 to $17,500.

5. Marketing

Marketing is a science that defines customers' needs and identifies how best to fulfill them. As American business has become increasingly sophisticated, salespeople have learned that their success can be greatly increased by advice and support from marketing experts.

Knowing the workings of the marketplace—which involves understanding factors such as the customers' demographic makeup, buying habits, and tastes and interests—is integral to the marketing function. Advertising and public relations are also involved.

Especially as more products and services must compete for customer attention, marketing will continue to be a high-growth area. The need for marketing expertise will exist on all levels of business and in all types of companies.

A few of the jobs where beginners can do particularly well:

Junior copywriters (see "Advertising Copywriters") learn to write advertising copy for print or broadcast media to promote the sale of goods and services. For the writer interested in steady work and good pay, this is an ideal job. Starting salaries range from $16,400 to $19,600.

Junior analysts (see "Market Research Analysts") assist senior analysts in researching market conditions to determine the potential sales of a product or service. They also help collect data on customer preferences and buying habits. Because market research will continue to be a way for businesses to explore a market without having to jump in feet first, the need for workers will continue to grow. Starting salaries range from $18,500 to $32,400.

Public relations assistants (see "Public Relations Workers") assist public relations representatives in the planning and execution of public relations campaigns designed to promote a product or service or build a positive company image. Companies are becoming increasingly aware of the importance of their portrayal in the press, which, of course, affects the public's view of them. This awareness will continue to create a need for public relations workers. Starting salaries range from $14,000 to $21,000.

6. Media and Communications

Whether at home or in the workplace, Americans have an unquenchable thirst for information. The print media have fed this need for years, and the newspaper, magazine, and book publishing industries continue to flourish. But new advances in technology are rapidly expanding the way we can receive information. The result is not only continued growth in radio and television but also continued development of cable television and the emergence of such new services as direct-to-home satellite transmission and low-power television broadcasting.

While competition in the field is tough, the broadcasting business holds some particularly good entry-level positions right now.

Broadcast technicians operate and maintain the electronic equipment used to produce and transmit radio and television programs. With the growing number of radio and television stations, there will be an increasing number of jobs available. Starting salaries range from $12,600 to $17,200.

News assistants perform all types of support tasks for the newsroom, from gathering copy from the news wires to running for coffee. For the person interested in a career with the electronic media, this is the bottom rung of the career ladder and an excellent place to learn. Salaries start at about $15,000.

7. Sales

The sales field is hot and getting hotter. By 1990, the number of salespeople is expected to increase from 6 million to 7.6 million. Across the United States, companies are making an all-out effort to find sales trainees. Those that are hired are moving quickly into management, making this an ideal field for a fast-moving career.

Sales openings exist in virtually every field, and starting salaries for sales trainees range from $15,000 to $30,000 a year. Salaries after several years' experience range from $35,000 to $60,000, and some salespeople's incomes exceed $100,000. Some companies supply a car, and most provide a full expense account.

Whether the title is sales trainee or client development specialist, take a look at it. The job is likely to be a good one with a promising future.

See "Careers in Sales" for a broad overview of the profession. Then pay particular attention to the following specialties that are offering excellent opportunities for beginning salespeople:

Advertising sales representatives sell commercial time on radio and television and advertising space in newspapers and magazines or on calendars and billboards. With the phenomenal growth of new media outlets such as cable TV and satellite broadcasting, advertising sales are bound to grow. Starting salaries range from $12,500 to $22,000, plus commissions.

Computer sales representatives sell products ranging from mainframes (large computers), minicomputers (small computers), or microcomputers (personal computers, automatic cash registers) to software (the packages that tell the computers what to do), as well as peripheral equipment such as printers. The boom in computers being used in business and in the home will mean definite growth in this field. Starting salaries range from $17,500 to $24,500.

Direct sales representatives represent companies selling everything from kitchenware to household products, jewelry, cosmetics, and clothing. They sell directly to the individual, sometimes on a one-to-one basis or via a sales party. Opportunities are unlimited for the motivated individual, and enthusiasm and sales ability are the main requirements. (Some companies do require an initial investment.) It's a great way to test one's taste for sales!

Food sales representatives sell food by the carload to wholesalers and large food and drug chains; or they sell directly to local stores, restaurants, schools, hospitals, and bakeries. A college degree is preferable but not required, and there will always be a need for these workers. Starting salaries range from $15,000 to $21,400.

Manufacturers' sales representatives sell a manufacturer's products to business, government and industry. Because product knowledge and expertise are needed (and can often be learned in the company's own training program), workers are very well paid. Top executives in this field frequently come from a sales background. Starting salaries range from $17,000 to $23,600.

Insurance agents sell life, property-liability (casualty), or health insurance in order to provide policyholders with financial resources in case of loss. Although ill-informed people have given what is the single largest business in the United States a poor reputation, the opportunities in the insurance industry are excellent nonetheless. Starting salaries range from $16,300 to $19,600.

What to Do Now

This book is like a map. It shows you major points of interest and little-known attractions, and it tells you what you ought to know to get where you're going. However, no one can choose your destination or map out the exact route you should follow to get there. That you must do yourself.

In addition to reading widely, asking questions of people you know with interesting jobs, and clarifying your interests and priorities, you will benefit from finding someone you can talk to.

Discuss your future with a competent employment or guidance counselor. You may want to start with your school or the school you are thinking of attending, an employment service, your local college or nearby university, or your alma mater. These people can direct you to sources of additional information in the fields that interest you. They can arrange for you to meet and talk with people who work in these areas, and may be able to introduce you to prospective employers as well. Such counseling will help you review your past education, experience, and desires, so that you can focus on both career goals and continuing education.

Keep in mind that parents, pastors, friends, relatives, and neighbors all mean well, but they are not you and they are usually not well versed in all phases of the job market. Thus, in seeking advice from them you get only part of the picture. Just as in most cases you would not ask your mother how to repair your car, or your father how to bake a cake, or a friend who doesn't water ski to teach you how, so you shouldn't depend solely on relatives and friends when choosing your life's work.

Gather facts from as many sources as you can, seek competent counsel, and then decide for yourself!

Careers in Agribusiness

In the days when the United States was an agricultural society, farmers harvested their crops and bartered what their families didn't need with neighbors or sold the produce at the nearest town market. We've come a long way since then, and today the development, production, and distribution of the products that meet our needs for food, clothing, and shelter have become elements of a very sophisticated business. From the agricultural engineer who designs machinery and improves farming methods to the food technologist who develops new ways to process the food we eat, there are many fascinating white-collar jobs for people interested in the field. Also important are positions such as the veterinarian who cares for livestock, the forester who maintains the trees that we need for many products, and the soil conservationist who plays a vital role in preserving our land and keeping the ground at its most productive.

In addition to the jobs described in the following section, there are many other ways to develop careers within the agricultural field. The skills of teacher, journalist, and salesperson, for instance, can be put to good use in agribusiness. Some of the other types of jobs people hold include:

Education. Constant technological innovations in production processes mean that *teach-* *ers* are important in instructing future farmers about the latest developments in successful farming methods. They work at the high school, vocational school, and college level.

Cooperative extension services workers do educational work in areas such as agricultural production, community development, natural-resource conservation, and home economics. They may conduct agricultural educational programs through youth groups such as the 4-H Clubs.

Agricultural communications workers keep farmers and others in the field up to date on current developments in farm research and technology. Crop reporters and market news reporters employed by the U.S. Department of Agriculture work from field offices throughout the country gathering the latest agricultural information.

Agricultural journalists collect farm news and data for publication in farm journals, magazines, and bulletins. Some work for radio and television stations or are employed by agribusiness firms to develop advertisements and public relations bulletins.

Management and administration. Many workers in managerial and administrative jobs are specialists in the agricultural field. *Agricultural accountants* prepare and analyze financial reports for farmers and farm supply businesses such as dairy equipment stores and farm machinery stores. *Agricultural financial experts* work closely with farmers in making loans and ensuring that borrowed money is put to constructive use. *Agricultural marketing specialists* prepare sales forecasts used by food businesses to make decisions relating to product design and advertising. *Agricultural economists* provide information about production, financing, and pricing to farmers, food processors and distributors, and government agencies.

Sales and service. There are many jobs for *salespeople* who can sell, maintain, and explain how to use machinery and supplies. Chemical sales workers and those who sell different types of feed, fertilizer, and seed are also needed.

As the need for feeding our nation and preserving our resources continues, well-qualified professionals will find agribusiness to be an important and growing field of the future.

AGRICULTURAL AND BIOLOGICAL SCIENTISTS

Duties and Responsibilities

Agricultural and biological scientists specialize in the study of life. They study all aspects of living organisms and the relationship of animals and plants to their environment. The knowledge they gain through their studies contributes to work done in many different fields.

Many of these scientists are primarily involved in research and development (R and D). Some conduct basic research to increase knowledge of living organisms. Others in applied research use this knowledge to accomplish goals such as increasing crop yields or improving the environment. Those who work in laboratories must be familiar with research techniques and the use of laboratory equipment and computers.

Some scientists work in management or administration, planning and administering programs for testing foods and drugs or directing activities at zoos or botanical gardens. Some teach in colleges and universities; others work as consultants to business firms or to government. Some work in technical sales and service jobs for companies manufacturing chemicals and other products. Still others write for technical publications or test and inspect food and drugs.

Scientists are usually classified by the type of organism they study or the activity they perform.

Botanists study plants and the environment. Some study all aspects of plant life, while others specialize in areas such as identification and classification of plants, the structure of plants and plant cells, and the causes and cures of plant diseases.

Microbiologists investigate the growth and characteristics of microscopic organisms such as bacteria, viruses, and molds. Some specialize in medicine, soil bacteriology (the effect of microorganisms on soil fertility), virology (viruses), or immunology (mechanisms that fight infection).

Zoologists study the origin, behavior, diseases, and life processes of animals. Some experiment with live animals in controlled or natural surroundings, while others dissect dead animals to study the structure of their parts. Zoologists are usually identified by the animal group studied—ornithologists (birds), entomologists (insects), mammalogists (mammals), herpetologists (reptiles), and ichthyologists (fish), for example.

Biological oceanographers study plant and animal life in the ocean. Their research has practical applications in improving and controlling commercial and sport fishing and in determining the effects of pollution on marine life.

Agricultural scientists apply scientific principles to problems related to food, fibers, and horticulture. *Agronomists* are concerned with the mass development of plants. They improve the quality and yield of crops such as corn, wheat, and cotton by developing new growth methods or by controlling diseases, pests, and weeds. They also analyze soils to determine ways to increase acreage yields and decrease erosion.

Animal scientists do research on the breeding, feeding, and diseases of domestic farm animals.

Horticulturists work with orchard and garden plants such as fruit and nut trees, vegetables, and flowers. They try to improve plant culture methods for the beautification of communities, homes, parks, and other areas, as well as for increasing crop quality and yields.

Ecologists study the relationship between organisms and their environments and the effects of influences such as pollutants, rainfall, temperature, and altitude on organisms. For example, ecologists examine plankton (microscopic water plants and animals) to determine the effects of pollution and measure the radioactive content of fish.

Biochemists specialize in the chemical composition and behavior of living things. Their work is vital for an understanding of reproduction, growth, and heredity. The methods and techniques of biochemistry are applied in areas such as medicine and agriculture. For instance, biochemists may investigate causes and cures for diseases or conduct research on transferring characteristics of one kind of plant to another. Some study the effects of food, hormones, or drugs on various organisms.

Most scientists work regular hours in offices, laboratories, or classrooms.

Colleges and universities employ over half of all agricultural and biological scientists. Many are employed by the federal government, primarily in the Department of Agriculture, with large numbers also in the Department of the Interior and in the National Institutes of Health. Many also work for local governments or in private industry, mostly in the pharmaceutical, industrial, chemical, and agricultural services fields. Some work for nonprofit organizations, and a few are self-employed as consultants to government and industry.

Those who have advanced degrees usually begin in research or teaching jobs. With experience, they may advance to jobs as supervisors of research programs.

Earnings and Opportunities

Over 125,000 people are employed as agricultural and biological scientists, and the job outlook for those with advanced degrees is very good, with a 36 percent increase in employment expected in the next decade. Salaries range from $24,000 to $48,000.

Training and Qualifications

A fascination with living things, curiosity, an analytical mind, and the ability to work independently or as part of a team are key qualities for future scientists. Being able to communicate well orally and in writing is also important.

Those with bachelors' degrees may be able to find starting positions in testing or inspecting jobs or as advanced technicians in medical research; however, promotions within the field are severely limited if no advanced degree is obtained.

A master's degree is sufficient for some jobs in applied research, but the Ph.D. is generally required for college teaching and is highly preferable for those who aspire to do independent research and seek advancement to administrative research positions and other management jobs.

For Further Details

American Institute of Biological Sciences, 1401 Wilson Blvd., Arlington, VA 22209. American Physiological Society, Education Officer, 9650 Rockville Pike, Bethesda, MD 20014. Secretary, Botanical Society of America, School of Biological Sciences, University of Kentucky, Lexington, KY 40506. American Society for Horticultural Science, 701 N. Saint Asaph St., Alexandria, VA 22314. American Society of Biological Chemists, 9650 Rockville Pike, Bethesda, MD 20014.

AGRICULTURAL AND BIOLOGICAL TECHNICIANS

Duties and Responsibilities

Agricultural and biological technicians are responsible for continuing the important work started by biologists and agricultural scientists in such areas as improving crop yield, preventing plant disease, and developing insecticides. It is the technician's job to apply the theoretical knowledge developed by engineers and scientists to actual situations.

Agricultural technicians work with agricultural scientists in food production and processing. They primarily work in fields, greenhouses, or barns, where they assist agricultural scientists in experiments conducted under actual growing conditions. There are several different specialties within the field. Plant technicians conduct tests and experiments to improve the yield and quality of crops. They also work to develop ways to increase the resistance of plants to disease, insects, or other hazards.

Technicians in soil science analyze the chemical and physical properties of various soils to help determine the best uses for them. Animal husbandry technicians work mainly with the breeding and nutrition of animals. Other agricultural technicians are employed in the food industry as food processing technicians. Those who work in quality control or in food science research help scientists develop better and more efficient ways of processing the food we eat.

Biological technicians work primarily in laboratories, where they perform tests and experiments under controlled conditions. Microbiological technicians study microscopic organisms and may be involved in immunology or parasitology research. Laboratory animal technicians study and report on the reactions of laboratory animals to certain physical and chemical stimuli. They also study and conduct research to help biologists develop cures for human disease. Technicians also assist biochemists in analyzing biological substances (blood, other body fluids, foods, and drugs) by conducting experiments and reporting results. A biological technician might also work with insects to study insect control, develop new insecticides, or determine how to use insects to control other insects or undesirable plants.

Technicians usually start as trainees and gain responsibility as they gain experience. They may eventually move into senior or supervisory positions.

Earnings and Opportunities

Over 885,000 people work as technicians, and employment opportunities are excellent. Salaries range from $17,500 to $32,000 and above.

Training and Qualifications

An aptitude for math and science, manual dexterity, and the ability to do detailed technical work accurately are key qualities for technicians. The ability to work both independently and as a member of a team is important.

Most employers prefer applicants who have completed specialized technical training, preferably programs in which students gain practical work experience. These programs are available at technical institutes, junior and community colleges, extension divisions of universities, vo-tech, and correspondence schools.

For Further Details

Engineers Council for Professional Development, 345 E. 47th St., New York, NY 10017. National Association of Trade and Technical Schools, 2021 K St., N.W., Washington, DC 20006. National Home Study Council, 1601 18th St., N.W., Washington, DC 20009.

AGRICULTURAL ENGINEERS

Duties and Responsibilities

The increasing demand for agricultural products, the need for modernizing American farm operations, and the increasing emphasis on conservation of resources are all contributing to a growing need for agricultural engineers who can help solve these problems.

Engineers in the field apply the theories and principles of science and mathematics to practical agricultural problems, and their work is often the link between a scientific discovery and its application. Agricultural engineers design agricultural machinery and equipment and develop methods that will improve the production, processing, and distribution of food and other agricultural products. They also design systems to improve the conservation and management of energy, soil, and water resources.

When developing a new product or piece of machinery, engineers must consider many factors. They must determine how the device will work, design and test all components, and fit them together in an integrated plan. They must also evaluate the overall effectiveness, cost, reliability, and safety of the item before deciding whether to put it into production.

Many engineers work in testing, production, operations, or maintenance. They supervise production processes, determine the causes of breakdowns, and test newly manufactured products to maintain quality. Some work in research and development, sales, administration, or management.

Engineers often use calculators and computers to create mathematical equations that describe how a machine, structure, or system operates. They spend a great deal of time writing reports and consulting with other engineers. Often they work on their own, but with complex projects they may work as part of an engineering team. Some work in offices most of the time; others work in research labs, industrial plants, or in the field.

Most agricultural engineers work for manufacturers of farm equipment, electric utility companies, federal and state soil and water management agencies, and distributors of farm equipment and supplies. Some work as consultants to farmers and farm-related industries; others are specialists with agricultural organizations or managers of agricultural processing plants.

Engineers with experience may advance to managerial or administrative positions.

Earnings and Opportunities

Over 15,000 people are employed as agricultural engineers, and the outlook for employment is excellent. Average salary in 1983 for agricultural engineers was $38,470.

Training and Qualifications

Creativity, an analytical mind and an interest in math and science and how they can be applied to our farming and agricultural systems are important qualities for agricultural engineers.

A bachelor's degree in engineering is generally acceptable for entry-level jobs, but many obtain a master's degree because it is helpful in gaining promotion.

For Further Details

American Society of Agricultural Engineers, 2950 Niles Rd., St. Joseph, MI 49085.

ANIMAL TRAINERS/HANDLERS

Duties and Responsibilities

While much of man's progress has unfortunately led to the disappearance of many of our wild animals, other aspects of progress have led to a new respect for how man and beast can and should work together. Partly because of this new understanding, the field of animal training, which is based on an understanding of animal behavior and uses a system of rewards and reinforcements, is an exciting one that is currently expanding into new areas.

Protective services is one area of new growth. Trainers and handlers are needed in the military, the U.S. Customs Service, and state and local law enforcement agencies. Some animals are specially trained to sniff out narcotics, while others work with their handlers and are used as attack dogs in areas where they can be more effective than man. Some work on local police forces, while others are employed by private protection services for such purposes as patrolling stores and industrial plants at night.

At some animal parks, the public is permitted to witness how science is benefiting from what can be learned from animals. Some trainers and handlers work with animals (e.g., elephants, dolphins, and whales) who learn to respond to commands. By observing these abilities and behaviors, scientists are better able to understand the ways of animals in the wild and are aided in their efforts to preserve them.

And, of course, who doesn't love to visit the circus or to watch an animal perform at the zoo? Training everything from llamas to lions, many animal trainers and handlers are employed by the entertainment industry. Some provide animals ranging from cockatoos to "killer" bees for use in motion pictures, television, and commercials, where the animals perform according to the script.

Trainers also work in the field of dog obedience, where they run classes or are hired privately to teach pets to be manageable and responsive to commands. Some work with guide dogs to teach them special commands and signals for use by blind people.

Earnings and Opportunities

Employment outlook is good. Earnings generally range from $10,000 to $15,000, though star circus trainers and those who work for films and TV command a great deal more.

Training and Qualifications

A special feel for animals and patience are important qualities for animal trainers and handlers.

Some workers are self-taught, but those who work with domestic animals have usually completed a two-to-six-month vocational program at a dog training academy. Some workers are trained in the military, and those who work in law enforcement are generally law enforcement officers who are selected to attend special training programs to learn to work with the animals. For the law enforcement people and for those who work with scientists, additional education may prove beneficial.

ENVIRONMENTALISTS

Duties and Responsibilities

Fresh air, pure water, preservation of the land, and industrial progress without damage to nature are among the goals of environmentalists, who work within business and government to study environmental needs and establish and comply with regulations that safeguard our environment.

Some environmentalists specialize in preserving our rivers, lakes, wetlands, and subterranean waters; others advise on the treatment and containment of waste water; still others monitor the air pollutants produced by cars, factories, mining, and other sources. Handling and disposal of solid and hazardous waste materials, including radioactive materials and many highly dangerous chemicals and poisons, is another area of specialization.

Whether employed by government or industry, most environmentalists are involved in governmental affairs and must be knowledgeable about government regulations and legislation. They may do environmental research, organize and chair various committees or civic groups, and plan and conduct meetings and training programs for staff and/or community organizations.

An environmentalist working in private industry might evaluate for his company the environmental impact of building on a specific site. Those who work for mining companies might be concerned with surface mining and the necessary reclamation of the land that must be done after the mining is completed. If dealing with subsurface drilling and mining, environmentalists have to be concerned with the results of the sinking of land areas caused by the removal of solids or liquids below the surface and must make recommendations on that subject.

Those employed by government might find themselves working for the Environmental Protection Agency, in a congressional office to oversee legislation concerning the environment, or working overseas teaching emerging countries how to handle their waste disposal problems.

Those environmentalists who move into management are usually responsible for the development and introduction of new programs in both public and private sectors. They also continually assess the legislative needs of the country in their area of specialty and monitor all upcoming legislation as to its effect on their employer. Overseeing the engineering or technological research necessary and making presentations to legislators, legislative committees, and other groups are also part of the job. Departmental budgets and the hiring, training, and supervision of other environmental professionals and technicians must also be taken care of.

In order to keep abreast of the field, most professionals find there is a continuing need for research and education on the university level.

Most environmentalists play an active role in civic committees—local, statewide, and national. They may also have the opportunity to publish in their area of specialization, which adds to job visibility and can be a contributing factor in getting promoted.

Earnings and Opportunities

The opportunities in this area will continue to grow as the amount of legislation for protecting our environment increases; in turn, this means that more and more companies must make impact studies before undertaking development that might affect the environment, all of which leads to an increase in the number of jobs available. Salaries range from $18,500 for trainees to over $50,000 for experienced professionals.

Training and Qualifications

Concern for the environment, an interest in the workings of government, a desire to see that our nation's business is not improperly restrained, and an eye for the future are helpful qualities for environmentalists.

Because of the need for various types of expertise, individuals enter this field from a wide diversity of backgrounds. Many have degrees in the environmental sciences; some come from civil, chemical, or mechanical engineering; others come from city planning; and a few have only a liberal arts degree, although additional education in the environmental sciences is recommended for those who wish to advance. In addition, an increasing number are coming in with backgrounds in law, owing to the need for people who can interpret and oversee the complex legislation concerning environmental issues.

FOOD TECHNOLOGISTS

Duties and Responsibilities

There was a time not too many years ago when a prime activity for the family in autumn was bringing in the produce from the garden and canning and preserving it for winter. Today we do little of that at home, and most of the foods that will see us through the winter as well as today's convenience foods are processed by industry.

Food technologists are part of this process. They study the chemical, physical, and biological nature of food to learn how to safely process, preserve, package, distribute, and store it and to ensure that it is nutritious and wholesome.

Almost one-third of all food technologists work in research and development. Others work in quality-assurance laboratories or in production or processing areas of food plants. Some teach or do basic research in colleges and universities or work for the government, and still others work in sales, advertising, market research, or management positions in business.

In research, workers study the structure and composition of food and the changes it undergoes in storage and processing. Those who work in applied research and development create new foods and develop new processing methods. They also work to improve existing foods by making them more nutritious and enhancing their flavor, color, and texture.

In quality control laboratories, technologists check raw ingredients for freshness, maturity, and suitability for processing. Periodically they inspect processing line operations to ensure conformance with government and industry standards.

Those who work in processing plants prepare production specifications, schedule processing operations, maintain proper temperatures and humidity in storage areas, and supervise sanitation operations, including the proper disposal of wastes. To increase efficiency, they advise management on the purchase of equipment and recommend new suppliers.

Workers are employed in every state; however, the product they work with varies by locality. For example, many technologists in Maine and Idaho work with potatoes, in the Midwest with cereal and meat products, and in Florida and California with citrus fruits and vegetables.

Workers with bachelors' degrees might start as quality-assurance or junior food chemists or assistant production managers. Those with advanced degrees might start in research or as food chemists in research and development. Advancement may mean moving up to become department or section head or to other research management positions.

Earnings and Opportunities

About 15,000 people are employed as food technologists, and employment opportunities are good. Earnings range from $17,600 to $52,000.

Training and Qualifications

An analytical mind, the ability to do detailed technical work and to communicate clearly are important qualities for food technologists.

A bachelor's degree with a major in food technology is generally the minimum requirement for beginning jobs. Advanced degrees are necessary for college teaching and many management and research positions.

For Further Details

Institute of Food Technologists, Suite 2120, 221 N. LaSalle St., Chicago, IL 60601.

FORESTERS

Duties and Responsibilities

While today's forester is more likely to be found in a four-wheel drive or a helicopter than riding on horseback, his or her job still provides the very special rewards of working close to nature. Forests are one of our most important natural resources, and it is foresters who manage, develop, and protect them for us, so that Americans can continue to enjoy them for generations to come.

Duties include making maps of forest areas, estimating the amount of timber and future growth, and managing timber sales, as well as protecting trees from fire, disease, and harmful insects. Other duties range from wildlife protection and watershed management to the development and supervision of camps, parks, and grazing lands. Others do research, provide information to forest owners and the general public, or teach at colleges or universities. Foresters often specialize in one area, such as timber management, outdoor recreation, or forest economics.

Nearly one-half of all foresters work for the federal government, primarily the Forest Service. About one-fourth work for state governments, while the remainder work in private industry, mainly for pulp and paper, lumber, logging, and milling companies, as well as for local governments, colleges, and universities. A few are self-employed either as consultants or forest owners.

Working conditions vary. Foresters spend a great deal of time working with people like landowners, loggers, forestry aides, and others. The work can be physically demanding. Many spend considerable time outdoors in all kinds of weather and often work in remote areas. They may work long hours on emergency duty like firefighting or search-and-rescue missions.

In the federal government, an experienced forester may supervise an entire forest area and may advance to regional forest supervisor or to a top administrative position. In private industry, foresters start by learning the practical and administrative aspects of the business. Some work their way up to top managerial positions within their companies. Many experienced foresters advance to office jobs, where they plan and organize the activities of the staff.

Earnings and Opportunities

Over 30,000 people work as foresters, and government employment is expected to grow slowly. Employment will probably grow faster in private industry. Salaries range from $15,300 to $48,000.

Training and Qualifications

The person well suited to forestry enjoys working outdoors, is physically capable, and likes living and working in remote areas. Foresters should be able to work well with people and express themselves clearly.

A bachelor's degree in forestry is the minimum educational requirement for a professional career. Because of keen job competition and the increasingly complex nature of the work, many employers require advanced degrees.

For Further Details

Society of American Foresters, 5400 Grosvenor Lane, Bethesda, MD 20814. American Forestry Association, 1319 18th St., N.W., Washington, DC 20036. U.S. Department of Agriculture, Forest Service, P.O. Box 2417, Washington, DC 20013.

FORESTRY TECHNICIANS

Duties and Responsibilities

Forestry technicians perform a wide variety of important tasks as they assist foresters in the care and management of forest lands and resources.

Specific duties may include estimating present and potential timber yield; measuring cut logs to determine actual yield; supervising survey and road building crews; protecting against flood damage and soil erosion; or inspecting trees for disease. They also help to prevent and control forest fires by leading firefighting crews and providing fire prevention information to forest users. After fires are extinguished, they take inventory of burned areas and supervise planting of new trees and shrubs.

Technicians also maintain forest areas for hunting, camping, hiking, and other recreational activities. They explain regulations to visitors and enforce them.

Jobs are located mainly in the Western and Southeastern states, where forest lands are most plentiful. Over half of all forest technicians work in private industry, mainly for logging, lumber, and paper companies. Mining, oil, and railroad companies employ some forestry technicians on reforestation projects; tree nurseries employ others.

Technicians do almost all of their work outdoors in all kinds of weather. Sometimes they work in remote areas for extended periods of time, as when controlling floods or fighting fires. The work can be physically and mentally demanding. Contending with snakes and insects is part of the job.

Earnings and Opportunities

An estimated 15,000 people work year-round as forestry technicians. Almost that many find temporary, seasonal employment—primarily with federal and state governments. Growth in employment is expected to be about as fast as the average for all occupations through the 1980s, and private industry is expected to provide a high proportion of these jobs. Applicants with specialized training and some practical experience on a firefighting crew, in a tree nursery, or in recreation work should have the best opportunities for employment.

Earnings: $14,000 to $18,600.

Training and Qualifications

Love of the outdoors, stamina, and the ability to carry out both supervised and unsupervised tasks are necessary for this job. Technicians should also be able to express themselves clearly both orally and in writing.

To qualify, candidates should finish high school and then apply for a specialized one- or two-year technical training course, preferably one that is approved by the Society of American Foresters. Most training schools require general education courses such as math and English; forestry-related courses, including biology and botany; and specialized forest technology courses like land surveying, tree identification, and timber harvesting. Most schools also provide practical experience working in a forest.

Forestry technicians generally begin work as trainees or with relatively routine assignments, working closely with an experienced technician or forester. As they gain experience, they are given more responsibility and often move into supervisory positions. Some technicians obtain bachelors' degrees in forestry and are promoted to the forester level.

For Further Details

Society of American Foresters, 5400 Grosvenor Lane, Bethesda, MD 20814; American Forestry Association, 1319 18th Street, N.W., Washington, DC 20036; U.S. Department of Agriculture, Forest Service, P.O. Box 2417, Washington, DC 20013.

RANGE MANAGERS

Duties and Responsibilities

Range managers—also called range scientists, range ecologists, and range conservationists—are responsible for managing and protecting the valuable natural resources found in the more than one billion acres of rangeland in the United States, most of it located in the Western states and Alaska. These resources include grass and shrubs for animal grazing, wildlife habitats, water from vast watersheds, recreation facilities, and mineral and energy resources. The range manager's job is to maximize the use of this land without damaging the environment. This might involve, for example, advising cattle ranchers on ways to utilize their land for grazing to achieve the best possible livestock production without sacrificing the soil and vegetation. Because of the multiple uses of rangelands, range managers often specialize in one area, such as wildlife or watershed management, forest management, or recreation.

Range managers spend much of their time outdoors in all kinds of weather, and they often must spend considerable time away from home. Travel is by car or small plane, and on rough terrain by four-wheel-drive vehicles, horseback, or on foot.

Their work involves a great deal of contact with people, including the general public, ranchers, government officials, and other conservation specialists. They often work as part of a team. In addition to outdoor work, they spend time preparing reports and performing other administrative duties.

Many range managers advance to managerial positions, where they write reports and plan and supervise the work of others. Those in private industry may move up to higher supervisory positions with their firms.

Earnings and Opportunities

Over 4,000 people work as range managers, and employment is expected to grow throughout the 1980s. Since the amount of land cannot be expanded, managers will be needed to increase range productivity while maintaining environmental quality. They will also be in great demand to manage large ranches, which are increasing in number. As oil and coal exploration accelerates, private industry will require many more specialists to reclaim or restore mined lands to a productive state. Salaries range from $14,400 to $28,600.

Training and Qualifications

Besides having a love of the outdoors, range managers must be able to write and speak effectively. They should be able to work alone or under direct supervision. Good physical health and stamina are also important.

A bachelor's degree in range management or range science is the usual minimum educational requirement. Graduate degrees in range management generally are needed for teaching and research positions, and they may be helpful for advancement in other jobs.

For Further Details

Society for Range Management, 2760 W. 5th Ave., Denver, CO 80204. Bureau of Land Management, Denver Service Center, Federal Center Building 50, Denver, CO 80225. U.S. Department of Agriculture, Forest Service, P.O. Box 2417, Washington, DC 20013. U.S. Department of Agriculture, Soil Conservation Service, P.O. Box 2890, Washington, DC 20013.

SOIL CONSERVATIONISTS

Duties and Responsibilities

Guarding against soil erosion, misuse, and exploitation is an essential part of our nation's overall responsibility to conserve our natural resources; and it is soil conservationists who perform this very important job, providing technical assistance to farmers, ranchers, and others concerned with the conservation of soil, water, and related natural resources.

Conservationists help farmers and land managers develop programs that make the most productive use of their land without damaging it. If a farmer is experiencing an erosion problem, for example, the conservationist will visit the farm, find the source of the problem and help develop a program to combat the erosion. Since the job involves convincing others to change their ways, sensitivity and tact can be very important when presenting the information.

Soil conservationists also inventory pastureland and rangeland, and recommend to farmers and ranchers areas where ponds can be constructed to provide water for livestock. They also suggest solutions to problems of overgrazing, such as seeding grassland or placing salt licks in undergrazed areas to keep the livestock away from areas that have been overgrazed. They pay close attention to weather patterns so as to be aware of possible conservation problems before they arise.

Most work for the federal government. Those employed by the Department of Agriculture work with Soil and Water Conservation districts throughout the country. Those employed by the Bureau of Indian Affairs generally work near or on Indian reservations, most of which are located in the Western states. Others are employed by state and local governments.

Rural banks, insurance firms, and mortgage companies that make loans for agricultural lands also employ conservationists. A few work for public utilities and lumber and paper companies that have large holdings of forested lands.

Those working at the county level may advance to the area or state level. Some transfer to related occupations such as farm management advisers, land appraisers, landmen for oil and coal companies, or to agricultural sales positions. Those with advanced degrees may accept teaching or research opportunities.

Earnings and Opportunities

An estimated 5,000 people work as soil conservationists, and employment is expected to change little through the 1980s. Average salaries range from $15,200 to $26,800.

Training and Qualifications

Soil conservationists must be able to communicate well, since much of their work consists of helping farmers and ranchers in planning and applying sound conservation practices. They must also be able to prepare written reports and programs to present to farmers, ranch managers, and Soil and Water Conservation districts.

Most who work in the profession have at least a bachelor's degree in agronomy, agricultural education, or general agriculture. A few have degrees in related fields such as wildlife biology, forestry, and range management. A knowledge of agricultural engineering is also very helpful, as are courses in cartography, or mapmaking.

For Further Details

U.S. Department of Agriculture, Soil Conservation Service, P.O. Box 2890, Washington, DC 20013.

VETERINARIANS

Duties and Responsibilities

Whether they are trying to help a rancher prevent a disease from spreading through a herd of cattle, treating a lion at the zoo, or helping your dog recover from a bout with bronchitis, veterinarians are an important part of the medical community. They not only help us care for animals we love, but they are an important reason why America's food chain is a strong and healthy one.

Veterinarians diagnose, treat, and control animal diseases and injuries. They help prevent the outbreak and spread of animal diseases, some of which can be transmitted to human beings. They also perform surgery on sick and injured animals and prescribe and administer medicines and vaccines.

Veterinarians usually treat pets in hospitals and clinics. Those who have a large-animal practice usually work out of a well-equipped mobile clinic and drive considerable distances between farms and ranches in order to care for animal patients. They often work long hours. Those in rural areas may have to work outdoors in all kinds of weather.

Most are in private practice. Over one-third of all veterinarians treat small animals or pets exclusively. Another one-third treat both large and small animals. Almost 10 percent specialize in the health and breeding of cattle, poultry, sheep, swine, or horses. Some inspect food; others work as part of a medical team investigating disease outbreaks. Others are employed in federal and state public health programs. Some teach in veterinary colleges, work in zoos or animal laboratories, or engage in medical research. Still others work for livestock farms, animal-food companies, and pharmaceutical firms.

Newly qualified veterinarians may enter the military services as commissioned officers or qualify for federal positions as meat and poultry inspectors, disease-control workers, epidemiologists, or research assistants, or they may obtain commissioned offices in the U.S. Public Health Service.

Earnings and Opportunities

Over 36,000 people currently work as veterinarians, and outlook for employment is excellent. The number of veterinarians is expected to rise 30 percent by 1995. Earnings: $22,000 to $45,000 and up.

Training and Qualifications

A love of animals, sensitivity, physical stamina, and the willingness to work hard are good qualities for future veterinarians.

To obtain the license which is required throughout the U.S., applicants must have a doctor of veterinary medicine (D.V.M. or V.M.D.) degree from an accredited college of veterinary medicine and must pass written and oral examinations.

For positions in research and teaching, a master's or Ph.D. degree is usually required in a field such as pathology, physiology, toxicology, or laboratory animal medicine.

The D.V.M. degree is offered as a four-year professional degree program and must be preceded by at least two years of preveterinary study. However, most applicants have obtained a bachelor's degree prior to being accepted.

For Further Details

For the free pamphlet *Today's Veterinarian* send a self-addressed, stamped business-size envelope to American Veterinary Medical Association, 930 N. Meacham Rd., Schaumburg, IL 60196.

VETERINARY TECHNICIANS AND ASSISTANTS

Duties and Responsibilities

Just as doctors require specially trained help to do their work well, so do veterinarians, and this is the very important role played by veterinary technicians and assistants, who aid in the diagnosis, treatment, and control of animal diseases and injuries.

Veterinary technicians are the most highly skilled of these workers, and they assist veterinarians by performing such tasks as giving medication and vaccinations, preparing animals for surgery, administering electrocardiograms and X rays, performing emergency first aid, collecting specimens for analysis, and performing some types of laboratory analysis. They may also be called upon to nurse very sick animals, keep records, and occasionally groom animals.

Veterinarian's assistants are not as highly trained, and most of their job involves basic animal care, working directly with the veterinarian. They aid with physical exams, administer medication, aid in parasite prevention and control, and help during surgery. They may also bathe, feed, and groom the animals and be responsible for cleaning cages and equipment. Sometimes they develop X rays, prepare samples for the laboratory, and answer the questions of the animals' owners. With further training, they may become technicians.

Animal care attendants clean, groom, feed, and exercise animals, as well as tend to the facilities. It is an unskilled job, but those who like it may decide to go on to get further training.

Veterinary technicians and assistants work with veterinarians in private practice, zoos, animal shelters, on farms, for kennels, and in diagnostic and research laboratories. Evening and weekend work is common since animals must be cared for daily, and illness or accident may occur at any time.

Earnings and Opportunities

Outlook for employment is quite good, reflecting the growing importance of veterinary medicine. Earnings range from $8,000 for animal care attendants to about $15,000 for veterinary technicians.

Training and Qualifications

A love of animals, stamina, and the willingness to work hard are good qualifications for these workers.

A high school diploma is advised for all workers. Post–high school vocational training is available for assistants, though many receive on-the-job training. Many technicians attend a two-year college program in animal technology.

For Further Details

American Veterinary Medical Association, 930 N. Meacham Rd., Schaumburg, IL 60196.

Careers in Architecture and Design

Man likes and needs to build things, and the history of civilization is replete with examples of this. From the Egyptian pyramids, Babylonian irrigation systems, Oriental terracing, and Roman amphitheaters to today's highways, bridges, and skyscrapers, people throughout the ages have performed amazing feats to build their dreams into reality.

Today those responsible for this work are generally employed in the field of architecture and design, and it is an area filled with opportunity. Surveyors and surveying technicians are needed to measure and lay out land boundaries and building sites and levels and elevations; architects are there to design and construct buildings that are safe and aesthetically appealing. Planners are responsible for urban and regional areas as well as for specialized work such as college and campus planning. Roadways, airports, bridges, dams, and manufacturing plants are just a few of the areas where civil engineers apply their knowledge. And finally, interior decorators are needed to create the interior environments we so enjoy.

Job growth in these areas is expected to be quite good, and so opportunities are promising.

ARCHITECTS

Duties and Responsibilities

While New York's Chrysler Building, San Francisco's Transamerica Building, and Chicago's Sears Tower exemplify architectural creativity at its best, architects design every home, school, and church with the same planning and care as the buildings that shape our cities' skylines.

Architects design a wide variety of structures, including houses, industrial plants, hospitals, shopping centers, hotels, and airports. They also design multibuilding complexes for urban renewal projects, college campuses, industrial parks, and new towns. Architects are involved in all phases of development, from the initial discussion of general ideas with the client through actual construction of the build-

43

ing. Their duties require knowledge of design and engineering, and they must be good at management as well.

No matter what is being built, there are three considerations that are of primary importance when designing a building: function (How will it suit the needs of the people who will use it?), safety, and aesthetics. To get a sense of these needs, architects first meet with the client to discuss the purpose, requirements, and estimated cost of a project. Scale drawings are then prepared by the architect to give the client a general sense of the mechanical and structural components of the building.

Next, working drawings are prepared, showing the exact dimensions of every part of the structure and the location of plumbing, heating units, electrical outlets, and air conditioning. Architects also specify the building materials and in some cases the interior furnishings.

After all plans are complete and any client requests for changes have been satisfied, the architect assists the client in selecting a contractor and negotiating the construction contract. As construction proceeds, the architect visits the building site from time to time to ensure that the contractor is following the design and using the specified materials. An architect's job is not finished until construction is finished, required tests are performed, construction costs paid, and guarantees received from the contractor.

Most architects work for architectural firms, builders, real estate firms, or other businesses with large construction programs. Some work for government agencies responsible for housing, planning, or community development.

Advancement may involve becoming an associate in the architectural firm for which the architect works, or it may involve starting one's own business.

Earnings and Opportunities

Over 79,500 people are employed as architects, and this number is expected to increase by 40 percent in the next decade, making the outlook for employment excellent. Income ranges from $17,500 to $100,000.

Training and Qualifications

A bachelor of architecture degree is advised, and most accredited schools offer either a five-year curriculum leading to that degree or a six-year program leading to a master of architecture degree. Although graduate education is not required for practicing architects, it is often helpful to those involved in research and teaching.

For Further Details

The American Institute of Architects, 1735 New York Ave., N.W., Washington, DC 20006. The Association of Collegiate Schools of Architecture, Inc., at the same address.

CIVIL ENGINEERS

Duties and Responsibilities

Civil engineering is the oldest branch of the engineering profession. The building you work in, the tunnel you drive through, and the system that brings your home its water supply are all examples of the work done by civil engineers. They design and supervise the construction of roads, airports, manufacturing plants, electric power generating plants, bridges, buildings, dams, railroads, and sewage systems. They also work on defense installations and synthetic fuel projects. In the process, they apply the theories and principles of science and mathematics to practical technical problems, such as how best to dig through a mountain in order to build a tunnel. They usually see a project through from the initial planning stages to completion and are responsible for its overall effectiveness, cost, reliability, and safety.

Major specialties within civil engineering

are structural, hydraulic, environmental (sanitary), transportation, highway, and soil mechanics.

Engineers often use calculators and computers to provide mathematical equations that describe how a structure or system operates. They may spend time writing reports or designing plans and consulting with other engineers. Though there is office work to be done, civil engineers also spend a great deal of their time working in the field on the site of a new highway or building.

Most civil engineers work in the construction industry or for federal, state, or local government agencies. Many work for consulting engineering and architectural firms or as independent consulting engineers. Others work for public utilities, railroads, educational institutions, and manufacturing industries.

Many civil engineers are in supervisory or administrative positions, ranging from supervisor of a construction site to city engineer or top-level executive. Others teach in colleges and universities or work as consultants.

Earnings and Opportunities

Over 165,000 people are employed as civil engineers, and employment opportunities are excellent, with a 47 percent increase in employment projected for the next decade. The median annual income for civil engineers is $38,845 for those who are generalists in the field. Those who specialize in structural civil engineering have median incomes of $41,000. Executives can earn in excess of $60,000.

Training and Qualifications

A fascination with math and science, as well as creativity, an analytical mind, and the capacity for detail are qualities possessed by good engineering candidates. Self-motivation combined with the ability to work well with others is also important.

A bachelor's degree in engineering is generally acceptable for beginning engineering jobs. Many engineers obtain a master's degree because it is desirable for promotion or for learning about new technology.

A number of colleges and universities offer five-year master's degree programs. Some longer programs also offer a work-study arrangement that offers useful experience as well as the opportunity for students to offset the cost of their education.

For Further Details

American Society of Civil Engineers, 345 E. 47th St., New York, NY 10017.

COLLEGE AND CAMPUS PLANNERS

Duties and Responsibilities

As colleges and universities expand in size and in diversity of programs offered, professional planners are needed to take into consideration the physical plant and surroundings and plan intelligently for expected growth.

Many colleges today are larger and more complex than some cities or towns, and college planners and campus planners are a highly specialized combination of city planner and landscape architect. How to house, feed, entertain, educate, exercise, and care for thousands of students, faculty, and operating personnel, while always taking the future into consideration, are the day-to-day concerns of these professionals. Architecture, construction, interior design, land usage, zoning, transportation, landscaping, demographics, and statistics are all important factors in the decisions they make.

Planners advise college presidents and boards of trustees as to what land must be acquired, when, and at what estimated cost. They study traffic flow, parking needs, housing requirements, and student trends in each area. They may make extensive drawings and models of alternative land and building uses. Their recommendations cover classroom, auditorium, and laboratory needs and design, building construction, demolition, and expansion, as well as interior and exterior treatment and beautification of new and existing buildings and their surrounding landscaping. In addition to planning for the main campus, they also make complete studies of alternative sites for satellite campuses and junior colleges.

Their role also extends into the community, where they represent the school at zoning and community planning meetings and other governmental hearings regarding land use, funding, and grants. They may also be required to prepare detailed documents to cover some issues.

Planners work a relatively normal forty-hour week, though sometimes they may need to attend evening or weekend meetings. Working in a college atmosphere can be exciting and stimulating, and it offers an ever-present opportunity for continuing education. Some planners take on limited teaching responsibilities or work as outside consultants.

Advancement for campus planners may consist of becoming head of the college planning department or starting one's own business to offer advice to smaller institutions on a consulting basis.

Earnings and Opportunities

There will always be a need for campus and college planners because of the increase in the number and size of colleges and the movement of existing campus planners into private practice or city planning. Earnings range from about $22,500 to $33,000, with the opportunity to do consulting or teaching for additional income.

Training and Qualifications

An analytical mind, creativity, and a love of the outdoors combined with an artistic bent are prime qualities for campus planners. Being able to deal with both the concrete and the abstract is also important in this job.

A bachelor of science degree in architecture or landscape architecture, in addition to a master's degree in college planning, is usually necessary for those who aspire to advance in the field.

For Further Details

American Planning Association, 1776 Massachusetts Avenue N.W., Washington, DC 20036.

DRAFTERS

Duties and Responsibilities

When workers build anything, from an office building to an airplane or a computer, they work from detailed drawings that show the exact dimensions and specifications of the entire object and each of its parts. The professionals who are responsible for creating these drawings are drafters.

Drafters work from rough sketches, specifications, and calculations given them by scientists, engineers, architects, and designers. Final drawings contain a detailed view of the object from all sides, as well as specifications for materials to be used, procedures to be followed, and other information to carry out the job. Drafters may also calculate

the strength, quality, quantity, and cost of materials.

To plan their work, drafters use compasses, dividers, protractors, triangles, and other drafting devices, as well as calculators, tables, and technical handbooks. In addition, today's drafters are increasingly making use of computer-aided systems and electronic drafting equipment to prepare drawings.

Drafters usually specialize in mechanical, electrical, aeronautical, structural, or architectural drawing; and workers are classified according to what they do. *Senior drafters* translate an engineer's or architect's preliminary plans into scale drawings of the object to be built. *Detailers* draw each part shown on the layout and give dimensions, materials, and other information to make the drawing clear and complete. *Checkers* carefully examine drawings for errors in computing or recording dimensions and specifications. Finally, *tracers* make minor corrections and trace drawings for reproduction on paper or plastic film.

New employees usually start out as tracers or junior drafters, depending on background, and may advance to checkers, detailers, and eventually senior drafters or supervisors. Some may become independent designers.

Earnings and Opportunities

Over 322,000 people are employed as drafters, and employment is expected to increase faster than the average because of industrial growth and the increasingly complex designs of new products and processes. Salaries range widely from $14,500 to $29,600 and up for supervisory positions.

Training and Qualifications

Good eyesight, manual dexterity, and the ability to work as part of a team are important, as is the ability to do freehand drawings of three-dimensional objects. Drafters must also be able to do detailed work carefully and accurately. Artistic ability is helpful in some specialized fields.

Employers prefer to hire applicants who have obtained specialized training in a technical institute, junior or community college, or a vocational or technical high school. Ideally, training should include mathematics, physical sciences, mechanical drawing, and drafting. Shop practices and shop skills are also helpful, since most higher-level drafting jobs require knowledge of manufacturing or construction methods. Many technical schools offer courses in structural design, architectural drawing, and engineering or industrial technology.

Holders of associate degrees in drafting and persons who are trained in the use of computer-aided drafting systems and electronic drafting equipment will have the best prospects for employment.

For Further Details

American Institute for Design and Drafting, 102 N. Elm Place, Suite F, Broken Arrow, OK 74012.

INDUSTRIAL DESIGNERS

Duties and Responsibilities

Just think of the comfortable fit of a pair of scissors or the handy way the cord reels into your vacuum cleaner. Coming up with product designs that are functional, attractive, safe, and easy to use is the job of industrial designers. They combine artistic talent with knowledge of product use, marketing, materials, and production methods to create the best and most competitive design possible.

When a new design is needed, the designer's first task is to research the project, which may involve making comparisons with competitive products, evaluating the needs of the product user, and taking into account fashion trends and the possible environmental effect of the product. Next the designer usually produces several sketches before meeting with a development team of product planners, engineers, production specialists, and sales and market research personnel about the feasibility of each idea. They consider performance, quality, visual appeal, convenience, utility, safety, and maintenance, as well as what the product cost will be to the manufacturer, distributor, retailer, and consumer.

Once the best design has been selected, a designer or a professional modeler makes a model for consumer testing, and there is an opportunity for final revisions. Finally, the approved product model is engineered, tooled, and manufactured.

Most industrial designers work in the field of product design; in some jobs, however, they may also assume other design responsibilities, such as developing company trademarks or corporate symbols that appear on products, advertising, brochures, and stationery, or designing containers for products.

Some designers work as freelance consultants, designing a wide range of products for a variety of clients.

Most designers work for large manufacturing companies or for design consulting firms. Some are on staff with architectural or interior design businesses.

Some designers become supervisors with major responsibility for the design of a product or a group of products. Some start their own firms.

Earnings and Opportunities

About 13,000 people are employed as industrial designers, and prospects are excellent. Earnings: $20,000 to $100,000 and more.

Training and Qualifications

Creative talent, drawing skills, and the ability to translate abstract ideas into tangible designs are key qualities for the industrial designer. Designers often work as part of a team, so working well with others is an asset.

Studying industrial design in an art school, university, or technical college is the usual requirement for this field. Most large manufacturing firms hire only those who have a bachelor's degree in industrial design. However, many schools do not allow formal entry into a bachelor's degree program until a student has successfully finished a year of basic art and design courses. Applicants may be required to submit sketches and other examples of their artistic ability.

Graduates seeking employment will need a portfolio of photographs, drawings, and sketches that demonstrate creativity, artistic ability, and the ability to communicate ideas.

For Further Details

Industrial Designers Society of America, 6802 Poplar Place, Suite 303, McLean, VA 22101.

INTERIOR DESIGNERS

Duties and Responsibilities

A well-designed home or office is a real pleasure. Not only pleasing to the eye, but functional and comfortable as well. Though some people are talented enough to create their own design schemes, most of us must turn to an interior designer to achieve the perfect combination of beauty and comfort.

Whether working on a home, an office, a restaurant, a theater or an airplane, interior designers plan and supervise every detail of an interior and its furnishings. First, the designer considers the uses of the space, and the client's needs, budget, and taste. Then he or she prepares color sketches and scaled plans of what he thinks the space should look like. These, along with photographs of furniture and accessories; samples of upholstery, drapery materials, and wall coverings; and

a budget estimate, must then be presented to the client. If the client approves, the designer orders the furnishings and contracts for painters, floor finishers, carpet layers, and other craft workers. He or she then supervises the work to see that all is accomplished according to plan.

Some designers may design entire office buildings, hospitals, or libraries. Some also design furniture and accessories and arrange for their manufacture.

Current trends are affecting the kind of work done by designers. More and more businesses are deciding to redesign or adapt existing office space rather than move, and homeowners are doing the same, redesigning or adding on to their houses. In the office, this frequently entails redesigning to accommodate computer and word processing equipment. The demand for redesigning in order to conserve energy is up by 72 percent since 1980, according to the American Society of Interior Designers.

Most designers work for design firms. They may work as part of a team that includes architects and engineers. Others work for large hotel and restaurant chains or builders who do a great deal of building or renovation. They also write for magazines that feature articles on home furnishings. Some designers run their own firms. A few design for theater, movies, and television. Still others work in large department and furniture stores, where they advise customers on design plans.

Work hours may be long and erratic. Since client convenience is important, designers may work on weekends or in the evenings. The ability to handle many details, even under pressure, is very important.

Earnings and Opportunities

Over 35,000 people are employed as interior designers, and employment outlook is very good. Designers receive compensation in a variety of ways. Some are paid straight salaries; some receive salaries plus commissions based on the value of their sales; and others work entirely on commissions. Income ranges from $15,000 for beginners to $30,000 for those with experience and $50,000 and over for the well known.

Training and Qualifications

Artistic talent, color sense, an eye for detail, and a sense of balance and proportion are important qualities for the aspiring designer. It is also important to be versatile and open to new ideas in order to keep current with changing trends.

Currently, most employers are looking for people who have professional training. Training is available in three-year certificate programs in professional schools of interior design and in four-year colleges or university programs offering that specialty.

For Further Details

American Society of Interior Designers, 1430 Broadway, New York, NY 10018. Institute of Business Designers, National Headquarters, 1155 Merchandise Mart, Chicago, IL 60654.

LANDSCAPE ARCHITECTS

Duties and Responsibilities

That inventive playground you wish they'd had when you were a child, the beautiful park you stroll in on Sundays, and the attractive plantings that surround the local shopping center are all the work of landscape architects, whose job it is to design outdoor areas in such a way that they are functional and beautiful.

In their work, they plan the location of buildings, roads and walks, and the arrangement of vegetation and other features in open spaces. When planning a site, the goal of the landscape architect is to establish the best possible physical relationship between people and buildings, trees, shrubs, water, roads, drainage, and lights. Sometimes, for example, streets are replanned to limit automobile access and make it more pleasant for pedestrians. Landscape architects must also consider natural resources and energy conservation. They evaluate the natural elements of the area such as climate, soil, slope of the land, and present vegetation. They also study the way the sun falls at given times of day and assess the usefulness of existing buildings, roads, walkways, and utility lines.

Next, detailed plans must be drawn up, and at this stage the landscape architect is likely to work as part of a design team or as a consultant to the project architect or engineer. The plans include reports, sketches, models, photographs, land-use studies, and cost estimates. Once the plans are approved, landscape architects prepare working drawings showing all existing and proposed features. They outline in detail the methods of construction and list necessary materials. Next, landscape contractors may be asked to bid for the work. After the contractor has been picked, landscape architects supervise the construction to ensure proper completion of the job.

Some landscape architects specialize in parks and playgrounds; others specialize in hotels and resorts, shopping centers, or public housing. Still others work primarily in regional planning and resource management, feasibility, site construction, environmental impact, and cost studies.

Most landscape architects have their own businesses, or they work for architectural, landscape architectural, or engineering firms. Others are employed by government agencies concerned with forest management, water storage, public housing, city planning, urban renewal, highways, parks, and recreation areas. Some work for landscape contractors and a few teach in colleges and universities.

Landscape architects spend much of their time in offices preparing drawings, models, and cost estimates and discussing them with clients. A good deal of time is also spent outdoors studying sites and planning projects.

Earnings and Opportunities

Over 15,000 people are employed as landscape architects, and employment opportunities are excellent. Earnings range from $18,500 to $75,000 and up.

Training and Qualifications

Artistic ability, creativity, and a love and appreciation of nature are important qualities for landscape architects. The minimum educational requirement is a bachelor's degree in landscape architecture, which takes four to five years to obtain.

For Further Details

American Society of Landscape Architects, 1733 Connecticut Ave., N.W., Washington, DC 20009.

SURVEYORS AND SURVEYING TECHNICIANS

Duties and Responsibilities

Surveying might just be the perfect combination of interesting work and mixture of outdoor and indoor responsibilities. Surveyors, aided by surveying technicians, are responsible for establishing legal land boundaries, researching deeds, writing descriptions of land for legal requirements, assisting in setting land valuations, measuring construction and mineral sites, and collecting information for maps and charts.

Usually working as part of a surveying party, land surveyors may locate boundaries of a tract of land for maps, deeds, leases, and other documents. Those doing topographical surveys determine elevations, depressions, and contours of an area and mark features such as farms, buildings, forests, roads, and rivers. A typical survey party consists of the *party chief* and one to six assistants known as *instrument assistants,* who adjust and operate the equipment and compile notes, sketches, and records from their findings.

Geodetic surveyors use techniques such as satellite observations to measure large areas of the earth's surface. *Geophysical prospecting surveyors* usually work in the petroleum field and mark sites for subsurface exploration. *Marine surveyors* survey harbors, rivers, and other bodies of water to determine shorelines, topography of the bottom, depth, and other features.

Photogrammetrists measure and interpret photographic images to determine the physical characteristics of natural or constructed features of an area. By applying analytical processes and mathmatical techniques to photographs taken from different locations, workers are able to make detailed maps of areas that are inaccessible or difficult to survey by other methods. *Mosaicists* and *map editors* develop and verify maps and pictures from aerial photographs.

About 40 percent of all surveyors work for construction companies and for engineering and architectural consulting firms. A sizable number either work for or own firms that conduct surveys for a fee. Some also work for oil and gas companies and for public utilities. The work can be rugged and may require travel or living away from home for a time. Workers may advance to instrument assistant, then to party chief, and finally to licensed surveyor.

Earnings and Opportunities

Over 61,000 people are employed as surveyors or surveying technicians, and opportunities are very good. Job opportunities are expected to increase 43 percent in the next ten years. Earnings range from $9,800 to $44,000.

Training and Qualifications

Being able to visualize distances and make mathematical calculations quickly are assets to surveyors and surveying technicians. Being in good physical condition with good eyesight and hearing is also important.

Most persons obtain training by combining post–secondary school courses in surveying with extensive on-the-job training. Some prepare by obtaining a college degree. Junior and community colleges, technical institutes, and vocational schools offer one-, two-, and three-year programs in surveying. Those interested in a career as a photogrammetrist usually need a bachelor's degree in engineering or a physical science. Most photogrammetry technicians have some specialized post-secondary training.

For Further Details

American Congress on Surveying and Mapping, 210 Little Falls St., Falls Church, VA 22046. American Society of Photogrammetry, 105 N. Virginia Ave., Falls Church, VA 22046.

URBAN AND REGIONAL PLANNERS

Duties and Responsibilities

Planning for the future and helping solve the social, economic, and environmental problems of the present are the business of urban and regional planners.

In order to provide for future growth and the revitalization of urban, suburban, and rural communities, these workers study and help prepare for situations that are likely to develop as a result of population growth or social and economic change. They must take into account an area's long-range needs for housing and business and industrial sites. Because the growth of many cities has led to transportation problems within the urban center, planners must often concentrate on new and better ways to transport people within a given area, such as the downtown district. Their ultimate goal, of course, is a more efficient and attractive urban area.

Studying in detail the current use of land is a very important part of being able to develop a long-range community plan. Such studies conducted by planners record such information as the location of streets and highways, water and sewer lines, schools, libraries, hospitals, and recreational sites. Working from this information, planners are then able to formulate ways to redesign certain areas or use undeveloped land. Finally, they must prepare materials that show how their programs can be carried out and what they will cost.

Urban and regional planners often confer with land developers, civic leaders, and other public planning officials. They may prepare materials for community relations programs, speak at civic meetings, and appear before legislative committees to explain their proposals.

Most planners work for city, county, or regional planning agencies. A number are employed by state or federal agencies dealing with housing, transportation, or environmental protection. Some do consulting work, either moonlighting or working full-time for a firm that provides services to private developers or government agencies. Planners also work for large land developers or research organizations and teach in colleges and universities.

Advancement often involves taking on greater responsibility for larger projects or taking over the design of a certain development. Some become planning directors, positions where a great deal of time is spent meeting with officials, speaking to civic groups, and supervising other professionals. For a planning director, future challenges might involve being transferred to a larger city with more complex problems.

Earnings and Opportunities

Over 23,000 people are employed as urban and regional planners, and the employment outlook is good, with a 15 percent increase in employment projected for the next decade. Earnings range from $18,500 to $44,000.

Training and Qualifications

Like designers, planners must be able to think in terms of spatial relationships and visualize the effects of their plans and designs. Creativity, farsightedness, and innovation are important; and being able to communicate well and develop good relationships within the community can be helpful in seeing plans through to completion.

For most entry-level jobs, applicants need a master's degree in urban or regional planning or the equivalent in work experience.

For Further Details

American Planning Association, 1776 Massachusetts Ave., N.W., Washington, DC 20036.

Careers in the Clergy

Whether they come to it right after school or when they are in their forties or fifties, those who decide upon a career in the clergy share a strong religious faith and a desire to help others.

For most, a religious career dictates one's entire work and personal lifestyle. Religious workers may be on call twenty-four hours a day, and they are expected to be models of moral and ethical conduct. Although some clergy may eventually attain a high degree of material comfort, the rewards of a religious career are primarily personal and spiritual.

When it comes to career growth, members of the clergy follow several different patterns. Often starting as a junior member of the clergy in a large church or temple, most hope to eventually head their own religious institution. Some will move ahead by advancing to minister to larger congregations; others are satisfied with blooming where they are planted, and they put all their efforts into building up the church they already head. Still others are called to be missionaries, in this country or abroad. A small number with more administrative leanings work in the headquarters of the larger denominations.

Some lay people also become religious workers. They usually work in an administrative capacity, coordinating activities of a congregation or school. In some positions, offering counsel and guidance is an important part of the work.

The jobs described here concern clergy in the three largest faiths in the United States, although there are also promising positions with other faiths. Information should be obtained directly from leaders of the respective groups.

PROTESTANT MINISTERS

Duties and Responsibilities

Leading souls to the Lord, Jesus Christ, providing spiritual leadership and offering counsel to people in need is a gratifying way to spend one's life, and those who choose to become ministers experience it.

The exact practices of Protestant ministers vary from denomination to denomination, but they all bear the same basic responsibilities.

They conduct worship services and administer rites of the Church, such as baptism and marriage, and for some, confirmation and holy communion. They write and deliver sermons and give religious instruction. They also conduct funerals, visit the sick, aged, and handicapped, and offer personal counsel to those who seek it. Ministers often create programs geared to specific groups within the congregation, such as young people, to keep the Church a meaningful part of modern day-to-day life. Many write articles, give speeches, and are active in their communities.

Those who serve small congregations generally work directly with parishioners. Those serving larger congregations have greater administrative responsibilities and may spend considerable time working with committees, church officers, and staff. They may be aided by one or more associates or assistants who assume responsibility for specific areas, such as the Sunday school.

Some ministers work as chaplains in hospitals, universities, correctional institutions, and the armed forces.

Ministers often work long and irregular hours. Most are married, and often their spouses actively assist them in their ministry, by teaching classes, leading music in the worship service, or preaching themselves, for example. Ministers are also on call for problems or emergencies that affect members of their church. In some denominations, they are subject to reassignment to a new pastorate every few years.

Men and women entering the clergy often begin their careers as pastors of small congregations or as assistant pastors in large churches. Some take jobs in parishes, working in youth counseling, family relations, or welfare programs, or as teachers in religious schools or organizations, until they have the opportunity to have their own congregation.

Earnings and Opportunities

Over 230,000 people are currently working as Protestant ministers, and the outlook is good. As the Bible says, "The harvest is great but the workers are few." Earnings: $12,500 to $44,000 and up.

Training and Qualifications

A burning desire to help save souls, a desire to first serve the Lord and then to serve others, and the ability to give of oneself are the best foundation for a life in the ministry.

Educational requirements vary by denomination. Many require a master of divinity degree from a three-year theological school or seminary, for which a bachelor's degree is a prerequisite. Candidates are usually ordained after graduation from the seminary.

Denominations that do not require seminary training ordain clergy at various times. For example, an Evangelical minister may be ordained with only a high school education.

RABBIS

Duties and Responsibilities

Rabbis serve as spiritual leaders, practical counselors, teachers and interpreters of Jewish law and tradition.

Rabbis may serve either Orthodox, Conservative, Reform, or Reconstructionist congregations. While all congregations preserve the essence of Jewish religious worship, they differ in the extent to which they follow the traditional forms of worship and Jewish laws.

Rabbis have the same basic responsibilities as other clergy members. They conduct religious services and deliver sermons on the Sabbath and on religious holidays; they conduct weddings and funeral services, visit the sick and help the poor, as well as supervising educational programs and taking an active part in community affairs.

Rabbis function independently and have a great deal of authority. They report directly to the board of trustees of the congregation they serve. Those who serve large congregations spend a considerable amount of time on administrative duties. They work with staff and with committees made up of members of the congregation. Large synagogues frequently have associate or assistant rabbis, many of whom serve as educational directors.

Rabbis also work as chaplains in the military, in hospitals, or in other institutions. Others work for one of the many Jewish community service agencies. Many are employed in colleges and universities.

Rabbis work long and irregular hours and are on call to visit the sick or help members of the congregation as needed. Community and educational activities may also demand extra time.

Newly ordained rabbis usually begin as leaders of small congregations, assistants to experienced rabbis, directors of B'Nai Brith/Hillel organizations on college campuses, teachers in seminaries and other educational institutions, or as chaplains in the armed forces.

Earnings and Opportunities

Over 3,000 people currently serve as rabbis, and the outlook for employment varies among the four branches of Judaism. It is most favorable for those in the Conservative, Re-

form, and Reconstructionist branches. Earnings: $20,000 to $50,000 and up.

Training and Qualifications

Deep religious commitment, a desire to serve the Jewish people, sensitivity to the needs of others, and leadership ability are good qualities for those who want to become rabbis.

To become eligible for ordination, students must complete seminary training. Entrance requirements vary, but all require applicants to have a college degree, high GRE scores and demonstrate maturity and intellectual capacity.

For Further Details

The Jewish Theological Seminary of America, 3080 Broadway, New York, NY 10027 (Conservative). The Rabbi Isaac Elchanan Theological Seminary, 2540 Amsterdam Ave., New York, NY 10033 (Orthodox). Hebrew Union College–Jewish Institute of Religion, whose three campuses are located at 1 W. 4th St., New York, NY 10012; at 3101 Clifton Ave., Cincinnati, OH 45220; and at 3077 University Mall, Los Angeles, CA 90007 (Reform). Reconstructionist Rabbinical College, 2308-10 N. Broad St., Philadelphia, PA 19132.

ROMAN CATHOLIC PRIESTS

Duties and Responsibilities

Moral and spiritual leadership, education in the doctrines of the Church, and counseling for those who desire it are the basic responsibilities of the Roman Catholic priest.

Priests fall into two main categories: diocesan and religious. Both are ordained with the same powers, but their ways of life and the work to which they are assigned can vary greatly.

Diocesan priests generally work in parishes assigned to them by the bishop of their diocese. Their work is much the same as any member of the clergy. They deliver sermons,

administer the sacraments, and conduct funeral services. They may preside over daily Mass and make regular visits to the sick and the poor. Most have set hours for hearing confessions. Many priests direct and serve on church committees, do civic and charitable work, and assist in community projects.

Religious priests generally work as members of an order such as the Jesuits, Dominicans, or Franciscans. They may lead a quiet life of prayer, or have special assignments such as teaching or doing missionary work.

Both religious and diocesan priests may hold teaching and administrative posts in Catholic seminaries, colleges, universities, and high schools. Members of religious orders do most of the missionary work conducted by the Catholic Church here and abroad.

Priests work long, irregular hours. They take a vow of celibacy and may not marry. Those assigned to be missionaries in foreign countries must adapt themselves to different cultures, sometimes under very difficult conditions.

The first assignment of a newly ordained diocesan priest is generally that of assistant pastor or curate. There are excellent opportunities to utilize your skills and abilities.

Earnings and Opportunities

Over 58,000 people currently serve as priests, and the outlook for employment is excellent, since the recent number of newly ordained priests has been insufficient for the number of openings. Priests generally have major expenses covered by the Church, and, based on limited information, spending money of diocesan priests ranges from about $2,000 to $4,000 a year. Priests who perform secular jobs for the Church, such as teaching, usually receive a smaller salary than a lay person would receive for the same work. Religious priests take a vow of poverty and are supported by their order.

Training and Qualifications

A deep commitment to serving the Lord, Jesus Christ, and sensitivity to others are necessary qualities for priests.

Preparation for the priesthood generally consists of eight years of study beyond high school. Preparatory study may begin the first year of high school, at the college level, or in theological seminaries after college graduation. Priests are encouraged by the Church to continue their studies after ordination, and postgraduate work in theology is offered at a number of Catholic universities. Many priests do graduate work in fields such as sociology or psychology.

Careers in Computers

A few years ago, computers and data processing were the special province of highly trained, technology-oriented individuals. But this is no longer true. When *Time* magazine puts a computer on its cover and labels it "Machine of the Year," you know times have changed.

Data processing—the compilation, analysis, and sorting of information through computer technology—is revolutionizing the way businesses and government handle operations. What began as an awkward, time-consuming system has been reduced to microchips and microseconds, and job growth and opportunity is on an exciting rise that shows no signs of stopping in this decade or the next.

Robotics will contribute greatly to this growth. In a new national study, the W. E. Upjohn Institute for Employment Research in Kalamazoo, Michigan, predicts that about 70,000 people will be involved in making, selling, and maintaining robots by 1990, up from about 5,000 today. The report sees a demand for 25,000 technicians, and 9,000 engineers, many employed by robot users to design automated manufacturing systems.

Within the field, the area of perhaps greatest expansion will be programming. For every application of the computer, a complex set of instructions, or software, must be written by someone who knows how to tell the machine what to do. Opportunities are burgeoning in many areas of both work and play, and the demand for programmers will only increase in business and industry, in all kinds of specialized areas.

Positions in computer operation range from simple data entry jobs to more sophisticated equipment operators. And as these systems get more and more use, there will be a growing need for skilled computer maintenance technicians to keep them running. Still others will be busy designing and planning new computer hardware (equipment) for the sophisticated software written by the programmers.

Perhaps because of the specialized and competitive nature of this booming field, the pay and perks at high-tech firms are quite good. One study indicates that 67 percent of companies use stock plans as incentives, which is more than double the rate found in industry generally. Front-end bonuses to recruits are popular, as are elaborate profit-sharing plans. Some companies even offer cash bonuses to workers who meet or beat deadlines.

While larger businesses and government have had computer operations for many years, the introduction of microchips has spawned a new generation of "micro" and "mini" computers in addition to the much-publicized home or personal computers. This recent growth has opened up computer accessibility to thousands and thousands of small businesses, schools, and other organizations. As these businesses become more sophisticated, it means more computers will be used in business management, accounting, inventory, sales forecasting, and countless other specialties. That, in turn, will call for more computer programmers, data entry operators, service technicians, and systems analysts. And many people in related fields, such as mathematicians, statisticians, and electronics technicians, will find new opportunities for employment.

As computers continue to be used in schools, and as America's young people become more computer-oriented, teaching and instruction will flourish too.

COMPUTER ENGINEERS

Duties and Responsibilities

While almost all engineers use computers in their work, some are specifically employed to design computers and/or study how they can best be used in various fields. These workers come from a variety of engineering backgrounds, with an emphasis on electrical, electronic, mechanical, and industrial engineering. They work with non-engineering members of a team that includes systems people, software specialists, and often scientists. Depending on the field for which the computer is being designed, other engineers, ranging from civil to petroleum engineers, may also be involved.

As a team, these workers do all that is necessary to build the optimum type of computer hardware for the software needed. Engineers bring their expertise to the mechanics of the design process as well as to the way the system is to be applied.

Computer applications engineers specialize in how a computer can be applied in various situations. Their work involves formulating mathematical models of systems and setting up controls in order to see that a particular computer system is capable of solving certain scientific and engineering problems. Part of their job often involves preparing technical reports describing step-by-step solutions to problems and developing new techniques for solving the problems.

Engineering managers are needed in the field and come from a variety of engineering backgrounds. Knowledge of computers is vital, as is strong management expertise and commitment, in order to head a team responsible for the design and development of the mechanical/electronic part of a computer.

Since computers can greatly simplify work involving mathematical and scientific thinking, they are perfect for engineers, who must constantly apply the theories and principles of science and mathematics to solve practical technical problems. For that reason, almost all engineers find themselves working with computers regardless of what their specific job entails.

Computer engineers are employed throughout government, and in businesses as varied as banks, telecommunications companies, and industrial plants.

Earnings and Opportunities

Outlook for employment is extremely strong throughout the 1980s. A shortage of about 113,000 computer science and electrical engineers is anticipated over the next five years, according to a survey conducted by the American Electronics Association. The industry expects to see a 46 percent increase in total employment through 1987. Salaries range from $35,000 to $60,000 or more.

Training and Qualifications

Mathematical ability, creativity, and an analytical mind are helpful qualities for computer engineers.

Since those who work in the field come to it from various specialties, candidates should assess their own skills and natural leanings and then select an engineering specialty such as electrical, mechanical, or electronic engineering for their field of study. They can then bring those talents and skills to the computer field.

COMPUTER OPERATORS

Duties and Responsibilities

Certainly computers are the wave of the future, and there will always be a need for people who can enter data and instructions, operate the equipment, and retrieve the results accurately and efficiently.

Information is put into a computer in a variety of ways. Most newer systems are capable of remote data entry, which is when the user sits at a regular computer terminal with a typewriter keyboard and an electronic display screen and enters information directly into the computer. Increasingly, data enter the computer at the source of the transaction being recorded. For example, inventory of grocery store items is taken right at the supermarket checkout line as the clerk records your purchase; and your airplane reservation may be entered into the computer by the person who sells you your ticket.

Console operators examine the programmer's instructions for processing the input and then make sure the computer has been properly loaded with the correct cards, magnetic tapes, or disks. Then they start the computer, carefully monitoring it to make sure that the material goes through correctly. If there is a problem, the operators may be able to solve it or will summon help.

Frequently the information on disks, magnetic tape, or punched cards is kept for future use, and *tape librarians* are responsible for classifying and cataloging this material.

Computer operating personnel are employed in almost every industry, but most work in manufacturing firms, wholesale and retail trade establishments, and consulting firms that provide data processing services for clients. Some work for insurance companies, banks, and government agencies.

Since many organizations use their computers twenty-four hours a day, some operators work evenings or night shifts. Increasingly, some operators are able to work at home with the new integrated office systems that allow managers to supervise and communicate constantly with workers who are not on site. (Productivity is way up, evidently as a result of this new work style!)

With additional training, data entry clerks can be promoted to console operators. Others may be promoted to supervisor. Console operators may also be promoted to supervisory positions, and through on-the-job experience and additional training some console operators advance to jobs as programmers.

Earnings and Opportunities

Over 558,000 people work as computer operating personnel, and employment opportunities are excellent. In fact, the number of jobs is expected to increase 27 percent in the next ten years. Earnings range from $10,200 to $34,000 and up for supervisory positions.

Training and Qualifications

For the console operator, independent problem-solving capability and the ability to reason logically are important. Data entry clerks and auxiliary equipment operators should be fast and accurate on the machinery and capable of working as part of a team.

Most employers require a high school education, and many prefer to hire console operators who have some junior college training in

For Further Details

For more information, see "Careers in Engineering" as well as the engineering field of specialty.

data processing. Many test applicants for their aptitude for computer work.

Computer operating training is available at many high schools, vocational schools, business schools, junior and community colleges, as well as computer schools.

Beginners are usually trained on the job. Auxiliary equipment operators can learn in a few weeks, but console operators require several months of training.

For Further Details

American Federation of Information Processing Societies, 1815 N. Lynn St., Arlington, VA 22209.

COMPUTER SERVICE TECHNICIANS

Duties and Responsibilities

Computers are becoming a part of many aspects of our lives—from the computer used to produce a paycheck to the cash machine we use at the bank. With our increasing dependence on this equipment comes a growing need for computer service technicians (also called field engineers or customer engineers) responsible for maintaining and repairing it.

Most systems are serviced at regular intervals when the mechanical and electromechanical parts of the central system, the remote terminals, and the high-speed printers are routinely adjusted, oiled, and cleaned. Technicians also regularly check the electronic equipment for loose connections and defective components or circuits.

Breakdowns can occur anywhere in the system—in the central processing unit, a reader, a printer, a remote terminal, or in the cables or data communications hookups that connect these machines. When the equipment does break down, the technician must quickly find the cause of the problem and make repairs. Determining the source of the malfunction can be a challenging and painstaking task and requires a logical, analytical mind as well as technical knowledge.

Computer technicians often help install new equipment. They lay cables, hook up electrical connections between machines, and thoroughly test the new equipment.

Computer technicians must keep up to date on technical information and revised maintenance procedures issued periodically by computer manufacturers. Some technicians specialize in a particular computer model or system or even in a certain type of repair.

Most technicians are employed by firms that provide maintenance services for a fee and by manufacturers of computer equipment. A small number are employed directly by organizations that have large computer systems.

Computers generally operate around the clock, and breakdowns can be expensive. For that reason, technicians may need to make emergency calls at any time of the day or night.

Advancement may consist of becoming a specialist or a troubleshooter assigned to help other technicians diagnose difficult problems. It may mean advancing to work with engineers in designing equipment and developing new maintenance procedures. Those with leadership ability may become supervisors or service managers. Others may qualify for jobs in equipment sales, programming, or management.

Earnings and Opportunities

Over 83,000 people are employed as computer service technicians, and the outlook for employment is one of the best in any field—the number of jobs is expected to increase by 97 percent by 1995. Earnings begin at $19,500 to $23,000 at the entry level, and range from $28,000 to $48,000 and up for experienced workers.

Training and Qualifications

Mechanical aptitude, patience, and analytical ability are key qualities for technicians, as are good vision and normal color perception for working with small parts and color-coded wiring.

Most employers require applicants for trainee jobs to have one to two years of post–high school training in basic electronics or electrical engineering. This training is available in vocational schools, the armed forces, colleges, and junior colleges.

Trainees usually attend company training centers for three to six months, and then generally complete six months to two years of on-the-job training.

For Further Details

Contact the personnel departments of computer manufacturers and computer maintenance firms in your area, or for information about schools offering training write: U.S. Office of Education, Division of Vocational/Technical Education, Washington, DC 20202. Or: Computer and Business Equipment Manufacturer's Association, 1828 L Street N.W., Washington, DC 20036.

ELECTRONIC AND MATHEMATICAL TECHNICIANS

Duties and Responsibilities

While scientists and engineers are experts at developing theoretical solutions to problems, much of the credit for the completion of this type of work must be given to the technicians whose job it is to apply that theoretical knowledge to actual situations. Two important categories are electronic and mathematical technicians.

In research and development, technicians set up experiments and calculate the results. They may also help to develop experimental equipment and models by making drawings and sketches and sometimes doing routine design work.

In production, they usually follow the plans given them by engineers and scientists. They may prepare specifications for materials, devise tests to ensure product quality, or study ways to improve the efficiency of an operation. They often supervise production workers to make sure all goes according to plan.

As sales workers or field representatives for manufacturers, technicians give advice on installation and maintenance of complex machinery and may write specifications and technical manuals.

Most technicians use calculators, computers, and technical handbooks in their jobs. Many also use complex electronic and mechanical instruments, experimental laboratory equipment, and drafting tools.

Specifically, electronic technicians develop, manufacture, and service electronic equipment and systems. The equipment they work on ranges from radio, radar, sonar, and television to industrial and medical measuring or control devices, navigational equipment, and computers. Because the field is so broad, technicians often specialize in just one area.

When working in design, production, or customer service, electronic technicians use sophisticated measuring and diagnostic devices to test, adjust, and repair equipment.

Mathematical technicians are especially likely to use computers. They work with scientific and engineering personnel to solve technological problems encountered in research and development and other areas. They apply standardized mathematical formulas to raw data to help translate these data into usable equations, graphs, and other forms.

Technicians usually start as trainees and gain responsibility as they gain experience. They may eventually move into senior or supervisory positions.

Earnings and Opportunities

Over 885,000 people work in the overall category of such technicians, and employment opportunities are excellent. The number of electronic technicians is expected to rise 61 percent in the next decade. Salaries range from $17,500 to $32,000 and above.

Training and Qualifications

An aptitude for math and science, manual dexterity, and the ability to do detailed technical work accurately are key qualities for technicians. The ability to work independently and to contribute to a team can be important.

Most employers prefer applicants who have completed specialized technical training, preferably programs in which the students gain practical work experience. These programs are available at technical institutes, junior and community colleges, extension divisions of universities, and vo-tech and correspondence schools.

For Further Details

Engineers Council for Professional Development, 345 E. 47th St., New York, NY 10017. National Association of Trade and Technical Schools, 2021 K St., N.W., Washington, DC 20006. National Home Study Council, 1601 18th St., N.W., Washington, DC 20009.

MATHEMATICIANS

Duties and Responsibilities

As a tool, mathematics is essential for understanding and expressing ideas in natural and social sciences. Mathemeticians not only study mathematics, but they use it to solve practical business or scientific problems.

Mathematical work generally falls into two broad classes: theoretical and applied.

Theoretical mathematicians advance the field by developing new principles and establishing new relationships among existing principles. They seek to increase basic knowledge of mathematical science, and their advances have been vital in producing many scientific and engineering achievements. For example, in 1854 Bernhard Reimann invented a seemingly impractical non-Euclidian geometry. However, it was to eventually become part of Albert Einstein's theory of relativity, and of course, years later, this theory contributed to the creation of atomic power.

Applied mathematicians use mathematics to develop theories, techniques, and approaches to solving practical problems in business, government, engineering, and the natural and social sciences. Their work ranges from analysis of the mathematical aspects of launching communications satellites to studies of the effects of new drugs on disease.

Almost three out of every four mathematicians work in colleges and universities. Most teach, but some work in research and development. Those who work in private industry and government are mainly employed by the communications, chemical, aircraft, and computer industries.

Earnings and Opportunities

About 40,000 people are employed as mathematicians, and the rate of growth in employment is expected to be above average, with a 28 percent increase in jobs in the coming decade. And opportunities for those with Ph.D. degrees who would like to teach at the graduate level is excellent. Because corporations siphon off many Ph.D. students before they gain their degrees, the American Assembly of Collegiate Schools of Business predicts seventeen openings for every Ph.D. candidate in 1985. Earnings range from $17,200 to $48,000.

Training and Qualifications

Good reasoning ability, persistence, communications skills, and the ability to apply basic principles to new types of problems are important to the mathematician. Knowledge of computer programming is now important as well, since most complex computations are done by computer.

In industry and government, a bachelor's degree may prepare applicants for jobs as assistants or in related fields such as computer science. However, most employers require an advanced degree.

In most four-year colleges and universities,

the Ph.D. degree is necessary for full faculty status. A master's degree is adequate for teaching in most two-year colleges and technical institutes.

For Further Details

American Mathematical Society, P.O. Box 6248, Providence, RI 02940. Mathematical Association of America, 1529 18th St., N.W., Washington, DC 20036. Society for Industrial and Applied Mathematics, 1405 Architects Building, 117 S. 17th St., Philadelphia, PA 19103.

PROGRAMMERS

Duties and Responsibilities

If you've ever had the opportunity to work on a computer, you have probably marveled at how "smart" these machines can be. It's difficult to remember that the computer is really no smarter than its programmer—the person whose task it is to write detailed instructions, called programs, that provide the machine with a step-by-step process for organizing data, solving a problem, or performing some other task.

Programs vary according to the problem to be solved. For example, the steps taken by a computer that keeps track of a retail store inventory are very different from the ones taken by a computer that helps to fly a 747. Programmers usually work from descriptions prepared by *systems analysts* (though sometimes a programmer may perform analyst duties as well), who study the task to be performed and list the general steps the computer will need to follow, such as retrieving data stored in another computer, organizing the material in a certain way, or performing certain calculations. An *applications programmer* then writes the specific program by breaking each step into a series of coded instructions using one of the languages developed especially for the computer. A programmer developing instructions for billing customers, for instance, would first tell the computer how to obtain old balances, locate new charges, calculate finance charges, and deduct payments before determining a customer's bill.

Next, the program must be tested to be sure that the computer will consistently perform the task correctly. If errors do occur during a test run, then the programmer rechecks and changes the program as needed. This is called "debugging." Finally, an instruction sheet is prepared for the computer operator who will run the program.

Systems programmers are responsible for maintaining the general instructions (the software) that control the operation of the entire computer system. Because of their knowledge of operating systems, systems programmers often help applications programmers determine the source of problems that may occur with their programs.

Most programmers are employed by manufacturing firms, data processing service organizations, government agencies, and insurance companies. Systems programmers usually work in research organizations, computer manufacturing firms, and large computer centers.

Prospects for advancement are excellent as the need for managerial help continues to grow.

Earnings and Opportunities

Over 228,000 people are employed as computer programmers, and the outlook for employment is excellent. The number of programming jobs is expected to increase a full 77 percent by 1995. Earnings: $22,500 to $50,000 and up.

Training and Qualifications

Being able to think logically and to perform exacting analytical work are important qualities for programmers. Patience, persistence, accuracy, and ingenuity are also vital in problem solving.

Most programmers are college graduates; others have taken special courses in computer programming to supplement work experience in fields such as accounting or inventory control.

Employers using computers for scientific or engineering applications prefer college graduates who have degrees in computer or information science, mathematics, engineering, or the physical sciences. Graduate degrees are required for some jobs.

For Further Details

American Federation of Information Processing Societies, 1815 N. Lynn St., Arlington, VA 22209.

STATISTICIANS

Duties and Responsibilities

From sales forecasts and population figures to the number of homes watching a particular television show on any given night, statistics have become an increasingly important part of our daily lives. They keep us informed as a society and can even help us understand the characteristics of our world and the people in it.

Statisticians are the people who devise ways to obtain the figures, oversee the research, and interpret the numerical results of surveys and experiments once they are in. What they study, of course, depends on where they are employed; and statisticians may apply their knowledge and skills to economics, politics, human behavior, natural sciences, or engineering. Statistical techniques may be used to predict population growth or economic conditions, develop quality control tests for manufactured products, or help business managers and government officials make decisions and evaluate the results of new programs.

Sometimes statisticians use a small sampling of people to study a certain piece of information rather than studying the entire group affected. Television rating services, for example, record data from only a few thousand families rather than all viewers in order to determine the size of the total audience. It is the job of the statistician to decide where and how to get the information, choose the size of the sampling, and develop a survey or a reporting form that will provide accurate figures. They also prepare instructions for workers who will tabulate the returns.

Over half of all statisticians can be found in private industry, mainly in manufacturing, business, finance, and insurance companies. About one-third work for federal, state, or local governments. Others work in colleges and universities and nonprofit organizations.

As they gain experience, statisticians may advance to positions of greater technical and supervisory responsibility. Opportunities for advancement are best for those with advanced degrees.

Earnings and Opportunities

About 26,500 people work as statisticians, and employment prospects are excellent as the growing use of computers in all fields and the increasing complexity of tax and pension laws contribute to the growing need. The National Science Foundation has projected a shortage of 11,000 statisticians between 1978–90, and overall employment is expected to increase 28 percent in the next decade. Earnings range from $14,500 to $48,000.

Training and Qualifications

Reasoning ability, communications skills, persistence, and the ability to solve new problems are important qualities for statisticians.

For some entry-level jobs, employers will hire applicants with bachelors' degrees, and they may prefer those who have a major in statistics or mathematics. Other employers look for a major in an applied field, such as economics or a natural science, with a minor in statistics. In addition, courses in computer uses and techniques are highly recommended.

For college and university teaching as well as for higher level jobs in government and industry, an advanced degree in mathematics or statistics is necessary.

For Further Details

American Statistical Association, 806 15th St., N.W., Washington, DC 20005. Institute of Mathematical Statistics, Department of Statistics and Probability, Michigan State University, East Lansing, MI 48824.

SYSTEMS ANALYSTS

Duties and Responsibilities

More and more problem solving of the future is going to be done by computer, and systems analysts, who devise efficient methods for processing the data needed to solve specific problems, will be in great demand in high-tech fields ranging from telecommunications to scientific research. Their tasks range from monitoring nuclear fission in a power plant to forecasting sales for an automobile manufacturer. Because the work is so varied and complex, systems analysts usually specialize in either business or scientific applications.

Analysts generally see a job through from start to finish. They first analyze a problem using various techniques such as cost accounting, sampling, and mathematical model building, and then devise a new system that will solve it. Once they hit upon one they feel will work, they must then prepare charts and diagrams and develop ways to describe the operation in layman's terms so that managers or clients will understand the system and how the process is to be accomplished. Analysts may also be responsible for preparing a cost-benefit analysis.

If the system is approved, analysts translate the requirements of the system into the capabilities of the computer. They also prepare specifications for programmers to follow, and they work with them to "debug" or eliminate errors from the system.

Most systems analysts work for manufacturing firms, government agencies, wholesale businesses, and data processing service organizations. Others are employed in large numbers by banks and insurance companies.

Systems analysts may work independently; or on major projects they may be part of a team.

Workers who begin as junior systems analysts may be promoted to senior or lead systems analysts after gaining several years of experience. Those who show leadership ability can also advance to jobs as managers of systems analysis or data processing departments.

Earnings and Opportunities

Over 205,000 people are employed as systems analysts, and job prospects are excellent, with a projected increase in employment of 85 percent by 1995. Salaries range from $22,500 to $28,500 for entry-level analysts, and go to $58,000 and up for those with experience.

Training and Qualifications

Logical reasoning, problem-solving ability, and the capacity to concentrate on details are assets to the systems analyst. Being able to communicate technical information to people who have no background in computer programming is also helpful.

Because of the number of fields in which systems analysts are employed, there are several ways to prepare for these jobs. In general, employers look for applicants who are college graduates. For work in a business environment, employers prefer those who have a background in accounting, business management, or economics. In scientifically oriented organizations, workers with a background in physical sciences, mathematics, or engineering are preferred. A growing number of employers are seeking those who have a degree in computer science or whose course work included heavy exposure to computer programming.

Prior work experience can also be important. Nearly half of all systems analysts have transferred from other positions, especially that of computer programmer.

For Further Details

American Federation of Information Processing Societies, 1899 Preston White Dr., Reston, VA 22091. Association for Systems Management, 24587 Bagley Rd., Cleveland, OH 44138.

Careers in Counseling

Helping people better understand themselves and their problems and guiding them toward possible solutions is the work of counselors, and there are several different areas of this field in which one can specialize.

Psychologists and social workers provide a valuable and much needed service, counseling people with personal problems that range from the mild to the severe. Working with individuals in group situations or privately, they help those who find themselves unable to cope with the pressures of modern day society. Alcohol and drug abuse as well as marital and family difficulties are some of the most common problems. Counselors also work with people who have attempted suicide and those who have been involved in cases of child abuse, rape, or family violence.

Rehabilitation counselors specialize in aiding emotionally or physically handicapped people in their efforts to lead as normal lives as possible.

Career and employment counselors are a fast-growing segment of the counseling field.

As this book indicates, career choices are increasing dramatically, and so too is the need for counselors who can help job seekers choose and prepare for certain careers. Counselors are needed at the high school and college level to help students select the appropriate education or vocational training necessary for specific career goals. Professional employment counselors work with a wide variety of job seekers, from recent high school grads and housewives returning to work to college graduates and the executive in the midst of a career change. Counselors are also important to businesses, since they can provide them with appropriately qualified workers as well as up-to-date information such as the prevailing wage rates for certain skills.

Counseling will continue to be an important part of American life as it helps smooth the way for individuals in their pursuit of a more rewarding life. At the same time, it will provide excellent jobs and career paths for those who are interested in counseling others.

SCHOOL GUIDANCE COUNSELORS AND CAREER PLANNING AND PLACEMENT COUNSELORS

Duties and Responsibilities

Whether's it's helping a high school student cope with a problem at home or guiding a college senior as he or she makes a career decision, counselors play an important role for today's students. They offer advice, expertise, and a willing ear to children and young adults whose problems or decisions are too difficult to be handled alone.

School counselors are primarily employed in public and private secondary schools, though some also work at the elementary level. Often working one-to-one with students, they devote time to the social, behavioral, personal, and career planning concerns of young people. In addition to talking to the students, counselors may consult with parents, teachers, or the school nurse or psychologist when appropriate. In some cases, they may refer students to other specialists within the school system or the community.

Counselors also deal with problems affecting the school as a whole. If drug abuse is widespread, for example, a counselor may set up group counseling and education sessions to make students aware of the dangers of drugs.

For students who are interested in furthering their education they provide information and advice on careers, colleges, scholarships, student loans, vocational training, part-time work, getting a job, and much more.

Those who work in elementary schools may counsel children and guide teachers on how to help individual students make the most of their abilities. They may help teachers in evaluating learning difficulties; sometimes they can spot the underlying cause of a problem, as when a family crisis is causing difficulties at school. Observation of classroom activity is a prime method of gathering clues about this age group.

Some counselors advance by moving to a larger school, becoming director or supervisor of counseling or guidance, or, with further education, becoming a college counselor, education counselor, vocational psychologist, or school administrator.

Career planning and placement counselors help students and alumni in all phases of career planning and job search. They may work alone or as part of a staff, and their task begins with helping to identify suitable fields of work. Once a choice has been made by a student, counselors may assist in resume writing and offer guidance in the job search. Counselors are also responsible for arranging for recruiter visits and keeping in touch with the business community.

They usually meet with students one-to-one, but it is also common practice to offer "career clinics" on topics such as resume writing and job hunting. All counselors maintain a library of career guidance and recruitment information.

Counselors must keep abreast of the job market, including salary information, training requirements, and job prospects.

Those at smaller two-year or community colleges may also advise administrators on curriculum and course content, which might help students be better prepared for the labor market. Some also teach.

They may advance to assistant director or director of career planning and placement, director of student personnel services, or other high-level administrative positions.

Earnings and Opportunities

Over 53,000 people work as school counselors, and approximately 5,000 are employed as college placement counselors. Little or no growth is expected in either field, though there will always be a need for workers because of job turnover. Earnings: $14,600 to $49,000.

Training and Qualifications

Respect and concern for young people, an open mind, and the ability to inspire confidence and trust are good qualities for counselors.

For years, most states required that school counselors have both counseling and teaching certificates. However, a growing number no longer require the teaching certificate, making the master's degree in counseling the primary credential needed in most places.

For college positions, applicants should have a master's degree in counseling in college student personnel work or in a behavioral science. Some enter the field after gaining a broad background in business, industry, government, or education.

For Further Details

American Personnel and Guidance Association, 2 Skyline Place, Suite 400, 5203 Leesburg Pike, Falls Church, VA 22041. The College Placement Council, Inc., P.O. Box 2263, Bethlehem, PA 18001.

PROFESSIONAL EMPLOYMENT COUNSELORS

Duties and Responsibilities

We spend half our waking hours working, so it is not surprising that our jobs are very important to us. And it's small wonder that we care so much about having the *right* job. This is, of course, where professional employment counselors (PEC's) come in—interviewing, counseling, and guiding individuals toward the right career path.

PEC's are also known as staffing specialists, recruiters, employment consultants, or personnel counselors. Their training and experience allow them to ascertain quickly what people have done, what they want to do, and ultimately what they are qualified to do based on job experience, education, and personal desire.

They spend a great deal of time searching out jobs and becoming familiar with the needs of hundreds of employers, both locally and nationwide. Those with real expertise may succeed in creating a job for the job seeker where none existed before. Some specialize, handling only salespeople or secretaries or engineers, for example.

Counselors often function as salespeople as well as advisers. For instance, an employer may need to be persuaded to pay more than he had intended to in order to find a candidate with a particular skill. Sometimes a job seeker and his spouse may have to be convinced that relocating is the best move for their future.

Counselors do research to locate certain types of jobs, write advertisements, keep records, set terms with companies and individuals, and collect fees. A great deal of the work is done by phone, with occasional personal visits to employers. Counselors frequently speak before business groups and high school and college students about the various aspects of jobs and job seeking.

Most counselors work for one of the approximately 12,000 private employment services throughout the country. Some firms employ fifty or more counselors, but most have staffs of under ten.

In large organizations, counselors can become senior counselors, training and supervisory personnel, department managers, branch managers, or area managers. Those who work for a franchised system may become field trainers, marketing consultants, and headquarters personnel. Some counselors start their own employment services.

Earnings and Opportunities

Over 50,000 people work as employment counselors, and employment is expected to double during the 1980s. Counselors are usually paid a base salary plus additional compensation based on sales. Earnings range from $10,000 to over $100,000, with the majority earning between $20,000 and $35,000.

Training and Qualifications

Most have worked in other fields prior to becoming counselors. Educational backgrounds range from high school graduates to Ph.D.'s, with most having at least two years of college.

Training is usually provided by the employer. Those who undergo special study and instruction through the National Association of Personnel Consultants may earn the designation of certified personnel counselor (CPC), a sign of achievement in the field.

For Further Details

National Association of Personnel Consultants, 1432 Duke St., Alexandria, VA 22314.

PSYCHOLOGISTS

Duties and Responsibilities

The mysteries of human behavior and the intricacies of the mind are the province of the psychologist, whose efforts to uncover the root causes of and solutions to people's problems inevitably lead to specialization.

Clinical psychology is by far the largest specialty. *Clinical psychologists* work with the mentally or emotionally disturbed and are generally employed by hospitals or clinics or maintain private practices. They provide psychotherapy or behavior modification programs for individuals or families. Sometimes they collaborate with physicians and other specialists in developing treatment programs. *Counseling psychologists* use interviewing and testing to advise people on how to deal with everyday problems ranging from the personal to the vocational. *Educational psychologists* design, develop, and evaluate educational programs. *School psychologists* work with students, helping to solve learning and social problems in school. *Industrial and organizational psychologists* apply psychological techniques to personnel and management problems in business. For example, an industrial psychologist may develop a training program or make recommendations about the working environment to increase productivity. *Engineering psychologists* work in factories and plants to develop and improve ways that workers use machines and industrial products. *Community psychologists* apply psychological knowledge to problems of urban and rural life. *Consumer psychologists* study the psychological factors that determine why people buy what they buy. *Health psychologists* counsel the public in health maintenance to help avoid serious emotional or physical illness.

Other specialties include *experimental psychologists,* who study behavior processes, including such research areas as motivation, learning and retention, and sensory and perceptual processes. They work with animals as well as humans. *Developmental psychologists* study the patterns and causes of behavioral change as people progress through life; some concentrate on certain periods such as infancy or old age. Other specialties include *personality psychologists, social psychologists, comparative psychologists,* and *physiological psychologists.*

In research, psychologists collect information and test its validity in order to develop theories. Research methods depend on the topic under study, but in general, psychologists use controlled laboratory experiments; performance, aptitude, and intelligence tests; observation, interviews, and questionnaires; and clinical studies or surveys.

The largest group of psychologists work in colleges and universities. Others work in health care facilities such as hospitals and rehabilitation centers; others are employed by the government and business; and many are self-employed.

Earnings and Opportunities

Over 106,000 people are employed as psychologists, and that number is expected to increase 33 percent in the next ten years, making the outlook for employment quite good. Income ranges from $29,000 to $80,000 and up.

Training and Qualifications

Sensitivity to others, emotional stability, patience, and perseverance are important qualities for psychologists.

A doctoral degree is required for employment as a psychologist. Either a Ph.D. or a Psy.D. (doctor of psychology) is acceptable.

People with masters' degrees in psychology can work as psychological assistants and may conduct research or administer and interpret tests working under the direction of psychologists. Some find jobs as school counselors.

For Further Details

American Psychological Association, Educational Affairs Office, 1200 17th St., N.W., Washington, DC 20036.

REHABILITATION COUNSELORS

Duties and Responsibilities

It is the job of a rehabilitation counselor to help the emotionally or physically handicapped person learn to lead as normal a life as possible. Perhaps its greatest reward is in the joy of helping a disabled person find a job or become more self-sufficient.

An increasing number of counselors specialize in a particular area of rehabilitation, such as working with paraplegics, the blind, deaf, mentally ill, retarded, or those who have been alcoholics or drug addicts.

The first step in the job of rehabilitation is to learn as much as possible about the client by interviewing his or her family, and conferring with medical personnel who can advise the counselor as to the kinds of tasks the client might be able to perform. Then the counselor begins a series of discussions with the client to explore and evaluate training and career options and to begin to develop a rehabilitation program.

Some programs begin with specialized training to help a disabled person live more independently. For example, this may involve teaching a blind person to work with a seeing-eye dog or read Braille.

A rehabilitation program generally includes training for a specific job, so counselors stay in touch with the business community to keep abreast of the types of workers needed by industry and the training required for various jobs. They also make an effort to publicize their programs so that industry will think of hiring the emotionally or physically disabled when openings occur.

Once training has been conducted and a placement made, the counselor often schedules follow-up meetings to be sure that all is going well. If problems have arisen, the counselor can help the employee and employer agree on adjustments that might be made.

More than a third of all counselors work in state and local rehabilitation agencies financed cooperatively with federal and state funds. Many work in Veterans Administration programs. Others are employed by rehabilitation centers, hospitals, special schools, and other public and private agencies with rehabilitation and job placement programs. Still others work in private industry, including insurance companies, manufacturing firms, and rehabilitation consulting firms.

Earnings and Opportunities

Over 25,000 people work as rehabilitation counselors, and the outlook for employment is quite good. Salaries range from $13,400 to $45,000.

Training and Qualifications

The ability to inspire, motivate, guide, and teach others is an important qualification for rehabilitation counselors. Patience and emotional stability in dealing with clients who may be discouraged or angry are also helpful.

Though some state agencies may hire applicants with bachelors' degrees in an appropriate field, a master's degree in rehabilitation counseling, counseling and guidance, or counseling psychology is generally considered the minimum educational requirement.

For Further Details

American Rehabilitation Counseling Association, 5999 Stevenson Ave., Alexandria, VA 22304. National Rehabilitation Counseling Association, Cary Building, Suite B-110, 8136 Old Keene Mill Rd., Springfield, VA 22152.

SOCIAL WORKERS

Duties and Responsibilities

Placing children in foster homes, working with juvenile delinquents, and assisting individuals and families whose lives are being destroyed by alcoholism, drug abuse, or illness —these are just a few of the jobs done by social workers, who, through counseling and referral, help individuals, families, and groups cope with their troubles.

Depending on the kind of problem and the resources available, social workers generally try to effect a solution using one of three approaches: *casework,* where they work directly with an individual and his or her family to assist with a specific problem; *group work,* where they plan and conduct activities for children, teenagers, adults, or other groups in community centers, hospitals, nursing homes, and correctional institutions; or through *community organization,* where workers help combat social problems by coordinating the efforts of political, civic, religious, business, or union groups.

Most social workers specialize. Some work primarily in family and child services, helping people cope with problems such as finding day care, learning about money management, or locating housing. Those who specialize in child welfare may advise mothers on child care or counsel children with difficulties. They may institute legal action to protect neglected ·or mistreated children, help unwed parents, and counsel couples about adoption. Social workers also work with probation and parole officers in helping parolees and ex-offenders re-enter society. Aging is a new area of specialization that is also attracting many social workers.

Two out of three social workers are employed in the public sector, mostly by state, county, or municipal governments. Those in the private sector usually work for voluntary nonprofit agencies, hospitals, nursing homes, and community and religious organizations. Some are employed in business and industry as industrial social workers. Others are in private practice.

Most social workers put in a forty-hour week, but many work evenings and weekends in order to match their schedules with those of the communities they serve. Many work part-time, particularly in private agencies.

Advancement for social workers consists of becoming supervisors, administrators, or directors. Some with advanced degrees go into teaching, research, or consulting.

Earnings and Opportunities

About 345,000 people are employed as social workers, and the employment outlook is very good. In the next decade it is estimated that the number of jobs for social workers will increase 21 percent. Salaries range from $13,500 to $29,000 and over $45,000 for executives.

Training and Qualifications

An understanding of human nature and the ability to be objective but caring when dealing with the problems of others are important qualities for social workers.

Minimum educational requirement is generally a bachelor's degree in social work, but the advanced degree is extremely important for advancement in the field.

Administrators generally have at least a master's degree and a background in social work, business or public administration, education, or health administration.

For teaching, an M.S.W. is required, and a doctorate is usually preferred.

For Further Details

Social Work Career Information Service, National Association of Social Workers, 7981 Eastern Ave., Silver Spring, MD 20910. Council on Social Work Education, 111 Eighth Ave., New York, NY 10017.

Careers in Education

While almost all of us went through a time in childhood when we wanted to become teachers, a surprising number of adults follow through on that dream, out of a sincere desire to teach and inspire others or because they enjoy the stimulation of an academic environment. Teaching is one of the largest occupations in the United States. More than 1.6 million people teach full- or part-time in kindergartens or elementary schools, and another 1.2 million teach in secondary schools. About 700,000 are college or university faculty members.

While little growth is expected in the teaching field during the 1980s except at the elementary school level, the field is so vast that some people will always be able to find jobs. Invariably, there are jobs available for people willing to teach in out-of-the-way spots, or in exceptionally difficult working environments. Those who want to accomplish their goals in a more traditional setting may have to look harder and apply a little creative thought to the problem.

Those who are more interested in the work environment than in teaching itself should read carefully through the descriptions of jobs connected with the administration of schools and colleges. Many of these positions combine an intellectually stimulating environment and the pleasure of working with young people with the challenge of seeing that a school or college is run in the best way possible.

Those who have their hearts set on teaching should remember that in addition to public and private elementary and secondary schools and colleges and universities, there are many other opportunities to use teaching skills. Some people offer instruction in preschool programs such as nursery schools and Head Start. Others work in business or vocational schools, teach adult education, or teach classes in art, dance, and music.

Training and human resource development in business are also attracting large numbers of former teachers who relish the opportunity to use their teaching skills in a business setting. Teaching everything from assertiveness to business writing and public speaking skills, they serve an important purpose and still enjoy the opportunity to do what they do best.

Others have started their own businesses, running everything from foreign language schools to exercise classes and seminars on how to make a career change. In addition, many tutor privately. If you have the skills and the motivation to teach and inspire others, chances are you'll be able to make use of them.

COLLEGE AND UNIVERSITY FACULTY

Duties and Responsibilities

Whether speaking to a large group of students in a lecture hall or sharing the give-and-take of a small seminar, faculty members are not just teachers—they are there to inspire and excite students to pursue the in-depth learning opportunities available to them in colleges and universities.

Faculty members are hired to be part of a specific department. A professor working in the history department may further narrow his specialty by teaching only the history of the United States after the Civil War. Or an English professor may teach a freshman composition class as well as a senior seminar in nineteenth-century English literature.

Faculty must suit their teaching methods to the subject, to the class size (seminar or lecture hall), and to the level of students. In subjects such as biology, engineering, or chemistry, instructors may work primarily in laboratories. Some have the help of teaching assistants, who may lead discussion sessions or grade exams. Closed-circuit television, tape recorders, computers, and other teaching aids are frequently used.

Faculty members are expected to keep up with developments in their fields by reading current literature, participating in professional activities, and conducting scholarly research. Publishing books or journal articles to build additional credentials is very important on some campuses.

In addition to time spent on class preparation, instruction, and research, faculty members work with student organizations and act as student advisers, work with the college administration, and serve the institution and the community in other ways as well. Department heads also have supervisory and administrative duties.

Almost one-third of all faculty members work part-time. Some of these are employed by more than one institution, while others are regularly employed in business or government.

Faculty members generally have flexible schedules, dividing their time among teaching, research, and administrative responsibilities. Vacation benefits are excellent. In addition to the summer months, when faculty may conduct research, prepare course materials, travel, consult, or pursue hobbies, they also have breaks during school vacations.

Earnings and Opportunities

Over 700,000 people are employed as faculty, and competition for future employment is expected to be keen. Salaries range from $17,500 to $48,000.

Training and Qualifications

The ability to inspire and encourage others, curiosity, and openness to new ideas are good qualities for those who pursue academic life. Being able to communicate well orally and in writing is also very important.

Most faculty members enter the profession as instructors and must have at least a master's degree. Some institutions will only consider applicants with doctorates.

Academic, administrative, or professional contributions also affect advancement opportunities. Research, publication, consulting work, and other forms of professional accomplishment all have a bearing on a person's ability to rise through the ranks.

For Further Details

American Association of University Professors, 1 Dupont Circle, N.W., Suite 500, Washington, DC 20036.

ELEMENTARY SCHOOL TEACHERS

Duties and Responsibilities

Introducing children to the basics of learning, helping them as they strive for early independence, and exposing them to the world beyond the family are some of the important responsibilities of elementary school teachers.

While teaching the basics of mathematics, language, science, and social studies is a vital part of their job, teachers also try to instill good study habits and create an excitement about learning that will stand the children in good stead throughout their school years.

Most elementary school teachers instruct a single group of children in several subjects. Currently, however, there is a trend toward specialization, and in some schools children may have one teacher for English and social studies and another for science and math. In addition to those who specialize by subject, some teachers specialize in order to meet the needs of certain groups, such as those with reading problems or speech difficulties.

Observing social development and health is also a teacher's responsibility. They watch how children interact with peers, what their attitudes are toward learning, and they watch for signs of learning difficulties that might indicate the need for remedial help or physical aids such as corrective glasses.

Today teachers may use everything from computers and videotapes to films and slides in order to enhance the classroom experience. Class trips, visiting speakers, and special projects are also an important part of learning.

Outside of the school day, teachers devote time to preparing lessons and grading papers. In addition, there are faculty meetings to go to, and at times most teachers must attend special workshops and classes in order to keep up to date on trends in education. Some teachers take on the supervision of extracurricular activities such as coaching team sports, sometimes for extra pay.

Many teachers work the traditional school year schedule with summers off. However, some school districts have converted to a year-round schedule where teachers may work for eight weeks, be on vacation for one week and have a five-week midwinter break.

Earnings and Opportunities

More than 1.6 million people work as kindergarten and elementary school teachers, and employment is expected to increase by 37 percent in the next ten years. Salaries range from $12,000 to $21,500.

Training and Qualifications

Prospective teachers need a bachelor's degree from an approved teacher training program. They must have completed student teaching and other education courses, and almost half the states require teachers to have graduate degrees. Specific information for your area is available from the state department of education or the local superintendent of schools.

For Further Details

National Education Association, 1201 16th St., N.W., Washington, DC 20036. National Council for Accreditation of Teacher Education, 1919 Pennsylvania Ave., N.W., Suite 202, Washington, DC 20006.

SECONDARY SCHOOL TEACHERS

Duties and Responsibilities

Working with teenagers—many of whom are questioning the world around them and delving into many issues as they prepare for adulthood—is the challenge that faces secondary school teachers.

At the high school level, teachers generally

have subject specialties, such as English, a foreign language, mathematics, social studies, or science. Within that specialty, they may teach several different types of classes. For example, the math teacher may teach algebra to one class, trigonometry to another, and geometry to a third. For each class, the teacher develops lesson plans, prepares and gives examinations, and arranges class projects and other activities.

In some cases, special arrangements may be needed for individual students. One student may need outside counseling or tutoring, while a particularly gifted youngster may take on additional work.

Teachers use a variety of instructional materials, including films, slides, and computer terminals. They also may arrange for outside speakers and trips to supplement the classroom work.

Some teachers give vocational education classes, such as business skills, welding, auto mechanics, or cosmetology, that train students for jobs after graduation.

In addition to their regular classes, secondary school teachers supervise study halls and homerooms, advise student groups, and attend meetings with parents and school personnel. Teachers also participate in workshops and college classes to keep up to date on their specialty and on current trends in education.

In addition to hours spent in the classroom, teachers spend time preparing lessons, grading papers, making reports, attending meetings, and supervising extracurricular activities. Some school districts have converted to a year-round schedule where teachers may work for eight weeks, be on vacation for one week, and have a five-week midwinter break.

With additional preparation and another certificate, experienced teachers may be able to move into positions as school librarians, reading specialists, curriculum specialists, or guidance counselors. For most teachers, however, advancement takes the form of a higher salary rather than a different job.

Earnings and Opportunities

About 1.2 million people work as secondary school teachers, and job opportunities are fair, with the number of jobs expected to increase 13 percent in the next decade. Salaries range from $15,200 to $48,000.

Training and Qualifications

The ability to work well with young people and to inspire enthusiasm for learning are good qualifications for teachers.

Prospective teachers need a bachelor's degree from an approved teacher training program with a prescribed number of credits in the subject they plan to teach. They must have completed student teaching and other education courses, and almost half the states require graduate degrees. Specific information is available from your state department of education or the local superintendent of schools.

For Further Details

National Education Association, 1201 16th St., N.W., Washington, DC 20036. National Council for Accreditation of Teacher Education, 1919 Pennsylvania Ave., N.W., Suite 202, Washington, DC 20006.

TEACHER AIDES

Duties and Responsibilities

The pleasure of being around young children is one of the bonuses of being a teacher aide, whose job is to assist in the classroom in whatever ways are necessary, so that the teacher is free to spend more time actually teaching.

Aides' responsibilities may vary greatly by school district. In some schools they work directly with the children. Under the supervision and guidance of the teacher, they may help students individually or in small groups. For example, an aide might help one child with arithmetic problems, listen to another give a book report or help a third learn to use the dictionary. Sometimes the teacher has an aide take charge of a special project for a group of students, such as preparing equipment for an art project.

In other schools, aides primarily handle routine non-teaching tasks. They may grade tests and papers, check homework, and keep health and attendance records. Secretarial duties such as typing, filing, and duplicating materials for the teacher may be part of the job. Sometimes they are expected to stock supplies, operate audiovisual equipment, and keep classroom equipment in order. They may also supervise students during lunch and recreation periods and during school bus loading.

Aides may also make special charts and other instructional materials, prepare bulletin boards, and work with art media.

In addition, they must also be familiar with the organization and operation of the school. It is good experience for those who aspire to become teachers, because aides learn the methods used to teach handwriting, reading, math, science, and other school subjects.

Teacher aides work both full- and part-time, and are mainly concentrated in the early grades. Recently, a substantial number have been hired to assist special education teachers who work with physically, mentally, or emotionally handicapped children.

Many school systems rely on volunteers who are willing to work as teacher aides. Some school districts provide release time so that aides may take additional courses and even-

tually earn bachelors' degrees and become certified as teachers.

Earnings and Opportunities

Over 415,000 people work as teacher aides, and the outlook for employment is quite good. A 28 percent increase in these jobs is projected for the next decade. Salaries run from $7,500 to $23,000.

Training and Qualifications

The ability to work well with young children, patience, and initiative, along with a willingness to follow the classroom teacher's directions, are important personal qualities for teacher aides.

Educational requirements vary widely. Some schools look for some college training, others require a high school diploma, while still others don't even require that. However, aides must have basic speaking and writing skills and be able to communicate effectively.

Teacher aides generally receive their training on the job. However, a number of two-year and community colleges offer associate degree programs that prepare graduates to work directly in the classroom as teacher aides.

For Further Details

American Federation of Teachers, 11 Dupont Circle, Washington, DC 20036. National Education Association, 1201 16th St., N.W., Washington, DC 20036.

COLLEGE PRESIDENTS

Duties and Responsibilities

At one time or another, almost every college student has wished he or she were the school president in order to change things to make the college a better place to live, study, work, and play.

And on certain days, most college presidents have probably wished they were students so they would not have to make some of

the tough decisions that face them: The faculty wants shorter hours, more teaching assistants, higher pay, and better facilities; the students want shorter hours, better teachers, nicer dorms, tastier food, fewer restrictions, and lower tuition; the board of trustees wants more funds raised, higher tuitions, and lower costs; and the president wants two more pairs of hands and a good night's sleep.

The position is challenging, rewarding, and

above all, busy. The president is expected to be everywhere. In addition to officiating at as many campus and community functions as possible and taking part in a great many fund-raising activities, he or she must also show the wisdom of Solomon in every decision made. Budgets, financing, fund raising, personnel, planning, construction, demolition, athletics, and the arts all must have presidential attention. Some presidents have large staffs and top-flight assistants to help them; those in smaller institutions do most of the work themselves.

College presidents spend much time in meetings with subordinates, committees, student groups, staff groups, boards of trustees, businesspeople, community organizations, and other educational bodies and associations.

The sheer size of some colleges and universities today makes the job of college president a demanding one. Many institutions are larger than a small city, with student bodies of 30,000 to 50,000 or more, staffs of thousands, physical plants worth hundreds of millions, and budgets in excess of $300 million.

Running such an organization certainly puts a college president on equal footing with presidents of Fortune 500 companies.

Advancement may mean moving to head a larger institution, or it may involve moving back into the business, political, or nonprofit world.

Earnings and Opportunities

Over 5,000 people are employed as college presidents, and job opportunities are expected to continue to grow. Earnings range from $40,000 to over $100,000.

Training and Qualifications

Management and administrative ability, enthusiasm, and a vision of what the future should hold are essential for this job.

Otherwise, there is no specific background that prepares someone to become a college president. Though some come from the academic world, others are hired for their public image; some are former presidents, cabinet members, or high-ranking government officials. Still others come from the business arena. The needs of the school, whether it is a public or private institution, its size, and the direction that the board of trustees wishes to take dictate the background and qualities of the individual they will ultimately select as president.

For Further Details

HEARS (Higher Education Administrators Referral Service), 1 Dupont Circle, Suite 510, Washington, DC 20036-1178.

COLLEGE ADMINISTRATORS

Duties and Responsibilities

While the faculty is responsible for what goes on in the classroom, it is the administrators who see to the overall management of a college—tending to everything from registration paperwork and assigning student housing to providing for the students' social, cultural, and recreational needs.

In large colleges and universities, a number of different individuals will usually take care of separate functions. In small colleges, however, a handful of people may be responsible for several different areas. Generally, the jobs include:

The *dean of students* (also called vice president or vice chancellor for student affairs) heads all nonacademic programs for students and is usually assisted by associate or assistant deans, who may be in charge of a specific area such as student life or housing. Planning, evaluating the changing needs of the student body, and helping to develop policy are among the dean's responsibilities.

The *director of student affairs* manages the student union and assists student groups in planning and arranging social, cultural, and recreational activities. The *director of resident life* is in charge of all aspects of student housing, including everything from room assignments to building maintenance. *Residence counselors* live in the dormitories and help the students as necessary. They may also manage the fiscal, food service, and housekeeping operations of their particular residence.

The *director of religious activities* coordinates the activities of the various denominations on campus. Counseling on marital, financial, or religious problems can be an important part of the job.

The *director of counseling* supervises *counselors, psychologists,* and other staff who help students with personal, educational, and vocational problems.

Foreign student advisers administer the services for students from other countries. They assist with admissions, orientation, financial aid, housing, job placement, and counseling. *Veteran coordinators* provide services to veterans and potential military enlistees.

Athletic directors administer intercollegiate athletic activities, hire and discharge coaches, schedule events, and control the budget. *Financial aid officers* help students obtain financial support for their education and usually direct a staff of *financial aid counselors.*

The *director of placement* assists students in career exploration and advises them on job search strategies.

The *director of admissions* directs the work of *admissions officers,* who interview, screen, and select future students.

The *registrar* directs and coordinates college and university registration, which means keeping accurate records of the academic career of every student. This office also establishes class schedules, coordinates room assignments, and prepares transcripts.

Earnings and Opportunities

Over 55,000 people are employed as college administrators, and employment is expected to decline. Salaries range from $15,600 to $47,000.

Training and Qualifications

Leadership ability, management skills, and the ability to work well with people are important qualifications for college administrators. Because of the diversity of duties, the requirements of these jobs vary considerably. However, schools usually prefer to hire those with a master's degree in student personnel administration. A master's degree in counseling or in clinical or counseling psychology is usually required for work as a college counselor. Directors of religious life are usually members of the clergy.

For Further Details

HEARS (Higher Education Administrators Referral Service), 1 Dupont Circle, Suite 510, Washington, DC 20036-1178.

ELEMENTARY AND SECONDARY SCHOOL ADMINISTRATORS

Duties and Responsibilities

Spiraling costs, declining enrollments, and contract negotiations with teachers are just some of the perennial problems that go with the school administrator's job, but these professionals also have the satisfaction of knowing that they are instrumental in providing the best education possible for the youth in their communities.

Planning, goal setting, staff management, and budget administration are very much a part of the job of school administrator. The *superintendent* is the chief administrator of a school district, and oversees and coordinates the activities of all the schools in the district.

He is selected by the board of education, and his duties range from routine administrative tasks to long-range planning and maintaining good relations with the public. On any given day, a superintendent may supervise the preparation of a budget; meet with parents, teachers, or citizens' groups; plan for changes in physical facilities or staff size owing to changes in enrollment; write reports to the school board; or consider future issues facing the school system.

Most superintendents have one or more assistants. In some districts, *assistant superintendents* oversee all the operations in a particular geographic area; in others, they have authority over specific areas—personnel, budget, or instruction and pupil services, for example.

Principals are the highest authority in a school. They are responsible for running the school according to standards set by the superintendent and the board of education. Improving the quality of education is the principal's most important responsibility. In addition to doing a great deal of paperwork, principals spend much of the day with people. They confer with teachers and administrative staff; they talk with parents and members of the community; and they meet with students, including those who cause disciplinary problems.

In some schools, *assistant principals* handle discipline. They may also provide individual or group counseling about personal, social, educational, or vocational matters; and they often coordinate social and recreational programs.

Earnings and Opportunities

About 150,000 people are employed in this field; about 23,000 are superintendents and their assistants, and about 127,000 are principals and assistant principals. Employment opportunities for school administrators are expected to increase 15 percent in the coming decade. Salaries range from $18,500 to $48,000.

Training and Qualifications

Leadership skills, managerial ability, and a personal, practical philosophy of education are important qualities for school administrators. Self-confidence and the ability to get along with diverse groups of people are also helpful.

A master's degree in educational administration is usually required for a principal or assistant principal. For superintendents, graduate study in educational administration, preferably at the doctoral level, is usually required. In some larger districts, candidates for positions in the district's central office may be expected to have a law or business degree in addition to a graduate degree in education.

Experience in education is a must. Superintendents are generally experienced school administrators; some are former principals. Most principals and assistant principals have worked as classroom teachers, though some move into the job from other administrative jobs, such as curriculum specialist, financial adviser, or department director.

For Further Details

American Association of School Administrators, 1801 N. Moore Street, Arlington, VA 22209.

LIBRARIANS

Duties and Responsibilities

The prim, bespectacled librarian behind a desk with a QUIET PLEASE sign on it is an image from the past. Today's librarian is more aptly thought of as an "information specialist" who is (or soon will be) as comfortable helping people find information on a computer as he or she is helping them find books on the shelves.

In small libraries, the librarian may handle

everything from buying the books and other materials to publicizing library services. By contrast, large libraries, headed by a chief librarian, have staffs of specialists who supervise major departments, run the branch libraries, and oversee technical and user services.

Under technical services fall such specialties as *acquisitions librarians*, who research, select, and order books, periodicals, films, and materials they determine will be of interest; *classifiers*, who classify the material by subject; *catalogers*, who supervise assistants who make complete records of all acquisitions.

Many librarians specialize in helping particular groups of people make use of the library. For example, there are *children's librarians; young adult librarians*, and *adult services librarians. Community outreach librarians* and *bookmobile librarians* develop ways to reach special groups within the community.

Some large libraries also have *special collections librarians*, who may collect and organize books, pamphlets, and manuscripts in a special field, such as women's history, art, or botany.

Bibliographers usually work in research libraries compiling lists of information on particular subjects.

School librarians help students find materials of interest, teach them research methods, and help develop in them a love of books; *academic librarians* serve the same purpose for college students, faculty, and researchers.

Collections of films, tapes, cassettes, and records are becoming increasingly important; and these are sometimes maintained by a *media specialist* or an *audiovisual librarian*.

Special librarians work for government agencies and corporate firms such as pharmaceutical companies, banks, and law firms, obtaining and making accessible information needed by the company or agency. In scientific and technical libraries in particular, computerized data bases are an important and much-used part of the collection.

The staff of a technical library or documentation center may also include *information scientists*, who have a more extensive technical and scientific background and can abstract complicated information into condensed, readable form for their clientele.

Many libraries are putting their own records and operations on computer, and more and more will be tying into remote computer data bases in order to give users access to all types of information that were formerly difficult to obtain. This will mean that librarians will increasingly need to be comfortable with computers and their operation.

School and academic libraries account for about 70 percent of all librarians. Pubic libraries and special libraries employ the remainder, with a few working as consultants, government administrators, or teaching.

Librarians typically work a forty-hour week. Public and college librarians may work some evenings and weekends.

Experienced librarians, primarily those who have specialized or completed graduate training in library school, may advance to administrative positions or specialized work.

Earnings and Opportunities

Over 135,000 people are employed as librarians, and though overall growth in the field is expected to be somewhat slow (13 percent increase in jobs by 1995), there will be an increasing need for those with specialized knowledge who can manage information for businesses and government as well as those with expertise in computerized library systems. Earnings: $12,500 to $48,000 and up.

Training and Qualifications

A love of books and information, organizational skills, and the ability to do detailed work are important qualities for librarians.

A master's degree in library science (M.L.S.) is necessary to obtain an entry-level professional position in most libraries. A degree from a school accredited by the American Library Association is preferable. A Ph.D. is advantageous for teaching or for a top administrative post. Those interested in special libraries or research libraries will benefit from a master's, doctorate, or professional degree in the appropriate field.

State certification requirements for public school librarians vary; most require they be certified as teachers, and a degree in library science may not be necessary. Some states also require certification for public librarians.

For Further Details

American Library Association, 50 E. Huron St., Chicago, IL 60611. Special Libraries Association, 235 Park Ave. S., New York, NY 10003. American Society for Information Science, 1010 16th St., N.W., Washington, DC 20036. Association of American Library Schools, 471 Park Lane, State College, PA 16801.

LIBRARY TECHNICIANS AND ASSISTANTS

Duties and Responsibilities

A resurgence of reading in our nation has brought our libraries alive again. Library technicians and assistants are the workers who help professional librarians keep the library running smoothly, and and they're the ones we usually ask for help in using the library's resources.

Like librarians, technicians usually work in either technical or user services. Those in user services work directly with the public, helping them find the information needed. They may do this by phone or in person. Requests may come from the general public, businesses, the news media, or legislators. Workers in the technical area are primarily concerned with acquiring and preparing materials for use, and they deal less frequently with the public. In many libraries, technicians may handle both types of duties.

Library technicians, also known as library technical assistants, answer questions about the use of the card catalog, direct library users to standard references, perform routine cataloging of new materials (books, magazines, audiotapes, videotapes, etc.), verify information on order requests, and sometimes supervise other support staff. Some operate and maintain audiovisual equipment such as projectors and tape recorders. They may also assist library users with microfilm or microfiche readers or retrieve information from a computer data base. They sometimes work on special projects such as planning displays or designing posters.

Library assistants, sometimes called library clerks or circulation clerks, check books in and out, sort and shelve library materials, repair damaged books, and answer routine inquiries. They may maintain special materials such as newspaper clipping files and pictures.

Those who are employed in government or special libraries such as those in business and law firms usually work a regular forty-hour week, but those in public libraries and college and university libraries may work weekend and evening hours.

Earnings and Opportunities

About 154,000 people are employed as library technicians or assistants, and continued employment growth is expected in business, medical, and law libraries. Salaries range from $9,800 to $17,400.

Training and Qualifications

A love of books and attention to detail are good qualities for those interested in this career.

To become a library assistant, a high school diploma is usually required, and typing ability is helpful. For a position as library technician, most employers prefer people with at least some college education. Over a hundred institutions offer special training for library technicians. These programs usually last two years and lead to an associate of arts degree in library technology. However, applicants should be aware that credits earned in an associate degree library program do not apply toward a professional degree in library science.

For Further Details

Council on Library Assistants, University of the District of Columbia, 4200 Connecticut Ave., N.W., Washington, DC 20008. American Library Association, 50 E. Huron St., Chicago, IL 60611.

Careers in Engineering

Engineering is a tremendously varied, challenging field that is experiencing a high rate of growth that shows no signs of stopping through the mid-1990s. Engineers of different disciplines are responsible for such diverse achievements as sending a man to the moon, developing ways to probe the ocean depths, building faster and smaller computers, designing defense systems, developing microwave ovens, and finding ways to build electronic games and pollution-free cars. They apply the theories and principles of science and mathematics to practical technical problems, and their work often provides the crucial link between a scientific discovery and its application.

Engineering is the second-largest profession, exceeded only by teaching. Most engineers specialize, and within each specialty there are subdivisions. For example, electrical, electronic, mechanical, chemical, and industrial engineering are all components of the aerospace engineering field.

When developing a new product, engineers must consider many factors. In the course of inventing a new piece of equipment to explore outer space, for example, engineers determine how the device will work, then design and test all components and fit them together in an integrated plan. They must then evaluate the overall effectiveness, cost, reliability, and safety of the item.

In addition to design and development, engineers may also work in testing, production, operations, or maintenance. In these areas they supervise production processes in factories, determine the causes of breakdowns, and test newly manufactured products to maintain quality. They also estimate the time and cost of completing projects. Some engineers combine their expertise with other skills to work in engineering administration, management, or sales.

About half of all engineers work in manufacturing industries—the majority in electrical and electronic equipment, aircraft and parts, machinery, chemicals, scientific instruments, metals, and motor vehicle industries. Others are employed by public utilities, engineering services, and business and management consulting services. Still others work for the departments of Defense, Energy, and Transportation and in the National Aeronautics and Space Administration (NASA), and many engineers go on to become high-level executives in government and industry. Some with advanced degrees teach in colleges and universities.

Beginning graduates usually work under close supervision and may also receive additional classroom training. As they gain experience, responsibilities increase and they may move to managerial or administrative positions. Some obtain graduate degrees in business administration to improve advancement opportunities; others obtain law degrees and become patent attorneys.

Because complex problems usually cut across traditional fields, engineers in one area often work closely with specialists in other engineering, scientific, and business occupations.

Engineers often use computers to create mathematical equations that describe how a machine, structure, or system operates. They spend a great deal of time writing reports and consulting with other engineers. At times, engineers work on their own; on complex projects, they may work as part of a team. The working environment depends on the specialty. Some engineers spend most of their time in offices; others work in research labs, industrial plants, or in the field.

Employment opportunities for engineers are expected to be excellent throughout the 1980s. Growth is expected in defense-related industries as a result of anticipated sharp increases in defense budgets. More engineers will also be required in energy-related fields to develop more sources of energy as well as to design energy-saving systems for cars, factories, homes, and other buildings. Shortages also are reported at state transportation agencies, where bridge engineers and middle managers are in particular demand.

Opportunities for women are favorable as more women join this male-dominated profession. According to the National Science Foundation, the number of women engineers is up to 34,500 in the early 1980s, from 11,400 in 1976. Despite these gains, women still compose only 2.3 percent of all engineers, up 1 percent from 1976.

Salaries range from $22,000 to $30,000 to start, and $40,000 to $80,000 and more for those with experience.

A fascination with math and science as well as creativity, an analytical mind, and the capacity for detail are essential for the engineering candidate. You should be self-motivated

but also have the ability to work well as part of a team. Being able to express yourself well, orally and in writing, is also important.

A bachelor's degree in engineering is generally acceptable for beginning engineering jobs. Many engineers obtain a master's degree because it is desirable for promotion or for learning new technology. Some specialties, such as nuclear or astrophysical engineering, are taught mainly at the graduate level, and graduate school is essential for most teaching jobs.

A number of colleges and universities offer five-year master's degree programs, and some schools have arrangements where students spend three years in a liberal arts college studying pre-engineering subjects and two years in an engineering school. They then receive a bachelor's degree from each. Some longer programs include a work-study arrangement that offers useful experience as well as the opportunity for students to offset the cost of their education.

Many colleges have two- or four-year programs leading to degrees in engineering technology that prepare students for practical design and production work rather than for jobs requiring theoretical knowledge.

To keep up with rapid advances in technology, engineers often continue their education throughout their careers by taking advanced study in evening classes or employer-sponsored programs.

Throughout the United States, licensing is required for engineers whose work may affect life, health, or property or those who offer their services to the public. Licensing generally requires a degree from an accredited engineering program, four years of relevant work experience, and passing a state examination.

For Further Details

Engineering Manpower Commission of American Association of Engineering Societies, 345 E. 47th St., New York, NY 10017. National Society of Professional Engineers, 2029 K St., N.W., Washington, DC 20006. Society of Women Engineers, 345 E. 47th St., New York, NY 10017.

AEROSPACE ENGINEERS

Duties and Responsibilities

Being a member of the team responsible for building the space shuttle, designing sophisticated navigational systems for our military aircraft, or improving the manufacturing technology of commercial and recreational aircraft are all jobs performed by aerospace engineers.

Aerospace engineers design, develop, test, and help produce commercial and military aircraft and space vehicles and often further specialize in areas like structural or engine design, navigational guidance, instrumentation, and communication.

Employment is mostly in private industry, working for aircraft and parts manufacturers, defense contractors, aerospace companies, instrument producers, and some airlines. Others work for the federal government, primarily in the Department of Defense and the National Aeronautics and Space Administration (NASA). Most of these jobs are concentrated in states where large aircraft, defense, and aerospace businesses are located, most notably in California and Washington.

Earnings and Opportunities

Over 68,000 people are employed as aerospace engineers, mostly in the aircraft and parts industry. Employment is expected to grow faster than the average for all jobs through the 1980s, with a projected increase in jobs of 41 percent by the mid-1990s, mostly as a result of more government spending on the military and defense. Aerospace engineers will also be needed to design and help produce new commercial aircraft, as well as to bring advances in technology—like fuel efficiency and noise reduction—to existing fleets of private and military aircraft.

Any further growth in the space program, with its emphasis on satellite launchings for commercial enterprise, will also call for more aerospace specialists. Note that since such a large number of these jobs depend on defense spending, cutbacks in that area can result in layoffs. Median annual income for aerospace engineers is $42,125, and can go over $90,000.

Training and Qualifications

Not all engineers who work in the aerospace field are aeronautical engineers. Many come from chemical engineering, metallurgical engineering, mechanical engineering, electrical engineering, and even from the petroleum and industrial engineering fields. This is because the aerospace field is so broad that many different technologies are brought to bear on the problems.

While some aerospace engineers get their masters or doctorates prior to beginning their careers full time, most enter with a B.S. and get their feet wet in the field before opting for further education.

For Further Details

American Institute of Aeronautics and Astronautics, Inc., 1290 Ave. of the Americas, New York, NY 10019.

BIOMEDICAL ENGINEERS

Duties and Responsibilities

The fact that so many people are living normal lives through the use of pacemaker heart implantations is largely due to the advances made by biomedical engineers, who use engineering principles to solve medical and health-related problems.

Biomedical engineering is a relatively new science whose potential has not yet been fully realized. Already, however, biomedical engineers have used their knowledge to remedy many inherited human physical disorders, to develop cures that never existed before, as well as to produce vastly improved vegetation for human consumption. Some foresee even greater advances in the field, including the development of artificial hybrid microbes, plants, and animals that could alleviate the world's food, health, and energy problems, and the prevention of genetic disorders such as sickle-cell anemia and Down's syndrome.

Working with life scientists, chemists, and members of the medical profession, many biomedical engineers do research on man and animals. Some design and develop medical instruments and devices, including artificial hearts and kidneys and lasers for surgery. Other biomedical engineers adapt computers to medical science and design and build systems to modernize laboratory, hospital, and clinical procedures.

Engineers often use calculators and computers to create mathematical equations that describe how a machine or system will operate. They spend a great deal of time writing reports and consulting with other engineers. At times they may work on their own, while with more complex projects they may work as part of a team.

Many biomedical engineers teach and do research in colleges and universities. Some work for the federal government, primarily in the National Aeronautics and Space Administration, or in state agencies. An increasing number work in private industry or in hospi-

tals developing new devices, techniques, and systems for improving health care.

Earnings and Opportunities

Over 4,000 people are employed as biomedical engineers, and the outlook for employment is excellent. Earnings range from $22,500 to $60,000 and up.

Training and Qualifications

A fascination with math and science as well as creativity, an analytical mind, and the capacity for detail are good qualities for future biomedical engineers.

Most engineers in this field have an undergraduate degree in one of the major engineering disciplines (mechanical, electrical, industrial, or chemical) and an advanced degree in some area of biomedical engineering. However, a growing number of colleges are offering undergraduate degrees in biomedical engineering, and others offer biomedical engineering as an area of specialization within a more traditional engineering specialty.

For Further Details

Alliance for Engineering in Medicine and Biology, Suite 311, 4405 East-West Highway, Bethesda, MD 20014. Biomedical Engineering Society, P.O. Box 2399, Culver City, CA 90230. Society of Women Engineers, 345 E. 47th St., New York, NY 10017.

CERAMIC ENGINEERS

Duties and Responsibilities

When someone mentions ceramics, you probably think of pottery and glassware—items associated with the home. But ceramics actually include all non-metallic, inorganic materials that require the use of high temperatures in their processing. Ceramics are widely used in the electronics field to make parts that house integrated circuits and other components in products such as calculators and computers;

and the energy industry uses ceramic materials for furnaces and nuclear reactors.

Ceramic engineers are instrumental in the design and development of these and other new products. They often specialize in one area, like electronics or energy. They also design the equipment used to manufacture these products.

Ceramic materials' resistance to high levels of heat makes them especially useful as protective coatings for metals or atomic fuel elements. The ceramics process is also used in forming brick or tile, as well as in products such as fire- and heat-resistant materials like firebrick. And of course, its role is well known in creating porcelain, glass, and china dinnerware.

Most ceramic engineers are employed in businesses, primarily in the glass, clay, and stone industries. Others work in fields that produce or use ceramic products such as the energy, iron and steel, electrical equipment, aerospace, and chemical industries.

Earnings and Opportunities

Over 15,000 people are employed as ceramic engineers, and employment is expected to grow faster than average through the 1980s. Growth in industries like electronics, defense, nuclear energy, medicine, pollution control, and energy conservation will lead to an increase in demand. Income for ceramic engineers is about on a par with that of most engineering professions, ranging from $24,000 to $30,000 to start, to $40,000 to $80,000 for those with experience.

Training and Qualifications

Like those who study chemistry or chemical engineering, ceramic engineers should have an interest in the structure of matter; and in fact, many start out in chemistry or chemical or mechanical engineering before specializing in ceramic engineering. Owing to the shortage of ceramic engineers, individuals from the aforementioned fields many times wind up handling these jobs, and some go back for further graduate study in order to progress in this profession.

For Further Details

National Institute of Ceramic Engineers, 65 Ceramic Dr., Columbus, OH 43210.

CHEMICAL ENGINEERS

Duties and Responsibilities

Chemical engineers working in research and development are on the cutting edge of exciting new developments and discoveries. They learn to understand the complex nature of chemicals and how they can be utilized in research, production and manufacturing. To invent the next nylon or other synthetic fabric, to improve the manufacture of rubber, find an economic way to get hydrogen from water, to create synthetic fuels and lubricants, or develop a new process to combat pollution—these are the goals of chemical engineers.

This area of engineering is very complex and frequently highly specialized. Because of the interrelation of different specialties, chemical engineering requires a high degree of knowledge of chemistry, physics, and mechanical and electrical engineering. Because of their expertise, chemical engineers are used in such diverse fields as computers, aeronautics, space, fluid hydraulics, and many others.

Most are employed in the chemical, petroleum refining, and related manufacturing industries, working on plastics, rubber, wire coatings, waxes, polymers, paint, fuels, oils, adhesives, and encapsulants. Some are employed in government agencies, working in nuclear and magnetic R and D; some are consultants; and still others teach and perform research at colleges and universities.

Earnings and Opportunities

Over 55,000 people are employed as chemical engineers, most in private industry. Employment is expected to grow about as fast as the national average for all occupations through the 1980s. A major boost to this growth is tied to the expansion of the chemical and energy industries.

More chemical engineers will be required to design, build, and maintain plants and equipment as they become more complex. Problems of environmental protection, the development of synthetic fuels, and the growth of nuclear reactors will also contribute to employment. The development of new chemicals used in manufacturing consumer goods, such as plastics and synthetic fibers, probably will create more jobs as well. Automation of these processes will also call for more experienced engineers to handle the load. Median income is $46,800.

Training and Qualifications

Most people agree that chemical engineering is the most difficult of the engineering disci-plines. Over 60 percent of those who start in the field do not complete it. As the name suggests, it combines chemistry and engineering, and strong math and science skills are a must. The minimum requirement is a B.S. degree, and many in this field go on for their masters and doctorates.

For Further Details

American Institute of Chemical Engineers, 345 E. 47th St., New York, NY 10017. American Chemical Society, 1155 16th St., N.W., Washington, DC 20036.

ELECTRICAL AND ELECTRONIC ENGINEERS

Duties and Responsibilities

Representing the largest branch of engineering, electrical engineers design, develop, test, and supervise the production of electrical and electronic equipment. Depending on the specialty, they work on anything from planning better equipment for power distribution, to designing sophisticated circuitry to test stereo receivers.

The kinds of equipment that electrical engineers work on include power generating and transmission equipment used by electric utilities, electric motors, machinery controls, lighting and wiring in buildings, automobiles, and aircraft. Electrical engineers who work in electronics are usually referred to as electronic engineers. Electronic equipment includes radar, computers, communications equipment, and consumer goods such as TV sets and stereo components.

Electrical engineers generally specialize in a major area like communications, aircraft, or automotives, or in an even more specific part of the field like microwave transmission, radar, or aviation electronic systems.

They research and design new products, test them, and play an important role in developing ways to manufacture them. As part of their jobs, they also attend and give seminars, exchange ideas with others, and write reports and articles.

The major employers of electrical engineers are the electrical and electronic equipment industries. In addition many electrical engineers work for manufacturers of aircraft and parts, business machines, computer and scientific equipment, as well as public utilities and power companies.

Earnings and Opportunities

More than 325,000 electrical engineers are employed in the field, and that number is expected to increase by 65 percent in the next ten years—considerably faster than the average for all occupations. The growing demand for electrical products will be spurred mainly by the computer and communications industries, but also by the military. (Keep in mind that electrical engineering positions in defense-related areas are subject to the rise and fall of defense-spending activity.) The market for electronic consumer goods will also grow, creating more jobs. The need for more efficient and more effective electrical power generation will also fuel the increase in such jobs. The median annual income for electrical and electronic engineers is $42,290. Some engineers earn in excess of $75,000, and managerial jobs can pay over $100,000.

Training and Qualifications

A strong grasp of mathematics and the sciences and the ability to focus on details are essential. A B.S. degree in electrical engineering is the minimum educational requirement. Many colleges today allow their electrical engineering students to specialize in either electronics or power, but you can also build credentials in your chosen specialty by taking electives and through graduate study. As in most other engineering fields, many enter the job market with a B.S. and go back for further training when they begin to specialize.

For Further Details

Institute of Electrical and Electronics Engineers, United States Activities Board, 1111 19th St., N.W., Suite 608, Washington, DC 20036.

ENGINEERING AND SCIENCE TECHNICIANS

Duties and Responsibilities

Employed as the right hand of various kinds of scientists and engineers, these technicians have the knowledge and ability to work in all phases of business and government—research and design, manufacturing, sales, and customer service. Their duties usually involve applying the theoretical knowledge developed by engineers and scientists to actual situations.

In their work, technicians use complex electronic and mechanical instruments, experimental laboratory equipment, and drafting tools. Most use technical handbooks, calculators, and computers in their jobs.

In research and development, technicians set up experiments and calculate the results. They may also help to develop experimental equipment and models by making drawings and sketches and sometimes doing routine design work.

In production, they usually follow the plans given them by engineers and scientists. They may prepare specifications for materials, devise tests to ensure product quality, or study ways to improve the efficiency of an operation. They often supervise production workers to make sure all goes according to plan.

As sales workers or field representatives for manufacturers, technicians give advice on installation and maintenance of complex machinery and may write specifications and technical manuals.

Specifically, technicians might work in one of the following areas:

In *aeronautical technology*, they help design and produce aircraft, rockets, guided missiles, and spacecraft. They may also serve as manufacturers' representatives, providing the link between customer and manufacturer concerning the use of equipment. In *civil engineering technology*, they assist in planning, designing, and constructing highways, bridges, dams, and other structures. In *industrial engineering technology*, they help with problems involving the efficient use of personnel, materials, and machines to produce goods and services.

Mechanical engineering technology technicians may work in automotive, diesel, and production technology or tool and machine design. In *instrumentation technology*, they help design and develop complex measuring and control devices such as those used in oceanographic and space exploration, weather forecasting, satellite communication systems, environmental protection, and medical research.

Chemical technicians work to develop, sell, and use chemical and related products and equipment. Most are involved in research and development, testing, or other laboratory work.

Meteorological technicians help in the study of atmospheric conditions. *Geological technicians* assist in evaluating the earth processes and are often involved in the research that is currently going into seismology, ecology, and petroleum and mineral exploration. *Hydrologic technicians* gather data to help predict river stages and water quality levels.

Technicians also specialize in fields such as metallurgical, electrical, and optical technology, in nuclear energy and environmental protection. (Check the index to find information on electronics, mathematical, agricultural, and biological, air-conditioning, and heating and refrigeration technicians.)

Working conditions vary depending on the job. However, most technicians work in laboratories and plants; others spend part or all of their time outdoors; and some are occasionally exposed to hazards from equipment or materials.

Technicians usually start as trainees and gain responsibility as they gain experience. They may eventually move into senior or supervisory positions.

Earnings and Opportunities

Over 885,000 people work as engineering and science technicians, and employment opportunities are excellent. Salaries range from $17,500 to $32,000 and up.

Training and Qualifications

An aptitude for math and science, manual dexterity, and the ability to do detailed technical work accurately are key qualities for technicians. The ability to work both independently and as part of a team is important.

Most employers prefer applicants who have completed specialized technical training, preferably programs in which students gain practical work experience. These programs are available at technical institutes, junior and community colleges, extension divisions of universities, and vo-tech and correspondence schools.

For Further Details

Engineers Council for Professional Development, 345 E. 47th St., New York, NY 10017. National Association of Trade and Technical Schools, 2021 K St., N.W., Washington, DC 20006. National Home Study Council, 1601 18th St., N.W., Washington, DC 20009.

INDUSTRIAL ENGINEERS

Duties and Responsibilities

While the focus of most engineers' work is on products and processes, industrial engineers are more concerned with people and methods of business organization in manufacturing and industry. They solve problems ranging from finding an ideal plant location to designing financial review procedures or product quality control systems. Their work centers on finding the most effective ways to use people and achieve greater productivity.

Industrial engineers work mostly for manufacturing companies, where their skills are used to help improve efficiency in management and production areas. This could include designing data processing systems, aiding in financial planning and cost analysis, designing production planning and control systems, and designing or improving systems for the physi-

cal distribution of goods and services. They also conduct plant location surveys in which they look for the best combination of sources of raw materials, transportation, and low taxes. In addition, they may develop wage and salary administration systems and job evaluation programs.

Other businesses employing industrial engineers include insurance companies, banks, retail businesses, and hospitals. These are all generally large operations where efficiency of business methods is especially important to the bottom line.

Earnings and Opportunities

Over 115,000 people work as industrial engineers, and this field is expected to grow faster than the average for all occupations through the 1980s. Industrial growth will spur the need for increased productivity and greater efficiency in business. As production and operating methods become more complex, and as automation becomes a larger factor in production, industrial engineers will find a growing need for analyzing and recommending better organizational and operating systems. Median salary for industrial engineers is $41,500. Those with experience in an area of high demand and those in supervisory positions can earn in excess of $60,000.

Training and Qualifications

At some time or other, engineers in every field have to deal with other people in their jobs, but industrial engineers usually have much more people contact than the others and therefore benefit from stronger interpersonal skills. So if you are good in math and science and are leaning toward engineering, but don't want to be buried in a laboratory somewhere, then this may well be the engineering field for you.

The minimum requirement is a B.S. degree in industrial engineering, obtainable in either a four-year or a five-year program. Graduate studies are available, but normally not recommended until after you have had some work experience to help define your goals more clearly.

For Further Details

American Institute of Industrial Engineers, Inc., 25 Technology Park/Atlanta, Norcross, GA 30092.

MECHANICAL ENGINEERS

Duties and Responsibilities

Mechanical engineers are today's highly trained and skilled counterparts of yesterday's tinkerer and inventor. They are responsible for thousands of patents and countless mechanical devices. They design power-producing machines, such as steam turbines that generate electric power, and they develop and refine everything from jet and rocket engines to electrically powered machines like elevators, refrigerators, and machine tools.

In a field this broad, there are a number of specialties—motor vehicles; marine equipment; energy conversion systems; heating, ventilating, and air conditioning; instrumentation; and custom machinery for industries like petroleum, plastics, and construction. The specific skills involved vary according to the specialty.

Most mechanical engineers work in manufacturing industries, including metals, machinery, transportation equipment, and electrical equipment companies. Many perform research, testing, and design work, while others work in maintenance, sales, production, and manufacturing operations.

Earnings and Opportunities

Over 213,000 people are employed as mechanical engineers, and a 52 percent increase in this number is projected by 1995. Because of a growing demand for machinery, the industry will need more and more people to design, manage, and maintain increasingly complex industrial machinery and processes. Areas like energy, environmental control, and transportation will see a continued demand for mechanical engineers to solve problems and increase efficiency. Median annual income is $43,000.

Training and Qualifications

Strong math and science skills, as well as imagination and creativity, are essential for those who would reach the top in this profession. A B.S. degree in mechanical engineering is a must; graduate work in one or more specialties is recommended, although such decisions would not be made until the senior year in college.

For Further Details

The American Society of Mechanical Engineers, 345 E. 47th St., New York, NY 10017.

METALLURGICAL ENGINEERS

Duties and Responsibilities

With their expert knowledge of the molecular structure of metals, metallurgical engineers are essential to the choice and design of materials in everything from the tremendously strong but extremely lightweight metals used for aircraft, to the huge weight-bearing structures of skyscrapers and soaring bridges. Their most important functions are to develop new types of metal with special properties for special uses and to devise new methods to convert metals into useful products.

There are three main branches of metallurgy in which an engineer might work: extractive, physical, and mechanical. Extractive metallurgists extract metals from ores and refine and alloy them to obtain useful metal. Physical metallurgists deal with the nature, structure, and physical properties of metals and their alloys. They also work on methods of converting refined metals into final products. Mechanical metallurgists develop methods such as casting, forging, rolling, and drawing to work and shape metals.

Scientists working in this field are known as *metallurgists* or *materials scientists*, and the difference between scientists and engineers in this specialty is small.

The metalworking industries, primarily iron and steel, are the major employers of metallurgical engineers. They also work in industries that manufacture machinery, electrical equipment, and aircraft and parts, as well as in the mining industry.

Earnings and Opportunities

Over 15,000 people are employed as metallurgical engineers or metallurgists, and employment is expected to grow faster than average through the 1980s. The metalworking industries will require more professionals to develop new metals and alloys as well as to adapt current ones to new uses. New ways to recycle waste materials will be needed as the supply of high-grade ores is exhausted. For the same reason, there will also be a need for new methods to process and make use of low-grade ores. The median annual income for metallurgical and materials engineers is $42,653.

Training and Qualifications

As with ceramic engineers, most of those who wind up in metallurgical engineering did not enter college with a burning desire to become metallurgists. They typically start out studying chemistry or another of the engineering sciences, then become interested in this specialty. A B.S. degree in metallurgy is the minimum requirement and a masters is recommended.

For Further Details

The Metallurgical Society of AIME, 420 Commonwealth Dr., Warrendale, PA 15086. American Society for Metals, Metals Park, OH 44073.

MINING ENGINEERS

Duties and Responsibilities

With pick and lantern in hand, the miner of yesterday descended into a rickety shaft in search of ore, unsure of his safety and what the day's efforts would bring. Today it's a different picture. Mining engineers are the professionals who help ensure both mine safety and the day's yield. Using advanced technology, engineers help locate minerals, and they develop the best methods for extracting them.

Mining engineers design mines, supervise their construction, and develop ways to transport minerals to processing plants. They are also responsible for the safe and efficient operation of mines, which includes ensuring proper ventilation, water supply, power, communications, and equipment maintenance. Some work with metallurgists and geologists to locate new ore deposits. Others are involved in the design and development of new mining equipment or mineral processing operations. They frequently specialize in a particular mineral, like coal or copper ore.

Mining engineers are generally employed at the sites of mineral deposits, which range from the rich coal lands of the Middle Atlantic states to the iron and copper deposits of the West. While most are employed by the mining industry, some work for mining equipment manufacturers.

Earnings and Opportunities

Over 6,000 people are employed as mining engineers, and employment opportunities are expected to increase faster than average through the 1980s. Much of this growth will be based on the demand for more technologically advanced mining systems that employ more efficient and economical ways of extracting ores. The need for less common ores for new alloys and specialty metals will also increase. Concern for the environment, particularly in relation to mined-land reclamation and water and air pollution, will create opportunities for mining engineers as well. Additionally, areas like undersea mining and the development of oil-shale deposits will call for their specialized knowledge and skill. Median annual income for petroleum and mining engineers is $52,500. This is the highest median income of the engineering groups polled.

Training and Qualifications

While a degree in mining engineering is preferred, it is also possible to enter this field with a degree in mechanical engineering or civil engineering. It is often just a matter of supply and demand. If you're the rough and rugged type and like pickup trucks as well as math and science, you stand a good chance of finding employment.

For Further Details

The Society of Mining Engineers of AIME, Caller Number D, Littleton, CO 80127.

PETROLEUM ENGINEERS

Duties and Responsibilities

Petroleum engineers are the people who develop ways of getting oil and gas out of the ground. With our natural resources growing scarcer, exploration and drilling become more competitive and there is an increasing need to improve production methods.

Since only a small proportion of the oil and gas in a reservoir flows out naturally, engineers must create artificial recovery methods to generate increased production. The best methods currently available recover only about half the available oil, so research and development will be directed at finding ways to recover a greater proportion of oil in each reservoir.

Engineers also supervise drilling, research drilling methods, and develop new ways to recover offshore oil and gas. As these resources become more difficult to find, methods of recovery from the ocean depths, or areas such as the Arctic, which have previously been considered inaccessible, will have to be developed.

Petroleum engineers are employed by major oil and gas companies as well as independent oil exploration, production, and service companies. They also work for drilling equipment and supply makers, and some serve as consultants to banks and financial institutions that need to assess the value of oil and gas properties.

Jobs are located where oil and gas are found, and almost three-fourths of all petroleum engineers work in Texas, Oklahoma, Louisiana, and California. Many American citizens can also be found on oil projects overseas.

Earnings and Opportunities

Over 18,000 people are employed as petro-leum engineers, and employment is expected to grow faster than average through the 1980s as economic expansion requires increasing supplies of petroleum and natural gas. With efforts to attain energy self-sufficiency and with high petroleum prices, increasingly so-phisticated and expensive recovery methods will be used. New oil and gas exploration—including new sources like oil shale—will also spur demand for more engineers. Median annual income for petroleum and mining en-gineers is $52,500. This is the highest median income of the engineering groups polled.

Training and Qualifications

While some people enter this profession from the mechanical or civil engineering fields, a degree in petroleum engineering is preferred, especially if you want to move into manage-ment. You should also enjoy rugged living and the outdoors and be willing to travel a great deal.

For Further Details

Society of Petroleum Engineers of AIME, 6200 N. Central Expressway, Dallas, TX 75206.

Careers in Finance

The world of finance is changing. Formerly a staid profession whose members thought it in bad taste to solicit another firm's customer, the financial community is entering a new era of competition where marketing is playing an increasingly important role. Spurred on by the continuing deregulation of the banking industry, banks, insurance companies, savings and loans, brokerage houses, and large retailing organizations are all crossing over into one another's turf, and all are responding by making aggressive changes in the way they run their businesses.

Marketing specialists, ranging from direct-mail experts to product development people, are sought after in growing numbers. Public relations and advertising people are also entering the financial community owing to a growing interest and need to convey more information to the public.

Lending money is not only more competitive but also more complicated. Real estate deals involving tens of millions of dollars require that lending institutions employ financial specialists capable of making difficult decisions. Billion-dollar loans to emerging third-world nations or financially strapped countries call for seasoned executives who can handle such situations diplomatically and soundly.

In addition, more people at all income levels need help managing their money as their investment options expand, so the demand for financial professionals such as accountants and financial planners is on the increase as well.

Huge financial institutions that employ thousands of people need workers at every level. High school graduates willing to be trained and to seek further education, college grads willing to do the same, and even Ph.D.'s will all be in demand as this segment of our economy continues its amazing growth. Housewives returning to the job market after raising families and men and women making mid-career job changes are also likely to find employment opportunities here.

In short, the world of finance will never be the same. Whether your interests lie in the area of the securities, banking, or insurance industries or whether you see yourself as a financial professional, the job opportunities in this field are more promising than ever before.

FINANCIAL ANALYSTS

Duties and Responsibilities

Financial fortune-telling is the work of analysts, who interpret industry conditions, economic and political trends (both national and worldwide), and the fluctuations on Wall Street and in the money markets in terms of what they will mean to specific businesses.

In today's competitive marketplace, financial analysts are becoming a very important part of the world of business, and they work for public, industrial, and financial institutions. Some senior financial analysts have become so well known for the accuracy of their predictions that a negative proclamation from them can send stock or bond prices tumbling.

Key to the success of any financial institution is a strong research department, where many analysts work. Most specialize in bonds, stocks, or commodities; and in larger institutions their specializations are broken down to specific industries such as communications, automobiles, oil, or steel. Their jobs consist of studying the financial health of these businesses to make statistical evaluations based on economic and political trends and a company's current financial standing. Using this information, analysts attempt to advise on the current worth of a company's securities and may try to predict the yield of various investment strategies. To companies whose stock trades on the open market the opinions of financial analysts are so important to stock prices that much time is spent keeping them informed as to the company's state of health.

Corporations and public institutions also need large numbers of financial analysts in order to help chart the company's path in the financial world, since almost every decision has to be evaluated in terms of its return on investment (ROI). Departments with large budgets will even have their own financial analysts who focus solely on the financial operations of that particular area. Risk management (making sure the company doesn't go out on a limb) is a very important part of their job.

On a day-to-day basis, analysts spend their time reviewing reports, performing analyses, and working with sophisticated computer models of various economic scenarios to make forecasts and recommendations.

Financial analysts generally start out as junior analysts or research assistants and receive on-the-job training.

Earnings and Opportunities

The outlook for financial analysts is excellent, and earnings are quite good. Junior analysts with M.B.A.'s generally start at about $18,000 to $22,500, and the industry average for all analysts is $40,000 to $45,000. Some senior analysts earn over $100,000 and some make as much as $300,000 including bonuses.

Training and Qualifications

An interest in finance, ease with statistics, and the ability to analyze and interpret facts are important qualities for financial analysts.

A bachelor's degree with a major in mathematics/statistics or business/finance is preferred, with strong emphasis on economics and computer usage. Many have earned their masters' degrees in business administration.

FLOOR BROKERS, TRADERS, AND COMMODITY TRADERS

Duties and Responsibilities

If you ever have the opportunity, go to the visitors' gallery of one of the stock exchanges and watch as floor brokers and specialists bargain face-to-face over hundreds of millions of dollars' worth of stock. Then make an effort to observe a commodity exchange, where negotiations take place in the "pit" (a wooden ring around which everyone gathers). Far from gentlemanly, deals are conducted by shouting —preferably a little louder than anyone else. It is a frenzy of activity as traders haggle over the price they'll pay for contracts on specific commodities.

If you like being in the center of fast-paced action then it's hard to beat having a job trading on a stock or commodity exchange.

Floor brokers are representatives of the brokerage companies (or individuals) who own seats on a stock exchange. They are usually salaried workers who conduct trading for the company they represent. For example, if they have an order to buy 10,000 shares of IBM, they go to the specialist in charge of that stock (where other buyers and sellers of that stock will have gathered) and make a deal. *Freelance brokers* handle the overflow of business from investment firms whose floor brokers are too busy at any given time.

Also present on the floor of a stock exchange are *specialists*, who are traders who have exclusive responsibility for a stock or group of stocks listed on that exchange. These workers match, buy, and sell orders and are supposed to make sure that trades are carried out with the smallest possible swing in the price of stock. If there's a seller and no buyer, the specialist must use his own money to buy and can then sell the next time a buyer appears. Because at times they must buy huge quantities of stock when no one else is buying, a great deal of capital is needed, so most specialists have been appointed to their jobs by the board of governors of the exchange for their ability to afford the position as well as handle the responsibility.

Floor traders are employed by companies who own seats on an exchange, and they use their firm's capital to buy and sell securities, earning money on the fluctuations of the marketplace. Traders usually specialize.

The commodities markets are where futures on commodities such as soybeans, cotton, cocoa, and pork bellies are sold. Recently, a booming interest in these exchanges has meant that people can now buy futures on an even wider variety of items, ranging from the price of foreign money or a Treasury certificate to frozen orange juice concentrate. Speculation in these markets involves participation in a win/lose situation. The risks are high, and the pressure is great. Handling these trades is the job of *commodity traders*, who may represent the major brokerage firms or the smaller investment companies who own seats on the exchange. While it is an exciting, hectic place to work and some people thrive on it, many report vocal cord damage and hearing loss because of the din.

The pressure in these jobs is great, but it is somewhat offset by the fact that the hours worked are primarily limited to the actual business hours that the exchanges are open.

Most workers take positions as clerks on an exchange in order to learn the business.

Exchanges are located throughout the country. The largest number of jobs on stock exchanges are in New York, home of both the New York and the American stock exchanges. The largest commodity exchanges are in Chicago.

Earnings and Opportunities

Opportunities for floor brokers are good, while the outlook for commodity traders is more limited. Earnings for floor brokers range from about $24,000 to $150,000. Average salaries for traders is between $60,000 and $100,000, including bonuses.

Training and Qualifications

A love of excitement, steady nerves, and a feel for the market are helpful qualities for these workers. For these jobs, an understanding of investment and a knowledge of the rules of an exchange are more important than special educational requirements. To qualify to become a broker or trader, candidates must pass the exams required by a particular exchange and are usually expected to spend a period of time in on-the-job training prior to assuming their full responsibilities.

SECURITIES BROKERS

Duties and Responsibilities

The exciting world of Wall Street, the Big Board, and high finance awaits those who choose to be securities salespeople. Securities salespeople—also called registered representatives, account executives, or brokers—are the ones through whom we buy and sell stocks, bonds, or shares in mutual funds or other financial products. They may trade for individuals with a few hundred dollars or for large institutions with millions to invest.

When an investor wishes to buy or sell securities, a broker usually relays the order through his firm's offices to a representative on the floor of a securities exchange, such as the New York or American Stock Exchange. That representative for the buyer then meets face-to-face with a representative for the seller and settles on a price for the security being traded. If a security is one that is not traded on an exchange, the broker sends the order to the firm's trading department, which trades it directly with a dealer in the over-the-counter market.

Brokers also offer advice and expertise. They may discuss an investor's financial goals with him. For example, some investors prefer long-term investments for capital gain or for providing income; others are looking for short-term investments and a quick profit. A securities broker may also put together a financial portfolio for a client which might include securities, tax shelters, annuities, and other investments.

In the beginning, brokers spend much of their time prospecting for clients. They may develop clients through business or social contacts, but many find it useful to gain additional exposure by teaching adult education investment courses or giving lectures at libraries or clubs.

Securities salespeople are employed by brokerage firms, investment bankers, and mutual funds. Most work in offices where there is a great deal of activity. When there is a major financial announcement or a significant news event that causes reaction in the financial community, the pace may become quite hectic.

To the securities broker, advancement is often in the form of continuing growth in size and volume of his or her client list. Some experienced brokers become branch office managers and supervise other salespeople while continuing to provide service for their own customers.

Earnings and Opportunities

Over 63,000 people work as securities brokers, and the number of jobs is expected to rise 36 percent in the next decade. Earnings for beginning brokers range from $14,500 to $25,000, but experienced brokers earn as much as $175,000 a year. Total income usually depends upon commissions, though trainees are generally paid a salary until they have met licensing and registration requirements.

Training and Qualifications

A competitive spirit and an interest in business and finance are important qualities for securities brokers. A college education is becoming increasingly important because of the growing importance of understanding economic trends. Brokers must also register as representatives of their firm. To do so, they must pass the Securities and Exchange Commission's General Securities Examination or other qualifying examinations.

For Further Details

Securities Industry Association, 20 Broad St., New York, NY 10005.

SECURITIES INDUSTRY OPERATIONS WORKERS

Duties and Responsibilities

While computers have greatly eased the work necessary to process and record hundreds of thousands of daily stock transactions, there is still much work that must be handled by people.

One important area of a brokerage house is where the securities are received, stored, and transferred. Because so many stocks and bonds are easily negotiable, security must be very tight, and *cage clerks* are the workers in this area who receive and deliver stocks and bonds, do stock recording, transfer securities, or box them for storage in the vault. (They are known as cage clerks because the area in which they work used to be encased in a metal cage for security reasons.)

Elsewhere in a brokerage firm, *margin clerks* keep track of customers' accounts to make sure they have not purchased more on credit (margin) than is legally allowed. *Compliance clerks* check to see that transactions are completed according to all rules and regulations. There are also *dividend clerks, clearance clerks*, and *purchase and sales clerks*, who work in the areas specified by their titles.

There are also numerous opportunities in middle management. The *stock loan manager* lends out the firm's excess securities to other houses. In addition to keeping tabs on stock sales, the *purchase and sales director* oversees the computing of taxes and commissions on all transactions. The *new accounts manager* is in charge of new accounts, and the *credit manager* supervises the amount of margin given.

On an exchange, there is also a great need for people who keep things running by helping to record transactions, balance accounts, and aid communications on the exchange floor. *Clerks* record, check, and deliver all transactions; while *pages* are very active on the floor of the exchange, running messages between brokers and their firms and from trader to trader.

Employment can be found in brokerage firms located throughout the United States, and on exchanges located in many urban areas.

Earnings and Opportunities

Employment opportunities are quite good, and earnings range from $7,000 to $8,500 for pages and from $9,000 to $15,000 for most brokerage clerks. Margin clerks generally earn a bit more, $15,000 to $20,000 for those with experience. Middle management workers generally average between $25,000 and $35,000.

Training and Qualifications

Accuracy and attention to detail, an ease with numbers, and the ability to work as part of a team are helpful qualities for these workers. A high school diploma is advised, and most clerks would benefit from courses in bookkeeping, typing, business arithmetic, and office machine operation. Those who aspire to middle management may want to work toward a college degree in order to further that goal.

BANK CLERKS

Duties and Responsibilities

Few of us are aware of all the work that must be done behind the scenes at a bank, savings and loan, or a small loan office. Who keeps track of your Christmas Club deposits? Who

sees to it that the check you wrote to a department store last month ends up in your bank statement this month? Who maintains the records for your mortgage, car payments or personal loan? All of these responsibilities belong to bank clerks, a group that includes secretaries, typists, bookkeepers, and office machine operators.

In a small bank, one clerk may do several jobs, but in a large bank, each usually has a specialty with a job title to match. Clerks known as *sorters* separate checks, deposit slips, and other items and see that they are charged and credited to the proper accounts. *Proof machine operators* use equipment that sorts, totals, and records checks and deposit slips. *Transit clerks* sort checks and drafts written on other banks and prepare documents to be mailed for collection. *Interest clerks* keep records on interest-bearing items, and *mortgage clerks* type legal papers dealing with real estate deals.

Bookkeeping specialties are also plentiful. A bank may employ a *Christmas Club bookkeeper,* an *interest-accrual bookkeeper,* and a *trust bookkeeper,* to mention a few. *Bookkeeping machine operators* run conventional or electronic posting machines to record financial transactions.

Banks now employ *electronic reader-sorter operators* who run electronic check-sorting equipment. A *check inscriber* operates machines that print the magnetic ink for machine reading on checks and documents.

Bank clerks may also do routine typing, calculating, and posting, and many use canceling and adding machines daily. Some clerks work evenings and weekends, but most work about thirty-six hours per week during normal business hours. They generally do not deal with customers, and though their jobs require specialized knowledge, much of their work can become routine.

A clerk may be promoted to a clerical supervisory position, to teller or credit analyst. Exceptional candidates who have college training or have taken specialized courses in banking may even advance to a bank officer position.

Earnings and Opportunities

Banks employ over 1 million clerks, and the employment outlook is very good. Earnings range from $8,000 to $18,200.

Training and Qualifications

Facility with numbers is important, as are accuracy and attention to detail, because mistakes can be costly. The clerk should be able to work rapidly, function well under close supervision, and work effectively as part of a team.

A high school diploma is generally required for employment at most banks. Courses in bookkeeping, typing, business arithmetic, and office machine operation are helpful. Most new employees receive on-the-job training.

For Further Details

American Bankers Association, Bank Personnel Division, 1120 Connecticut Ave., N.W., Washington, DC 20036. National Association of Bank Women, Inc., National Office, 500 N. Michigan Ave., Chicago, IL 60611. National Bankers Association, 499 S. Capitol St., S.W., Suite 520, Washington, DC 20003.

BANK OFFICERS

Duties and Responsibilities

The staid image of the genteel banker who starts work at 9 A.M. and leaves for home by 5 P.M. is quickly becoming a thing of the past. With the continuing deregulation of the banking industry and the resulting availability of more and more banking services, today's bank officers are aggressive marketers who are helping to make banking an industry of the future.

Within the field there are a wide variety of specialties, but regardless of the department in which an officer works, his or her prime responsibilities involve promoting and managing the financial services offered by the bank. Officers make decisions within a framework of policy set by the bank's board of directors and existing federal and state laws and regulations.

Banks make part of their money by making loans for which they charge interest, and *loan officers* are in charge of deciding to whom the bank lends money. Officers generally specialize in either consumer (personal) loans, commercial (business) loans, or mortgages. All loan officers base their decisions on the customer's credit rating, financial statement, and overall ability to pay back the loan. The job is a challenging one, because if the officers are too conservative, they may lose business to their competitors; but if they are too lenient, the bank may lose money on a bad loan.

There are several ranks of loan officer, from the junior loan officer who works with small loans that can basically be decided by formula, to middle management officers who oversee consumer and business loans that require some subjectivity. At the top are loan officers who give approval to loans in the hundreds of thousands of dollars.

In order to have money to lend out, banks must have money coming in, and that's where the *new accounts officer* (or *business development officer*) comes in. These workers function as sales representatives for the bank, soliciting new accounts and selling new services to both old and new accounts. This is such an important area that members of the board, the president, and other senior officers also participate.

Branch officers (or *managers*) manage the local branches of major banks. They are responsible for integrating the branch office into the neighborhood and soliciting local business. They also supervise tellers, oversee daily operations, and offer financial advice to customers.

Administrative efficiency is the domain of *operations officers,* who plan, coordinate, and control the bank's work flow, update systems, and strive for expeditious handling of the paperwork that travels between departments. *Electronic data processing managers* work in this area, and with the advent of electronic banking it is an important field of the future.

Trust officers are responsible for managing the trusts and estates that customers have en-trusted to the bank. They must see to the proper execution of legal agreements and details regarding the investment and distribution of funds, and they must be knowledgeable about probate and tax laws. Often, investment decisions are made solely by the trust officer, so investment strategies and financial planning are an important part of the job.

Financial planning officers are responsible for charting the future of the bank. Performance planners work with top management to determine goals and strategies, while officers in corporate finance oversee the bank's acquisitions and decide on the investment of bank funds—in government securities, Eurodollars, bonds, etc.

One need only read the headlines to realize the importance of the *international banking officer,* who plans the overall policy for the international division and develops new and existing services for this market. Should more money be lent to a foreign country? Should a current loan be restructured or taken as a bad debt? These are the kinds of questions that often must be resolved.

Correspondent bank officers establish relationships and coordinate the business that takes place with their correspondent banks (out-of-town banks with whom a bank chooses to do regular business). Other specialties for bank officers include auditing, economics, site selection, real estate and construction, and personnel administration.

Bank officers typically work a forty-hour week, although those in middle and top management may also have outside business responsibilities and community commitments that require extra time.

Workers generally enter the field by being accepted as *bank officer trainees* in a management training program. From there, beginners become junior members of various departments and may hold titles such as *junior trust officer* or *loan officer trainee.* At smaller banks that have no formal training program, new employees start out as junior officers or in assistant positions.

Advancement generally involves progressing through the ranks to the position of senior officer. Those intent on staying on the fast track often find that an international assignment is a quick way to get overall management experience. Some bank officers transfer to closely related positions in other areas of finance or to positions within other industries, such as manufacturing, where bank expertise is needed.

Earnings and Opportunities

Over 400,000 people are employed in bank management, and the outlook for employment is excellent, with a 45 percent increase in the number of jobs projected in the next ten years. Earnings range from $14,000 to $21,400 for trainees, and to $60,000 and up for officers. Some of the major commercial banks that are expanding into corporate investment banking are offering rich pay packages to attract and keep top talent. Base pay ranges up to $125,000, and bonuses sometimes increase the package by 50 to 100 percent.

Training and Qualifications

Good judgment and the ability to analyze detailed information are key qualities for bank officers and managers. Communications and sales skills are also important.

Those who enter management training programs offered by many banks are generally college graduates in finance or business administration, and a master's degree in business administration (M.B.A.) degree provides an even stronger background.

Some bank clerks and tellers move into management ranks, and banks also have room for some people with diverse backgrounds and education, such as in chemical engineering, nuclear physics, agriculture, and forestry. Expertise in these areas helps them meet the needs of the businesses and industries with which banks are involved.

For Further Details

American Bankers Association, Bank Personnel Division, 1120 Connecticut Ave., N.W., Washington, DC 20036. National Association of Bank Women, Inc., National Office, 500 N. Michigan Ave., Chicago, IL 60611. National Bankers Association, 499 S. Capitol St., S.W., Suite 520, Washington, DC 20003.

BANK TELLERS

Duties and Responsibilities

Most of us have more frequent personal contact with bank tellers than with any other person at the bank, and our overall impression of a bank may be based largely on how the tellers treat us. Because of their high visibility, tellers' jobs are very important.

In smaller firms a teller is likely to perform all types of functions, but at larger banks they may specialize. One may sell savings bonds, another may accept Christmas Club payments, while a third keeps records on customer loans. Still others handle foreign currencies, sell travelers' checks, or compute interest on various types of savings accounts.

Commercial tellers, the most common kind, cash customers' checks and handle deposits and withdrawals from various types of ac-

counts. Before cashing a check, the teller must compare the written and numerical amounts on the check, verify the identity of the person receiving payment, and be certain that the account has sufficient funds. Cash must be counted out carefully to avoid errors. Occasionally a cashier's check must be drawn. When accepting a deposit, the teller checks the accuracy of the deposit slip and enters the total in a passbook or on a deposit receipt. In many banks, tellers use computer terminals to record deposits and withdrawals.

Before banking hours begin, tellers receive and count the working cash for their drawer and verify the amount with their supervisor. They will be responsible for the safe and accurate handling of their drawer throughout the day. After hours, tellers count cash on hand, list the currency-received tickets on a settlement sheet, and then balance the day's accounts. They also sort checks and deposit slips.

Some tellers work evenings or on Saturdays, but most work Monday through Friday during normal business hours. In addition, a new move is afoot that is making part-time work very attractive. In an effort to attract older, better-educated workers for part-time assignments, Cincinnati's Provident Bank began paying "peak time" tellers from $7.59 per hour for a twenty-hour week to $9.39 per hour for a nine-hour week. (Pay for full-timers is usually $4.50 to $5.00 plus benefits.) The bank has found a drop in absenteeism and turnover and reports that cash shortages have shrunk and continuity of service is up. Many banks have observed the experiment and are expected to follow suit.

While the banking community has been encouraging increased customer use of automatic teller machines, this is not bad news for tellers. Overall employment of tellers is not likely to be adversely affected. Instead, they will become more specialized and will work with more complex matters that require personal attention.

After gaining experience, a teller may advance to head teller, and one who has had some college or specialized training may be promoted to officer or to a managerial position.

Earnings and Opportunities

Over 480,000 people work as tellers, many of them part-time, and this number is expected to increase by 29 percent in the next ten years. Earnings: $7,800 to $25,000, with a few over $40,000.

Training and Qualifications

Because there is a great deal of customer contact, the person who is neat, friendly, courteous, and attentive has excellent personal qualifications. He or she should enjoy working with numbers and feel comfortable handling large amounts of money. Clerical skills are also important.

A high school education is preferred. Training may consist of a few days to three weeks of on-the-job training or taking part in a formal training program at larger banks. Beginners usually start as commercial tellers, or in larger banks as savings tellers.

For Further Details

American Bankers Association, Bank Personnel Division, 1120 Connecticut Ave., N.W., Washington, DC 20036.

COLLECTORS

Duties and Responsibilities

A company that has extended credit to a customer expects to be paid on time. Unfortunately, it doesn't always work that way, and collection workers, also called bill collectors or collection agents, are responsible for bringing in a company's delinquent and bad debts. The job offers an excellent opportunity for a quick-witted person who is skilled at the art of persuasion.

The collector, either employed by a third party, such as a bank or collection agency, or working directly for the company itself, usually receives a bad debt file after the com-

pany's regular monthly statements and collection form letters have failed to elicit payment. The collector then contacts the debtor by phone, mail, or in person and inquires about why the bill has not been paid. When customers have financial emergencies or have mismanaged their money, collectors may work with the company and customer to outline a new payment schedule satisfactory to both.

Sometimes collectors find that people have not paid because they feel they have been wrongly charged or because they are dissatisfied with services or merchandise. Then collectors encourage debtors to contact the company to resolve the disagreement. If a collector finds a customer is fraudulently avoiding payment, he or she may recommend that the files be turned over to an attorney.

Sometimes collectors find that a debtor has moved without leaving a forwarding address. Then the collection worker becomes a detective of sorts, contacting all available sources in an effort to locate the person. This job is known as *skip tracing.*

Some collectors work as repossessors and are employed by creditors to locate and return goods that have not been paid for, such as automobiles or television sets.

Most collectors are employed by commercial banks, finance companies, credit unions, and collection agencies, and some work for retail and wholesale businesses and public utilities.

Contact with the debtor is usually by telephone, so most of a collector's time is spent in the office.

Workers with above-average abilities may become collection managers or may supervise a staff of collectors. A few collection workers progress to other positions in the credit field, such as credit authorizer, bank loan officer, or credit manager.

Earnings and Opportunities

Over 90,000 people are employed as collectors, and the employment outlook is good. Earnings range from $12,000 to $18,500, and over $36,000 for management.

Training and Qualifications

Collectors must have the ability to talk to strangers in a tactful, persuasive manner in order to encourage them to fulfill their financial obligations. They should be alert, imaginative, and quick-witted in order to handle whatever situations may arise.

Employers usually look for applicants with a high school diploma and then provide on-the-job training in collection procedures and telephone techniques.

For Further Details

American Collectors Association, 4040 W. 70th St., P.O. Box 35106, Minneapolis, MN 55435.

ECONOMISTS

Duties and Responsibilities

The economy has always had a major effect on everyone's life, but the public interest in economics is a recent phenomenon. Economic news has moved from academic journals and the business page to best-selling books and the front page. We're realizing that business news affects our jobs, our ability to get a mortgage, and whether or not we can buy that new TV we've been wanting.

The work of economists is to study the way a society uses its resources. By analyzing the results and determining the costs and benefits of using certain resources in a particular way, they try to advise business firms, insurance companies, banks, and government so that each of these groups might use the informa-

tion to plan properly. When economists come out with a new prediction about interest rates, for example, this may affect how banks choose to handle upcoming loans.

Some economists are theoreticians, using mathematical models to develop theories that attempt to explain things like the causes of inflation. Most economists, however, are concerned with practical applications of economic policy in a particular area. They may study such topics as energy costs, inflation, business cycles, unemployment, tax policy, or farm prices.

Economists who work for business firms may be asked to provide management with information to make decisions on marketing and pricing of company products; to look at the advisability of adding new lines of merchandise, opening new branches, or diversifying the company's operations; or to prepare economic and business forecasts.

Those who work for government agencies assess economic conditions in the U.S. and abroad and estimate the economic impact of specific changes in legislation or public policy.

Economists in colleges and universities teach the theories, principles, and methods of economics. They may also serve as consultants to businesses or government agencies.

Experienced economists may advance to managerial or executive positions in banks, industrial concerns, trade associations, and other organizations to formulate business and administrative policy.

Earnings and Opportunities

Over 44,000 people are employed as economists, and job prospects are promising through the mid '90s, with an increase in employment of 27 percent projected. Salaries generally range from $35,000 to $55,000, though a considerable number of base salaries are over $75,000. Economists in general administration and economic advisers command the highest

salaries, while econometricians and teachers have the lowest base.

Training and Qualifications

Since much time is spent on data analysis, future economists should enjoy working with numbers and detail, and they should be objective and systematic in their work. Patience and persistence are also helpful.

A bachelor's degree with a major in economics is sufficient for many beginning jobs. In most jobs, however, a graduate degree usually qualifies one for more responsible research and administrative positions. A master's degree is generally the minimum requirement for a college instructor at a junior college or a small four-year school, while a Ph.D. is usually required at the larger colleges and universities.

For Further Details

American Economic Association, 1313 21st Ave. S., Nashville, TN 37212. National Association of Business Economists, 28349 Chargin Blvd., Suite 201, Cleveland, OH 44122.

ACTUARIES

Duties and Responsibilities

Why do you pay one rate for your car insurance while your neighbor pays another? The answer has to do with the amount of risk the company must assume by insuring either one of you, and insurance workers known as actuaries use statistics to assess the amount of risk involved in each case. They also calculate the costs associated with insuring such risks.

Actuaries calculate the probabilities of death, sickness, injury, disability, unemployment, retirement, and property loss for all different kinds of insurance. For example, an actuary at a company offering homeowners' insurance may calculate how likely it is for a person living in Pueblo, Colorado, to be burglarized. He or she then calculates a price for

the insurance that would enable the insurance company to pay all claims and expenses if necessary, while still keeping the rate competitive with other insurance companies.

Most actuaries specialize in either life and health insurance or property and liability (casualty) insurance; a growing number specialize in pension plans.

Actuaries must keep informed about general economic and social trends and legislative, health, and other developments that may affect insurance practices.

Actuaries in executive positions help determine company policy. They may be called upon to explain complex matters to company executives, government officials, policyholders, and the public.

More than half of all actuaries work for private insurance companies. Most work for life insurance companies, and the rest work for property and liability companies. In addition, a growing number of actuaries are employed by consulting firms, rating bureaus, and accounting firms.

Advancement from assistant to associate and chief actuary depends largely on job performance and the number of actuarial examinations passed. Many actuaries are selected for administrative positions in underwriting, accounting, or data processing departments. Some advance to top executive positions.

Earnings and Opportunities

Over 8,000 persons are employed as actuaries, and job prospects are very good, as the number of actuaries is expected to increase 33 percent by the mid '90s. Earnings: $24,000 to $44,000, with some over $60,000.

Training and Qualifications

A strong background in mathematics and statistics as well as a basic fascination with num-

bers is important for the person considering this career.

A degree in actuarial science is the best educational background to have, but a bachelor's degree with a major in mathematics or statistics is acceptable. Students who pass one or more of the examinations offered by professional actuarial societies while still in school will have the best opportunity for employment.

Once employed, actuaries are encouraged to complete the entire series of exams in their specialty as soon as possible.

For Further Details

American Society of Pension Actuaries, 1700 K St., N.W., Washington, DC 20006. Casualty Actuarial Society, 1 Penn Plaza, 250 W. 34th St., New York, NY 10119. Society of Actuaries, 208 S. LaSalle St., Chicago, IL 60604. American Academy of Actuaries, 1835 K St., N.W., Suite 515, Washington, DC 20006.

CLAIM REPRESENTATIVES

Duties and Responsibilities

If your car is damaged in an accident or your basement floods during a rainstorm, you'll want to collect from your insurance company as soon as possible. Before receiving payment, however, you will be contacted by a claim representative (either a claim adjuster or a claim examiner) who will investigate your claim, negotiate settlement with you, and finally authorize payment.

Whenever a casualty insurance company receives a claim, the *claim adjuster* determines whether the policy covers the loss and the amount of the loss. Claim adjusters' responsibilities are to protect their companies from false or inflated claims and to settle valid claims fairly and promptly. Some adjusters are generalists, while others specialize in fire damage, marine loss, automobile damage, workers' compensation loss, or product liability.

Most adjusters are employed by insurance companies, some by independent adjusting firms, and a few, known as public adjusters, are retained by the insured (business, government, or individual) to negotiate claims with the insurance company.

Adjusters plan and schedule their own investigations, keep accurate records, and prepare written reports. They are away from the office most of the time and may be called to the site of an accident, burglary, or disaster. Evening and weekend work is common.

In life and health insurance companies, the counterpart of the adjuster is the *claim examiner*, who investigates questionable claims or those exceeding a specific amount. The examiner may interview medical specialists, consult policy files to verify information, and calculate benefit payments.

Examiners work primarily by mail and by phone, and rarely travel to do personal interviews. On occasion, both adjusters and examiners must testify in court on contested claims.

Advancement may mean becoming department supervisor in a field office or moving to a managerial position in the home office. Some go into underwriting or sales.

Earnings and Opportunities

Over 210,000 people work as claim representatives, and the outlook for employment is very good. Earnings range from $16,200 to $17,600 at the entry level, and go to $20,500 and higher for supervisory positions.

Training and Qualifications

Claim representatives work closely with people under all kinds of circumstances, sometimes difficult ones. They may have to question witnesses to an accident, for example, or explain to someone why his claim will not be honored. For this reason, the ability to establish a good rapport and communicate clearly is very important. In addition, a facility in mathematics is helpful.

Though no specific major is recommended, a college education is preferred. However, people with special expertise sometimes can qualify without a college degree. For example, a person knowledgeable about car repair might become an auto adjuster. Most large insurance companies provide on-the-job training.

For Further Details

Insurance Information Institute, 110 William St., New York, NY 10038. Alliance of American Insurers, 20 N. Wacker Dr., Chicago, IL 60606. The National Association of Independent Insurers, 2600 River Rd., Des Plaines, IL 60018. National Association of Independent Insurance Adjusters, 175 W. Jackson Blvd., Chicago, IL 60604.

UNDERWRITERS

Duties and Responsibilities

When someone is refused an insurance policy or has difficulty getting a particular kind of coverage, it's not the local insurance agent who is responsible—those decisions are made by an underwriter who usually represents a national insurance company. It is the underwriter's job to appraise and select the risks his company will insure.

Underwriters analyze information on insurance applications, reports from loss control consultants, medical reports, and actuarial studies (reports that describe the probability of insured loss) in order to decide whether their companies will write a policy. It is an important responsibility, because if they appraise risks too conservatively their companies may lose business to competitors, but if they are too liberal in their appraisal the company may end up having to pay additional claims.

Most underwriters specialize in one of three major categories of insurance: life, health, or property and liability. They further specialize in group or individual policies, and many specialties are broken down still further. For example, fire risk may be one underwriter's area of expertise, while another knows automobile risk or workers' compensation.

When deciding that an applicant is an acceptable risk, an underwriter may also outline the terms of the contract, including figuring the amount of the premium, since it varies according to the risk involved. Underwriters frequently correspond with policyholders, agents, and managers about policy cancellations or other requests for information.

An increasing amount of insurance is being sold through group plans. Here an underwriter must analyze the overall composition of the group to be sure that the total risk is not more than he or she feels the company will want to handle. Some underwriters meet with group representatives in order to discuss the types of policies available to the group.

Over 75 percent of underwriters specialize in property and liability, and they generally work out of regional or home offices; most life insurance underwriters are employed in home offices in a few large cities. They generally work a standard forty-hour week.

Experienced underwriters may advance to chief underwriter or underwriting manager. Some underwriting managers are promoted to senior managerial jobs.

Earnings and Opportunities

Over 76,000 people work as underwriters, and the outlook for employment is good. The number of jobs for underwriters is expected to rise 21 percent in the next ten years. Earnings: $19,600 to $46,000 and up.

Training and Qualifications

Decisiveness, communications skills, and the ability to do detailed work accurately are im-portant qualities for underwriters. Most large insurance companies seek college graduates, but some small companies hire people without a college degree for trainee positions. New employees learn the job by working under the close supervision of an experienced worker until they develop the necessary ability to ap-praise risk.

For Further Details

American Council of Life Insurance, 1850 K St., N.W., Washington, DC 20006. Insurance Information Institute, 110 William St., New York, NY 10038. Alliance of American Insurers, 20 N. Wacker Drive, Chicago, IL 60606. The National Association of Independent Insurers, Public Relations Dept., 2600 River Rd., Des Plaines, IL 60018.

ACCOUNTANTS AND AUDITORS

Duties and Responsibilities

The day of the nose-to-the-ledger accountant with the green eyeshade has passed. Today accounting is an exciting profession that can lead to the president's chair of a major corporation, a partner's seat in an accounting firm, or to owning your own business.

Accountants are some of the finest sales-people you'll find. Whether they are selling their clients on new accounting or tax tech-niques or their employers on cost control and budgeting, they have to know how to persuade as well as how to figure.

Accounting is a growing field, with many types of specialties and responsibilities. *Management accountants,* also called industrial or private accountants, work on staff at major companies and provide the financial in-formation executives need to make business decisions. They may work in areas such as tax-ation, budgeting, costs, investments, or inter-nal auditing.

As a *public accountant,* one might work for an independent accounting firm or be self-employed. Clients would include individuals and small-to-medium-sized businesses. Many spe-cialize in traditional areas, such as taxes or au-diting (examining a client's financial records and attesting to them). But as a growing num-ber of accounting firms take on pension and trust work and other management advisory jobs, public accountants increasingly serve as management consultants, offering advice to businesses on improving their accounting and financial systems or on financial applications of computers or electronic data processing sys-tems. And the demand for middle managers to help handle these expanded services has in-creased dramatically.

Thousands of *government accountants and auditors* are employed by such agencies as the IRS and GAO. They examine the records of government agencies and audit private busi-nesses and individuals whose dealings are subject to government regulations.

During tax season, tax accountants work long hours under heavy pressure. Accountants employed by large firms may travel exten-sively in their work. Those who teach on the staffs of universities and business and profes-sional schools have more flexible schedules.

Those who are self-employed may even set up offices at home. Part-time work is often available, because the field is growing and because of the seasonal nature of tax work.

Earnings and Opportunities

About 900,000 people are employed as accountants, and job prospects are excellent, with a projected increase in jobs of 40 percent in the next decade. Earnings: $15,400 to $22,500 for entry level, and to $54,000, with some over $100,000, for experienced accountants.

Training and Qualifications

Though many who do not have a college degree do land junior accounting positions, most public accounting and business firms require at least a bachelor's degree and many prefer a

master's degree. Some also require a law degree for highly technical tax accounting.

Certification or licensing is also extremely valuable. Anyone working as a *certified public accountant* must hold a certificate and a license issued by a state-run board of accountancy.

For a *public accountant* or *accounting practitioner* license or registration, some states require only a high school diploma.

For Further Details

American Institute of Certified Public Accountants, 1211 Ave. of the Americas, New York, NY 10036. National Association of Accountants, 919 Third Ave., New York, NY 10022. National Society of Public Accountants, 1010 N. Fairfax St., Alexandria, VA 22314. Institute of Internal Auditors, 249 Maitland Ave., Altamonte Springs, FL 32701.

BOOKKEEPERS AND ACCOUNTING CLERKS

Duties and Responsibilities

Business would come to a standstill if there weren't people to keep track of daily business transactions, company financial records, and customer accounts. Bookkeepers and accounting clerks are the workers who bear this responsibility.

In a small firm, general bookkeepers may handle most of the company bookkeeping. They analyze and record all financial transactions such as orders and cash sales. They balance accounts, calculate payrolls, and issue employee paychecks. They also prepare and mail bills and answer customer telephone requests for information about orders and bills. A full-charge bookkeeper is also able to balance the books at the end of the month, reconcile bank statements, prepare profit and loss statements, and update the company's balance sheet.

In large companies, several bookkeepers and clerks work under the direction of a head bookkeeper or accountant. Each worker tends to have a specialty. Some prepare income

statements or tally daily operating expenses. Others enter accounts receivable and accounts payable data into a computer and review printouts. Business transactions, payroll deductions, and bills paid and due may be handled by other workers, while still others may type vouchers, invoices, and other financial records. Most use calculating machines, some use check-writing and bookkeeping machines, and many are learning to work with computers.

Most bookkeepers and accounting clerks work for business firms, but they are also needed in schools, hospitals, nonprofit organizations, and government agencies.

They work a standard forty-hour week, and the day involves a great deal of desk work with long periods of time spent concentrating on figures.

Newly hired workers begin by recording routine transactions such as accounts receivable or accounts payable. As they gain experience, they may advance to more responsible assignments such as preparing income statements, reconciling accounts, and reviewing computer printouts. Some bookkeeping workers are promoted to supervisory jobs. Others who enroll in college accounting programs may advance to jobs as accountants.

Earnings and Opportunities

Almost 2 million people are employed as bookkeepers and accounting clerks, and the outlook for employment is good, with a 16 percent increase in jobs projected in ten years. Salaries range from $9,500 to $21,000 and can go in excess of $44,000 for supervisory positions.

Training and Qualifications

Bookkeepers have to be good at working with numbers and concentrating on details. Small mistakes can mean big problems, so accuracy is vital.

The minimum requirement for most book-keeping jobs is a high school diploma, with courses in business arithmetic, bookkeeping, and the principles of accounting, though many employers prefer applicants who have taken some additional training.

Training for the occupation is widely available in high schools, community and junior colleges, and business schools. Business education programs typically include courses in bookkeeping-accounting, business law, business arithmetic, office practices, and principles of data processing and computer operation.

For Further Details

A directory of private business schools located throughout the country can be obtained at no charge from: Association of Independent Colleges and Schools, 1730 M Street N.W., Suite 600, Washington, DC 20036.

FINANCIAL PLANNERS AND BUSINESS MANAGERS

Duties and Responsibilities

Managing money—from the family budget to the investment portfolio—is one of the most important areas of our lives. No matter what kinds of financial resources we have, whatever the size of our salaries or bank accounts may be, we all share an interest and concern in this area, and that's where professional financial planners come in. Their job is to advise people on how to invest their money, handle their finances, and establish financial goals based on personal needs.

Though this is a relatively new field, the number of financial planners is growing at an amazing rate, and the public has been utilizing their services more and more. While planners used to work mainly with the wealthy, middle class people are now turning to them in order to take advantage of their financial expertise. In addition, financial counseling has become a fast-growing executive perk, with a good percentage of companies now offering it, which contributes to the demand for financial planners. Interest in benefiting from tax-sheltered income has also spurred the popularity of financial planning services.

Financial planners meet with individuals and review their holdings, their financial commitment, their family and personal needs, and their investment goals. They then make recommendations and tailor investment strategies to fit those particular needs. A family with children, for example, will need to begin saving for college, while a middle-aged couple with no family will need to focus on retirement planning. All these aspects are carefully reviewed and recommendations varying from stocks and bonds to real estate and tax shelters are made.

Business managers combine financial planning knowledge and skills with day-to-day management of someone's finances. Managers allocate cash, establish living-expense budgets, provide for retirement plans, and handle all tax responsibilities as they take charge of all the client's financial dealings.

Planners sometimes work for financial institutions. However, many are self-employed. The work involves following the investment markets closely and spending a great deal of time doing financial analysis. Time is also spent counseling individuals, and long-term clients may phone for advice on a regular basis.

Earnings and Opportunities

Planners generally charge a basic rate for a consultation—usually a flat fee or an hourly charge. Some charge commission fees from the investments they recommend. Earnings range from $30,000 to $150,000.

Training and Qualifications

Financial planners and business managers must be knowledgeable about the ins and outs of today's fast-paced economy. A solid business education is a plus, as is specialized work in accounting, investment, insurance, law, and finance. Some planners and managers are C.P.A.'s, while others earn certification from the Denver-based College of Financial Planning or the American College, a school for insurance professionals in Bryn Mawr, Pennsylvania.

For Further Details

Institute of Certified Financial Planners, 3443, S. Galena St., Suite 190, Denver, CO 80231. The International Association for Financial Planning, 5775 Peachtree Dunwoody Rd., N.E., Suite 120-C, Atlanta, GA 30342.

INCOME TAX PREPARERS

Duties and Responsibilities

It is said that death and taxes are the only things certain in life, and since this seems to be so, and we can't avoid them, many people decide the least they can do with the latter is seek help.

Professional income tax preparers are becoming increasingly important because of our complex tax systems. Sometimes people turn to preparers because they simply can't understand how the tax codes apply to them; other times they want to learn more about how they can take advantage of recent changes that might help them save money. As inflation pushes more people into higher tax brackets, more and more will seek help.

Tax preparers are knowledgeable in federal, state, and local tax codes, and up to date on all changes. Some now use computers to aid in completing and verifying the forms.

In their work they help clients gather the needed financial information, complete the necessary forms, determine their tax liability (or refund), and file within the deadline. They can also advise on tax-saving ideas to use all year round, and may provide other related financial counsel. Many tax preparers will also assist with and accompany clients on an audit when necessary.

Most tax preparers work for themselves as independents or franchisees of large income tax preparation firms, generally in local offices where clients come in to discuss and have their returns prepared. The bulk of this work falls between February and April 15. Though there is full-time work available for some income tax preparers (who assist people who file late, receive delays, or have to go through audits), many who enter this field of work do so for the advantages of the three-to-four-month work schedule. Because of the short tax period and clients' work schedules, much work is done in the evening and on weekends.

Many accountants, lawyers, and C.P.A.'s moonlight as tax preparers or go into the business on a full-time basis. Much of their work is done in their home or office or in the client's office.

Earnings and Opportunities

Opportunities in this field should continue to be good as the tax laws continue to change, requiring the public to turn to professionals for assistance. Earnings vary from $5,000 to $25,000.

Training and Qualifications

An ability to work with numbers, good organizational skills, strong reading comprehension, and analytical ability are helpful qualities in this field.

A degree in accounting is not vital, but certainly it is helpful, particularly for those who aspire to make it a full-time career.

Those who work seasonally should have a high school diploma and take the tax courses provided by large income tax preparation firms or other education and training centers. Job applicants will generally be expected to pass an exam covering the current tax code prior to being hired.

For Further Details

Federated Tax Service, Dept. MM-9, 2021 Montrose Avenue, Chicago, IL 60618.

Careers in Federal and Municipal Government

The government employs almost every type of worker imaginable. This includes the chef who prepares the meals for the Senate, the curator in charge of colonial furniture at the Smithsonian, air controllers, construction inspectors, and CIA operatives investigating foreign espionage, to name just a few.

On the federal, state, and local levels there are probably job possibilities you've never thought of, and for the most part, government employees are well paid for their efforts. Benefits are also quite good.

The process of promotion can be frustrating, because it may be contingent on a number of considerations—time in grade, civil service exams, education, experience—not to mention politics, unions, and the economy. However, giving something back to your nation and your community should give you a sense of pride, a feeling of worth, because you're useful and involved in helping your fellow citizens.

The jobs listed here are just a sampling of career opportunities with the government, and are limited to those occupations found solely in government agencies. Bear in mind, however, that virtually every job listed in this book could be found at some level of government. The government is the country's largest employer and needs people with all manner of business, managerial, technical, and professional backgrounds.

AIR TRAFFIC CONTROLLERS

Duties and Responsibilities

When it comes to the job of taking responsibility for hundreds of lives on a moment-to-moment basis, Americans want the best talent available. The position of air traffic controller is just such a job, and it requires a keen mind capable of processing many items of information at once, a decisive spirit, and nerves of steel.

Air traffic controllers are responsible for shepherding hundreds of planes through the airways daily. Some controllers regulate airport traffic; others regulate flights between airports. For all controllers safety is paramount, but efficiency and on-time service are always on their minds too.

At airports, controllers rely on radar and visual observation to monitor all planes that pass through airport airspace. During arrival and departure, each plane is handled by several controllers. For the initial approach, a pilot radios the *arrival controller,* who will direct him to a holding pattern or to a runway when one is free. As the plane nears the runway, the pilot then works with a *local controller,* who monitors the aircraft during the last mile or so, delaying any departures that would interfere with the plane's approach. Once the plane lands, the *ground controller,* working almost entirely by sight, directs it along the taxiways. For departure, a similar process occurs in reverse.

Once on its way, a plane is monitored by *enroute controllers* at one of the twenty-five enroute control centers throughout the country. All controllers are usually in charge of several planes at one time, and often have to make quick decisions simultaneously. In addition to working at airports and enroute centers, controllers are also employed at flight service stations operated at over 300 airports, where pilots can obtain up-to-date information about the local area.

Controllers work a basic forty-hour week. There is overtime, however, and since air travel is a twenty-four-hour-a-day process, they should expect to work some nights and weekends.

To advance, controllers can transfer to jobs at different locations or move up to supervisory positions, including management or staff jobs in air traffic control and top administrative jobs with the Federal Aviation Administration (FAA).

Earnings and Opportunities

Over 29,000 people are employed as air traffic controllers, and employment opportunities are fair. Earnings: $22,500 to $40,000.

Training and Qualifications

Air traffic controllers must have an excellent memory for keeping track of detailed information. They need to be decisive and able to communicate clearly with pilots.

They must have three years of general work experience or four years of college or a combination of both. They must pass physical and psychological examinations and have eyesight correctable to 20/20.

Those who qualify get on-the-job and classroom training. They receive approximately sixteen weeks of intensive training, including practice on simulators. Some learn their trade in the armed forces.

For Further Details

Contact the U.S. Office of Personnel Management Job Information Center nearest you. (Check the phone book under U.S. Government.)

FEDERAL AGENTS

Duties and Responsibilities

Tracking down kidnappers, investigating political corruption, stopping counterfeiting, or nabbing spies are the kinds of cases assigned to federal agents. Whether they work for the FBI or the CIA, their primary function is to investigate violations of federal laws and matters involving national security.

Each group has jurisdiction over a different area of federal investigation; and within their divisions, special agents are generally assigned to cases that relate to their background. A computer expert, for example, might be assigned to investigate computer crime. In fact, the workers currently in greatest demand by the FBI have backgrounds in electrical engineering or computer science, and many are employed doing acoustical and video research. An example of this is the re-examination of the Kennedy assassination gunfire tapes, in which experts study the timing and origin of the gunfire. Now undergoing a four-year staffing buildup, the agency is hiring up to forty such workers a year.

Other areas of specialization include theft of government property, organized crime, foreign espionage, drugs (alcohol, tobacco, marijuana, and narcotics), terrorism, racketeering, smuggling, bank robberies, and protection of the President and other government officials.

Though the stories that make headlines are usually elaborate sting operations like ABSCAM, there is also a lot of day-to-day fact gathering that never makes the news. One job of the special agent is to collect evidence in cases where the U.S. government is or may be an interested party. In their casework, agents conduct interviews, examine records, observe the activities of suspects, and participate in raids or arrests. Frequently agents must testify in court about cases they investigate. However, the work is highly confidential and agents may not disclose any of the information gathered in their official duties to unauthorized persons, including members of their families.

Agents often work alone, but are usually teamed with other agents when performing potentially dangerous duties such as arrests or raids. Agents are based in offices, but much of their time is spent doing fieldwork—visiting homes, offices, or industrial plants, and interviewing all kinds of people.

Special agents are on call twenty-four hours a day, and the job may require travel. Agents are trained in the use of firearms, and there is sometimes the risk of personal injury.

Earnings and Opportunities

Over 20,000 people are employed as federal agents, and the outlook for employment is good. Earnings: $28,500 to $48,000.

Training and Qualifications

An analytical mind, the ability to pay close attention to detail and perseverance are important qualities for federal agents. Being capable of handling firearms and fully exerting oneself physically in dangerous situations, excellent hearing and vision, and normal color perception are also vital. Applicants must be U.S. citizens between the ages of twenty-three and thirty-five and must be willing to serve anywhere in the world.

From an educational standpoint, the needs of the government vary greatly. The minimum is usually a college degree. Additional schooling in law is usually helpful, as is fluency in a second language.

All applicants must pass a rigid physical examination and fitness tests as well as written and oral examinations testing their aptitude for meeting the public and conducting investigations. Background and character investigations are also made of all applicants.

For Further Details

Federal Bureau of Investigation, U.S. Department of Justice, Washington, DC 20535. Central Intelligence Agency, Washington, DC 20505. U.S. Secret Service, 1900 G Street, Washington, DC 20223.

REGULATORY INSPECTORS

Duties and Responsibilities

Protecting the public welfare is the duty of regulatory inspectors, who ensure that laws and regulations in their fields are obeyed. These workers fall into several different categories:

Immigration inspectors interview and ex-amine people who want to enter the United States. Checking passports and verifying the person's citizenship, identity, and legal eligibility are all part of the job. They also process petitions for immigration or temporary residence in the United States.

Customs inspectors are stationed at airports, seaports, and border crossing points, and they are responsible for counting, weighing, and sampling commercial cargos entering and leaving the United States to determine the amount of tax to be paid. If you return to the U.S. from a foreign country, your bags and belongings will also be inspected by these workers to be sure that all merchandise is properly declared and taxes are paid on it.

Air safety inspectors work for the Federal Aviation Administration to see that the quality and safety of aircraft and equipment are maintained. They also certify aircraft pilots, pilot examiners, flight instructors, schools, and instructional materials.

Occupational safety and health inspectors visit all types of worksites to detect unsafe or unhealthy working conditions. They check machinery and equipment and observe employees at work to see that proper safety precautions are taken.

Mine inspectors visit mines and related facilities to enforce safety laws and regulations. They also investigate accidents and direct rescue and firefighting operations.

Wage-hour compliance inspectors inspect employers' time, payroll, and personnel records to ensure compliance with federal law on such matters as wages and equal employment opportunity.

Alcohol, tobacco, and firearms inspectors inspect facilities where these products are made and sold, to check compliance with revenue laws and other regulations on operating procedures, unfair competition and trade practices, and to determine that the proper taxes are paid.

Most inspectors spend a great deal of time in the field, and employment is divided nearly evenly among the federal, state, and local governments.

Earnings and Opportunities

About 112,000 workers are employed as health and regulatory inspectors, and employment is expected to grow rather slowly. Earnings range from $21,500 to $44,000.

Training and Qualifications

The ability to accept responsibility, pay close attention to detail, and communicate well orally and in writing are important qualities for regulatory inspectors.

Specific qualifications vary according to the job, but the federal government requires a passing score on the Professional and Administrative Career Examination (PACE) for several inspector occupations, including immigration; customs; wage-hour compliance; alcohol, tobacco, and firearms; and occupational safety and health. To qualify to take the exam, applicants must have a bachelor's degree, three years of responsible work experience, or a combination of the two.

Air safety inspectors and mine inspectors should have experience in their fields.

For Further Details

Contact the local office of your state employment service, the area office of the U.S. Office of Personnel Management (see your white pages) or the Federal Job Information Center (in large cities only) for further information on federal government jobs. Contact the state civil service department in your state capital for state jobs and contact your local government for local government jobs.

Or contact: U.S. Customs Service, 1301 Constitution Ave., Washington, DC 20229. Occupational Safety and Health Admin. (OSHA), 200 Constitution Ave., N.W., Washington, DC 20210. Federal Aviation Administration (FAA), Independence Ave., S.W., Washington, DC 20591. Department of Labor, 200 Constitution Ave., N.W., Washington, DC 20210. Bureau of Alcohol, Tobacco and Firearms, 1200 Pennsylvania Ave., Washington, DC 20226.

CITY-COUNTY MANAGERS AND ASSISTANTS

Duties and Responsibilities

If you have ever thought about what fun it would be to run your own business, then imagine the challenge that's in store for the person who runs an entire city.

A city manager is usually appointed by a community's elected officials and reports directly to them. The job involves administering and coordinating the day-to-day operations of the city. This includes such management duties as hiring department heads and their staffs, and preparing the annual budget for approval by elected officials. City managers are also responsible for overseeing departments involved in tax collection, disbursement, law enforcement, and public works. In addition, they study and try to correct existing problems, such as housing, traffic congestion, crime, and pollution, while planning for future development in the face of population growth and industrial expansion.

City managers work closely with their own department heads and elected officials and often make public appearances to discuss government operations and special programs with local citizens.

In many cities, city managers are aided by *management assistants*. These people work under the direction of the city manager and generally help to keep the government running smoothly. *Assistant city managers* organize and coordinate city programs, supervise city employees, and act for the city manager in his or her absence. They may assume full responsibility for certain projects. *Department head assistants* are generally responsible for one area, such as personnel, finance, or law enforcement, but they may also get involved in other projects. *Management analysts* study and recommend possible changes in organizational or administrative procedures.

Some city managers work for county governments, metropolitan or regional planning organizations, or councils of government. About four-fifths of all city managers work for cities having fewer than 25,000 inhabitants. However, one-half of all cities with populations between 10,000 and 500,000 have city managers, and the trend toward the council-manager form of city government is increasing.

Nearly all city managers begin as management analysts or assistants. Some work directly for a city manager, while others work in a government department to acquire experience. For a city manager, advancement may come in the form of moving on to manage the government of a larger city.

Public managers are also in demand in the private sector, and many go on to successful careers there. City managers' experience with bureaucracies and special interest groups, as well as their knowledge of how to obtain public funds, makes them highly sought after by private groups, such as redevelopment and arts organizations, and nonprofit groups of all types. One city manager says that in his ten years as a city manager he got about six offers a year from private groups.

Earnings and Opportunities

Over 3,300 people are employed as city managers, and several times that number work in various assistant positions. Earnings range from $20,000 to $100,000.

Training and Qualifications

Administrative ability, sound judgment, and the capability to work well under stress are important qualities for city managers. They should also be able to communicate well and work effectively with other people, since coordinating efforts with elected officials is vital to success in the job. A master's degree, preferably in public or business administration, is an asset.

For Further Details

Contact the personnel offices of local governments in your area, or the International City Management Association, 1120 G St., N.W.,

Washington, DC 20005. For information about educational programs for careers in public management, send $10 to receive *Programs in Public Affairs and Administration* to: National Association of Schools of Public Affairs and Administration, 1225 Connecticut Avenue, N.W., Suite 306, Washington, DC 20036.

CONSTRUCTION INSPECTORS

Duties and Responsibilities

Bridges, highways, and skyscrapers come under our government's system of inspection, and construction inspectors are the people who make sure that construction, alterations, and repairs of roadways, buildings, and sewer and water systems comply with building codes and ordinances, zoning regulations, and contract specifications.

Construction inspectors usually specialize. *Building inspectors* may even specialize in a particular type of building, such as structural steel or reinforced concrete. Before construction, inspectors review blueprints to determine that they comply with regulations. They visit the site prior to the pouring of the foundation, again after the foundation is completed, and numerous other times depending on the type of building and its rate of progress.

Electrical inspectors inspect the installation of electrical systems and equipment. They visit worksites to inspect new and existing wiring, lighting, sound, and security systems, generating equipment, and the wiring for appliances and heating and cooling systems.

Plumbing systems—including septic tanks, plumbing fixtures and traps, and water, sewer, and vent lines—are inspected by *mechanical inspectors*. They also check the installation of the mechanical components of kitchen appliances, boilers, heating and air-conditioning equipment, gasoline and butane tanks, gas piping, and gas-fired appliances.

Public works inspectors ensure that federal, state, and local government construction of water and sewer systems, highways, streets, bridges, and dams conforms to specifications. They also record the amount of work performed and materials used so that contract payment calculations can be made.

Whether working alone or as part of a team, an inspector may spend time outside at the construction site but also works in an office reviewing blueprints, writing reports, and scheduling inspections. For certain types of inspections, inspectors may need to climb ladders or crawl beneath buildings.

Advancement usually involves taking on responsibility for more complex types of inspection assignments. For those who wish to advance to the job of supervisory inspector, an engineering degree is frequently needed.

Earnings and Opportunities

Over 48,000 people are employed as construction inspectors, and employment opportunities are limited. Earnings vary from $15,600 to $35,000.

Training and Qualifications

Good physical condition for getting around worksites and the ability to pay close attention to detail are important qualifications for inspectors. Several years' experience working as a construction contractor, supervisor, or craft worker is desirable. Many employers prefer applicants to be graduates of an apprentice program, to have studied at least two years toward an engineering or architectural degree, or to have a degree from a community or junior college, with courses in construction technology, blueprint reading, technical mathematics, English, and building inspection.

For Further Details

International Conference of Building Officials, 5360 S. Workman Mill Road, Whittier, CA 90601. U.S. Office of Personnel Management, 1900 E St., N.W., Washington, DC 20415.

HEALTH INSPECTORS

Duties and Responsibilities

Protecting us from health hazards is the responsibility of health inspectors who enforce the laws and regulations that govern food, drugs, cosmetics, and other consumer products. Health inspectors work with engineers, chemists, microbiologists, and health workers, and there are several specialties within the field:

Within the field of consumer safety, *consumer safety inspectors* usually specialize in food, feeds, and pesticides; weights and measures; or drugs and cosmetics. Working individually or in teams under a supervisory inspector, these workers periodically check companies and look for inaccurate labeling and for decomposition or contamination that could result in a health hazard to the public.

Food inspectors inspect meat, poultry, and their byproducts to be sure they are safe for public consumption. Working as part of a constant on-site team that includes a veterinarian, they inspect meat and poultry slaughtering, processing, and packaging operations.

Agricultural quarantine inspectors inspect aircraft, railroad cars, ships, and cars entering the U.S. for hazardous plant or animal materials that should not be brought into the country.

Environmental health inspectors, sometimes called sanitarians, primarily work for state and local governments, and their job is to see that food, water, and air meet government health standards. They check cleanliness and safety of food and beverages produced in dairies and processing plants, as well as food and drink served in restaurants, hospitals, and other institutions. They inspect for water pollution and oversee the treatment and disposal of sewage, refuse, and garbage.

When you buy "AA" eggs, you know they have been checked by *agricultural commodity graders,* who usually specialize in one area such as eggs and egg products, processed or fresh fruits and vegetables, grain or dairy products.

Most inspectors spend a great deal of time in the field. Employment is almost evenly divided among federal, state, and local governments.

Earnings and Opportunities

About 112,000 people are employed as health and regulatory inspectors. The employment outlook is poor. Earnings: $20,500 to $34,000.

Training and Qualifications

A good head for detail work, the ability to communicate well, and the willingness to accept responsibility are important qualities in future health inspectors. Qualifications vary depending on the job. The federal government requires a passing score on the Professional and Administrative Career Examination (PACE) for consumer safety inspectors and some other federal jobs. To qualify to take the exam, applicants must have a bachelor's degree, three years of responsible work experience, or a combination of the two. Food inspectors must have related experience and pass an examination based on specialized knowledge.

At the state and local level, environmental health inspectors must usually have a bachelor's degree in the field or in the physical or biological sciences.

All inspectors are trained in applicable laws and inspection procedures through a combination of classroom and on-the-job experience.

For Further Details

Department of Agriculture, Food and Consumer Services, Federal Grain Inspection Service, Animal and Plant Health Inspection Service, Food Safety and Quality Service, 14th St., S.W., Washington, DC 20250. Environmental Protection Agency (EPA), 401 M St., S.W., Washington, DC 20460. Food and Drug Administration (FDA), 5600 Fishers Lane, Rockville, Md. 20852.

RECREATION WORKERS

Duties and Responsibilities

Perhaps the perfect combination of work and play for an active person is the job of recreation worker. Recreation workers are employed by local governments and voluntary agencies to provide craft and sports activities at schools, playgrounds, and recreation centers. They may work with people of any age and socioeconomic background. Some direct recreation at correctional institutions.

Under the supervision of a camp director, counselors lead and instruct campers in such group activities as swimming, hiking, and horseback riding or in specialized areas such as music, drama, or tennis. In industry or the armed forces, personnel direct leisure-time or recreational activities, athletic programs, and social functions.

A rapidly growing area of specialization is that of therapeutic recreation, where the activities are designed to help individuals recover or adjust to illness, disability, or other specific problems. *Recreational therapists* work in hospitals, correctional institutions, health and rehabilitation centers, nursing homes, private schools, and camps for the mentally retarded, emotionally disturbed, and physically handicapped.

There are a variety of positions within the field. *Recreation leaders* are responsible for the day-to-day activities and instruct and supervise groups as needed. *Activity specialists* are those who have a specific specialty such as dance, swimming, or tennis in which they conduct classes or coach teams.

Recreation supervisors plan the overall program for the population they serve. They supervise the recreation leaders and may direct certain activities. *Recreation administrators* or *directors* manage recreation programs. They have overall responsibility for program planning, budget, and personnel.

Most workers put in a forty-hour week. However, the hours are sometimes irregular in order to best suit the group served.

To advance, recreation leaders may become supervisors, but advancement to administrative positions usually requires graduate work as well as experience.

Earnings and Opportunities

About 135,000 people are employed as group recreation workers and camp directors. Employment opportunities are average, with a 23 percent rise in the number of jobs projected for the next ten years. Salaries range from $16,800 to $60,000.

Training and Qualifications

Good health, physical stamina, creativity, and resourcefulness are good qualities for recreation directors, as is the ability to motivate people while still remaining sensitive to their needs and capabilities.

A number of recreation leader positions are currently filled by high school graduates. Those seeking a career in the field should obtain at least an associate degree, however, and a college degree with a major in parks and recreation is preferable. For jobs directing a specific activity, specialized training may be required.

A bachelor's degree and work experience are the minimum requirements for administrators, but more and more of them go on for a master's degree in parks and recreation or related fields. Those interested in recreational therapy will need a college degree in that specialty or a related field of therapy.

For Further Details

National Recreation and Park Association, Division of Professional Services, 3101 Park Center Dr., Alexandria, VA 22302. National Industrial Recreation Association, 20 N. Wacker Dr., Chicago, IL 60606. American Camping Association, Bradford Woods, Martinsville, IN 46151.

Careers in Health Services

Most of the jobs in this section involve a great deal of one-to-one contact with patients. These positions have developed largely out of a need to expand the roles of auxiliary workers in order to free medical practitioners such as doctors and dentists to perform the highly skilled tasks only they are qualified to do.

Responsibilities vary. The optometric assistant may perform some clerical duties and also assist the optometrist as he or she works with patients. The assistant may also take on the job of teaching patients to care for their contact lenses. By contrast, paramedics or emergency medical technicians function not as assistants but as fully trained professionals prepared to handle emergency situations in the absence of a physician.

In addition to the jobs we list, *nurses' aides* and *orderlies*, about 1.2 million of them, are employed in hospitals, nursing homes, and rehabilitation centers; and they provide important patient care. *Psychiatric aides* work primarily in mental hospitals, where they help patients with bathing, dressing, grooming, and meals. *Ambulance attendants* and *drivers* also provide essential services.

For the most part, employment in these occupations is expected to grow faster than average throughout the 1980s. These can be permanent jobs or stepping-stones to careers in health or medicine, depending on individual desires.

DIETITIANS

Duties and Responsibilities

In the last ten years there has been an increasing awareness of the importance of good nutrition among most of us. The caffeine-free drinks and growing number of health food stores are proof of it. Yet this awareness is something dietitians have always maintained in order to plan nutritious meals for groups of people who have specific dietary needs. Dietitians are trained to provide counseling, set up and supervise food service systems, and promote sound eating habits through education and research.

Administrative dietitians are responsible for the kind of large-scale meal planning and preparation provided in hospitals, prisons, company cafeterias, schools, and other institutions. They supervise the planning, preparation, and service of meals; select, train, and direct food service supervisors and workers; budget for and purchase food, equipment, and supplies; and enforce sanitary and safety regulations.

Clinical dietitians, sometimes called therapeutic dietitians, work in hospitals, nursing homes, and clinics. They assess nutritional needs, develop and implement dietary plans, and evaluate and report the results. In a small institution, a dietitian may perform both administrative and clinical duties.

Community dietitians or *nutritionists* work mainly for public and private health and social service agencies such as "meals-on-wheels" and maternal-infant nutritional programs. They may counsel individuals or groups on sound nutritional practices, or be responsible for the actual planning, developing, and administering of a nutrition program.

Research dietitians study nutrition from all angles and seek ways to improve nutrition for both the healthy and the sick. They may work in medical centers, educational facilities, or in community health programs.

Dietetic educators teach nutrition to health care teams, consumer groups, and adult education groups.

Although most dietitians work forty hours a week, some jobs may involve weekend work or irregular hours. Part-time work is available, and a growing number are working as self-employed consultants to institutions and companies. While much of their time is spent in research laboratories, classrooms, or offices near food preparation areas, dietitians may also be on their feet a lot in hot, steamy kitchens.

Dietitians may advance to assistant or associate directors or directors of dietetic departments. Advancement to higher level positions in teaching, research, or public health usually requires graduate education. Those interested in administrative dietetics may find that graduate study in institutional or business administration is valuable.

Earnings and Opportunities

About 44,000 people are employed as dietitians, and the job outlook is excellent, with a 40 percent increase in this number projected by the mid '90s. Earnings: $16,800 to $38,500.

Training and Qualifications

Scientific aptitude, organizational and administrative talent, and the ability to work well with all types of people are good personal qualities to bring to this field.

The basic educational requirement is a bachelor's degree with a major in foods and nutrition or institution management. For professional certification—an advantage—the American Dietetic Association recommends completion of an approved dietetic internship.

For Further Details

The American Dietetic Association, 430 N. Michigan Ave., Chicago, IL 60611.

HOSPITAL AND HEALTH SERVICE ADMINISTRATORS

Duties and Responsibilities

The hushed hustle and bustle of a hospital, nursing home, or clinic sometimes lulls us into forgetting that running one of these facilities is as complex as managing a small city. The patients' needs and the doctors' and nurses' work requirements must be met without fail.

Usually operating under the general guidance of a board of directors, hospital and health service administrators have overall management responsibility for preparing a budget, establishing rates for health services, directing the hiring and training of personnel, coordinating activities of the medical and nursing staff, and overseeing maintenance of the physical plant.

In a small organization they may operate alone, but in large operations they may be responsible for millions of dollars' worth of facilities and hundreds of employees, and most likely direct a staff that in turn manages the day-to-day operations of the various departments.

Administrators are frequently visible within the community, taking part in fund-raising drives and promoting public participation in health programs. They may speak before civic groups, arrange publicity, and coordinate the activities of the organization with those of other health agencies.

Increasingly, the need for cost cutting is spurring health care institutions to seek administrators who have business backgrounds. C.P.A.'s and bankers turned administrators are not unheard of. In addition, new positions in marketing, corporate planning (to develop cost controls), and industrial engineering (to study productivity) are being added to administrative staffs in order to improve efficiency.

Most administrators work in patient care facilities, including hospitals, nursing homes, rehabilitation centers, home health agencies, and health maintenance organizations. Some work for state and local health departments. Others work for voluntary health agencies that support medical research into causes and treatments of particular diseases or impairments. Still others are employed by consulting firms that provide management services for a fee.

The job is demanding and the responsibility great. Administrators may be called on at any time whenever an emergency arises. However, the rewards of a job well done offset the hours and possible inconvenience.

Earnings and Opportunities

Over 220,000 people work in some phase of health administration, and employment is expected to continue growing at a very rapid pace, with a 58 percent increase in the number of jobs expected in ten years. Salaries range from $25,000 to $120,000 and more. More than

one-quarter of not-for-profit hospitals now have some type of executive incentive pay linked to productivity, up from 1 percent of hospitals only a few years ago. Other bonuses are tied to a facility's improved market share for a service.

Training and Qualifications

Health administrators need to be self-motivated people with a talent for managing others. These workers should have excellent communications skills and a high degree of self-confidence.

In the next few years the minimum academic requirement will likely be a master's degree in hospital administration or an advanced degree in business administration.

Candidates may be hired by hospitals as associate or assistant administrators, department heads, or project directors. A doctoral degree is usually required for positions in teaching or research and is an asset for those seeking administrative jobs in larger health organizations.

Those with a business or management background will find good job opportunities in nursing homes and other long-term-care facilities.

For administration jobs in nursing homes and long-term-care facilities, licensing is required throughout the United States.

For Further Details

American College of Hospital Administration, 840 N. Lake Shore Dr., Chicago, IL 60611. Association of University Programs in Health Administration, 1 Dupont Circle, N.W., Washington, DC 20036. National Health Council, Health Careers Program, 70 W. 40th St., New York, NY 10019. American College of Nursing Home Administrators, 4650 East-West Hwy., Washington, DC 20014.

MEDICAL OFFICE ASSISTANTS

Duties and Responsibilities

The person in the crisp white uniform who weighed you and updated your file the last time you were at the doctor's may well have been a medical office assistant. These are workers who aid physicians in examining and treating patients and perform most of the administrative tasks needed to keep an office running smoothly.

In small offices, assistants typically handle both clerical and clinical duties. In large offices, assistants usually specialize in either office duties or patient care.

Clinical duties may include taking temperature and blood pressure, obtaining medical histories, performing simple laboratory tests, preparing patients for examination or treatment, and assisting a doctor during an examination. They may also apply dressings and instruct patients about medication and self-treatment.

Assistants are responsible for sterilizing and arranging instruments and equipment in the examining room, maintaining supplies, and keeping the office neat and orderly.

Clerical duties may include greeting patients, answering the phone, recording and filing medical information, filling out insurance forms, typing correspondence, scheduling appointments, and arranging for hospital admission and laboratory services. They may also include bookkeeping and billing.

Medical assistants with leadership ability may rise to the position of office manager. Further training is usually necessary for advancement into a health care occupation.

Most assistants work for physicians in private practice, though some are employed in clinics, nursing homes, and hospitals. Saturday or evening hours are sometimes part of the schedule.

Earnings and Opportunities

Over 90,000 people are employed as medical assistants, and employment opportunities, especially for graduates of accredited training programs, are expected to be excellent in the coming decade. It is estimated that the number of jobs should increase by 47 percent. Earnings vary greatly, and range from $9,600 to over $16,600.

Training and Qualifications

Assistants have a great deal of contact with patients, many of whom may be nervous, so a conscientious attitude, a neat personal appearance, and a warm, pleasant manner are assets. They must have the ability to explain information clearly to patients and to follow doctors' orders precisely. Typing is often required.

Assistants should have a high school diploma, and while most will receive on-the-job training, an increasing number have attended one of the formal training programs available. Most community colleges offer two-year associate degree programs in medical assisting.

The American Association of Medical Assistants and the American Medical Technologists offer certification programs. Certification is not required, but it does indicate to a physician that the applicant is highly qualified.

For Further Details

The American Association of Medical Assistants, 1 E. Wacker Dr., Suite 2110, Chicago, IL 60601. Accrediting Bureau of Health Education Schools, Oak Manor Office, 29089 U.S. 20 West, Elkhart, IN 46514. American Medical Technologists, Medical Assistant Program, 710 Higgins Rd., Park Ridge, IL 60068.

MEDICAL RECORDS ADMINISTRATORS

Duties and Responsibilities

In the medical records field, there is no room for lost files or mistaken information. The administrator in charge of medical records has the important job of organizing and overseeing what must be a virtually error-free department.

Up-to-date records of patient case histories; reports on physical examinations, X rays, and laboratory tests; doctors' orders; and nurses' notes are absolutely necessary for prompt diagnosis and treatment of illnesses and injuries. These records are also used for research, insurance claims, legal actions, and evaluation of treatment in the training of medical personnel.

The medical records administrator is the person responsible for this department and for the workers who verify, transcribe, code, and maintain patient files. The administrator directs activities of the department and develops systems for documenting, storing, and retrieving the medical information. He or she also serves as a department head and is a part of the hospital management staff. Since administrators are responsible for the medical information system, they may also be required to testify in court about records and procedures. The increasing use of computers for storing medical information means that more and more of an administrator's job involves working with computer systems.

At a large hospital, a chief medical records administrator may supervise other administrators as well as technicians and clerks. At smaller hospitals, an administrator may be responsible for only two or three people.

Most administrators work in hospitals, and others are employed in nursing homes, clinics, group practices, public health departments, and university medical centers. Health insurance companies employ medical records administrators to help determine liability for payment of clients' medical fees. Some work for manufacturing companies to help them develop better processing equipment and improved medical forms.

As in any other management job, administrators must be good at organizing and analyzing departmental procedures and directing the staff to carry them out. Most work a standard forty-hour week, and because the department is seldom involved in emergencies, the pace of the work is predictable.

Earnings and Opportunities

Over 15,000 people are employed as administrators, and employment is expected to grow faster than average. Part-time opportunities should continue in teaching, research, and consulting work. Salaries range from $18,600 to $35,400.

Training and Qualifications

A bachelor's degree in medical records administration is recommended. Medical schools offer many of these programs. Those who already have a bachelor's degree in another discipline may qualify for a one-year certificate program if they already have the required courses in the liberal arts and biological sciences.

Graduates of approved schools are eligible for the national registration examination given by the American Medical Record Association (AMRA). Passing this exam gives professional recognition as a register record administrator (RRA), which can be helpful in advancement.

For Further Details

American Medical Record Association, John Hancock Center, Suite 1850, 875 N. Michigan Ave., Chicago, IL 60611.

MEDICAL RECORDS TECHNICIANS AND CLERKS

Duties and Responsibilities

The careful and accurate recording of a patient's medical information is a vital job at any hospital, clinic, or health care institution; and medical records technicians and clerks are the ones responsible for transcribing, analyzing, and coding the files that doctors, hospital administrators, public health authorities, and insurance companies rely on.

Medical records *clerks* assemble information, check all forms, signatures, and dates and locate previous medical records. Basic information is coded and recorded. Clerks may also answer routine requests and gather statistics for reports. Some transcribe reports of operations, X rays, laboratory examinations, and special treatments given to the patients.

Technicians perform the duties that require more technical knowledge. They code and record diseases, operations, and special therapies according to recognized classification systems for easier review of patient histories. Analyzing records and cross-indexing medical information is also part of the job. Records are also reviewed for consistency, completeness, and accuracy.

Technicians gather statistics and prepare periodic reports on types of diseases treated, surgery, and use of hospital beds in response to inquiries from the medical staff, law firms, insurance companies, and government agencies.

In large hospitals, technicians and clerks are supervised by a medical administrator, but in smaller hospitals experienced technicians are often in charge of the department.

Although most clerks and technicians are employed by hospitals, a growing number work in nursing homes, clinics, community health centers, group practices, and health maintenance organizations. Some work for insurance companies and public health depart-

ments, and others work for small health care facilities as consultants. A few are self-employed and provide medical transcription services.

Medical records personnel generally work a standard forty-hour week in comfortable surroundings. Part-time work is available.

Clerks with experience can advance to the technician level upon completion of the AMRA Independent Study Program and obtaining thirty credit hours in medical records technology.

Earnings and Opportunities

Approximately 20,000 people work as medical records technicians and 35,000 as clerks. Salaries range from $12,500 to $24,900.

Training and Qualifications

A medical records clerk must pay close attention to detail and enjoy organizing and assembling information. High school graduates with basic secretarial skills can enter the field as clerks and learn on the job. In addition, the American Medical Record Association (AMRA) offers a correspondence course in medical transcription, and the certificate earned can be helpful in being hired.

There is also demand for technicians who have associate degrees earned in two-year American Medical Association (in collaboration with the AMRA) accredited programs. Candidates can then take the Accredited Record Technician (ART) exam.

For Further Details

American Medical Record Association, John Hancock Center, Suite 1850, 875 N. Michigan Ave., Chicago, IL 60611.

NURSES

Duties and Responsibilities

Nurses are responsible for the day-to-day care of the physically or mentally ill or infirm, and they perform a wide variety of tasks within this framework. While the work can become routine at times, it is a challenging profession that can make the difference between life and death.

Nurses fall into one of two categories depending on background and training: licensed practical nurses (LPN's) and registered nurses (RN's).

Licensed practical nurses, sometimes called licensed vocational nurses, work under the direction of physicians and registered nurses and provide nursing care that requires technical knowledge but not the professional education and training of an RN. They work in hospitals doing such tasks as recording temperatures, administering medicines, assisting doctors, and helping patients with bathing and other tasks. In private homes they provide nursing care and may prepare meals and instruct the family in ways to keep the patient comfortable. In doctors' offices and in clinics, LPN's prepare patients for examination and treatment, administer medications, apply dressings, and teach patients health care regimens.

Registered nurses work in a variety of settings. *Hospital nurses* provide skilled bedside nursing care and carry out the medical regimen prescribed by physicians. They may supervise LPN's, aides, and orderlies. Usually they work with a specific group of patients who require similar nursing care, such as children, the elderly, or in a post-operative-care unit.

Private duty nurses give individual care to patients who need constant attention. They may work in a home, a hospital, or a convalescent institution.

Community health nurses care for patients in clinics, homes, schools, and other community settings. They may instruct patients and families in health care and proper diet and may arrange for immunizations.

Office nurses assist physicians, dental surgeons, and occasionally dentists in private practice or clinics. Sometimes they perform routine laboratory and office work in addition to their nursing duties.

Occupational health or industrial nurses provide nursing services to employees in industry and government. They may treat minor injuries and illnesses occurring at the workplace and arrange for further medical care if necessary. They may also assist with health examinations and inoculations.

Nurse educators teach students the principles and skills of nursing, both in the classroom and in direct patient care.

Two out of three RN's and three out of five LPN's work in hospitals. Others work in nursing homes, doctors' offices, schools, community health programs, in business and industry, or as private duty nurses. A good number of RN's work in education, research, or administration.

Nursing can be quite taxing emotionally and physically because you frequently must deal with people in crisis, but there are definite rewards when patients make recovery. Hours usually involve a normal forty-hour week, but because care is needed round the clock, this may involve nights and weekends. Part-time work is available.

Advancement for LPN's may consist of gaining the additional training needed to become an RN.

In hospitals, registered nurses may be promoted to head nurse, assistant director, and eventually, director of nursing services. A growing number of hospitals are using a career planning system called clinical ladders to reduce turnover and satisfy nurses who want to advance in patient care rather than administration. According to Wharton School's Institute of Health Economics, careers are typically divided into five levels based on expertise. After screening by supervisors, nurses advance to take on more duties for greater pay. Some programs let nurses develop highly specialized skills like cardiac nursing. In other instances, nurses become nurse practitioners who can perform physical examinations and use diagnostic and health assessment skills beyond those of regular nurses. Graduate education is sometimes necessary for advancement.

Earnings and Opportunities

Over 550,000 people are employed as LPN's, and over 1,105,000 work as RN's, and the outlook for employment is excellent. Nurses will be in great demand in the next decade, as the number of jobs for LPN's is expected to increase by 37 percent, and for RN's by 49 percent. Salaries range from $15,600 to $34,000.

Training and Qualifications

A desire to help others, good judgment, initiative, and the ability to follow instructions precisely are important qualities in the nursing profession.

Both LPN's and RN's must be licensed. LPN's must complete a state-approved practical nursing course and pass a written exam. Courses generally last a year and are available through trade, technical, or vocational schools or community and junior colleges, hospitals, and health agencies. Many schools do not require—but prefer—high school graduates.

Registered nurses must graduate from a state-approved school of nursing and pass a state board examination to qualify for a license. The educational program chosen by an RN will affect her future opportunities. While a two-year associate, three-year diploma, or four-year bachelor's degree will each satisfy basic licensing requirements, a bachelor's degree is usually necessary for supervisory or administrative positions, for jobs in public health agencies, and for admission to graduate nursing programs. Those considering research, consulting, teaching, or a clinical specialization should also start their nursing education in a bachelor's degree program.

For Further Details

Career Information Services, National League for Nursing, 10 Columbus Circle, New York, NY 10019. National Association for Practical Nurse Education and Service, Inc., 254 W. 31st St., New York, NY 10001. National Federation of Licensed Practical Nurses, Inc., 250 W. 57th St., New York, NY 10106.

OCCUPATIONAL THERAPISTS AND ASSISTANTS

Duties and Responsibilities

One of the fastest-growing fields of employment in the United States is occupational therapy. Using vocational and recreational activities to help patients who are mentally, physically, or emotionally disabled, the occupational therapist works as a member of a medical team that may include a physician, physical therapist, vocational counselor, and other professionals. Together they evaluate the patient in terms of capacities and abilities. Depending on need and patient ability, therapists select activities that are suited to the developmental level, physical capacity, intelligence, and interest of each patient. The activities are designed to develop independence, prepare patients to return to work, develop or restore basic functions, or aid in adjustment to disabilities.

The therapist's primary tools are activities of various kinds. They may use woodworking, weaving, or other therapeutic activities to help patients improve motor skills, strength, endurance, concentration, motivation, or other physical and/or mental capacities.

Most occupational therapists work with persons who suffer physical disabilities, and the rest work with patients who have psychological or emotional problems or developmental deficiencies. Some work exclusively with children and young adults; others work only with the elderly.

Assistants work under the supervision of a therapist. Most work very closely with patients, helping them, observing them, and making reports to the occupational therapist on progress and development.

The chief occupational therapist in a hospital may teach medical and nursing students the principles of occupational therapy. Many supervise occupational therapy departments, coordinate patient activities, or are consultants to public health departments and mental health agencies.

More than half of these workers are employed by hospitals; and many work for nursing homes. A number are employed by school systems and schools for the handicapped. Most of the rest work in rehabilitation centers, clinics, community mental health centers, home health agencies, and adult day care programs. Some work in vocational rehabilitation programs. Many work part-time.

Earnings and Opportunities

Over 19,000 people are employed as occupational therapists, and over 8,500 work as assistants. The outlook for employment is excellent, with a projected growth of 60 percent by 1995. Salaries range from $22,000 to $34,000; less for assistants.

Training and Qualifications

A warm and friendly personality, emotional stability, patience, and the ability to inspire others are prime qualities in this field. Manual dexterity for teaching patients to work with their hands, and ingenuity and imagination for adapting activities to individual needs are also important.

To qualify, applicants must have a degree or certificate from an accredited educational program and pass a state licensing exam.

Graduates of accredited programs are also eligible to take the American Occupational Therapy Association certification examination to become a registered occupational therapist (OTR).

Assistants may obtain initial training at a community college or a vo-tech school offering such a program.

For Further Details

American Occupational Therapy Association, 1383 Piccard Dr., Rockville, MD 20850.

PHYSICAL THERAPISTS AND ASSISTANTS

Duties and Responsibilities

It is the job of physical therapists to restore bodily functions, relieve pain, or help to prevent permanent disability following a disabling injury or disease. Physical therapy is among the fastest-growing occupations in the United States, and demand for physical therapists and their assistants is expected to be great.

Their patients include accident victims, handicapped newborns and children, and stroke victims, as well as people suffering from multiple sclerosis, cerebral palsy, nerve injuries, amputations, fractures, and arthritis. Therapists must have detailed knowledge of human anatomy and physiology.

After evaluating a patient, going over medical records, and performing tests, therapists develop a course of treatment in cooperation with the physician. Therapy may include exercises for increasing strength, coordination, and expanding the range of motion of an arm or a leg. Therapists also apply massage, heat, cold, light, and water in special treatments in order to relieve pain or improve the condition of muscles or skin.

Gaining the trust of patients and the aid of their families can be an important part of making the therapy succeed, so workers also spend time developing a relationship with patients and instructing patients and families how to carry on prescribed treatment programs at home.

Therapists may treat people with a wide variety of problems; or they may specialize in pediatrics, geriatrics, orthopedics, sports medicine, neurology, or cardiopulmonary disease.

About half of all workers are employed in hospitals; a substantial number provide services in nursing homes, rehabilitation centers, schools, and residential facilities for handicapped children, home health agencies, outpatient clinics, and physicians' offices. Some teach, conduct research, or serve as consultants. A number of physical therapists are in private practice.

Evening and weekend hours are sometimes required, and the job can be physically exhausting and emotionally tiring.

Assistants may gain more responsible duties as they gain experience; those with an associate degree from an accredited program sometimes advance to physical therapist by earning a bachelor's degree in the field. For therapists, a graduate degree combined with clinical experience increases opportunities for advancement into teaching, research, and administrative positions.

Earnings and Opportunities

Over 34,000 people are employed as physical therapists, and 11,500 as assistants. The number of jobs for physical therapists is expected to increase 58 percent in the next ten years, making employment prospects excellent. Starting salaries range from $16,700 to $22,300; those with experience earn up to $35,000.

Training and Qualifications

Key qualities for working in this field are emotional stability for helping others cope with problems, resourcefulness for creating ways to help different individuals, patience, and tact. Manual dexterity and physical stamina are also important.

Licensing for physical therapists is required throughout the United States. To qualify, applicants must have a degree or certificate from an accredited physical therapy educational program and pass a licensing exam.

Those considering the field may want to do summer or part-time volunteer work to gain a better understanding of what is entailed.

For Further Details

American Physical Therapy Association, 1156 15th St., N.W., Washington, DC 20005.

SPEECH PATHOLOGISTS AND AUDIOLOGISTS

Duties and Responsibilities

What could be more rewarding than teaching a partially deaf child to overcome a speech difficulty suffered since birth, or helping an adult relearn articulation after a brain injury? Diagnosing speech or hearing disorders and aiding in treatment is the province of speech pathologists and audiologists, whose work is of tremendous importance.

One American in ten is unable to speak or hear properly, and today there is a growing trend toward earlier recognition and treatment of hearing and speech problems. Children who formerly were thought to have learning disabilities or mental problems were later found to have speech or hearing disorders that—when properly diagnosed—could be treated.

Speech pathologists and audiologists use diagnostic procedures to identify and evaluate disorders ranging from deafness to problems caused by mental retardation, emotional disturbances, or a cleft palate. It is the job of the audiologist to assess and treat hearing problems, sometimes correcting them through fitting a hearing aid. If the problem is with speech, the pathologist takes over. These professionals may then work with physicians, psychologists, physical therapists, and counselors to develop and implement a therapy program.

About half of all pathologists and audiologists work in public schools. Others work for colleges and universities as professors, at clinics, or in research centers. Others work in hospitals, speech and hearing centers, government agencies, industry, and in private practice.

As in most fields, there are some supervisory positions available. However, most gravitate to private practice for greater personal flexibility and higher earnings.

Earnings and Opportunities

Over 35,000 people are employed as speech pathologists, and 29 percent growth in employment is expected in the next ten years. Currently, school systems are increasing their speech, language, and hearing staffs to comply with the requirements of the Education for All Handicapped Children Act of 1975. Earnings range from $17,600 to $32,400.

Training and Qualifications

Taking pleasure in one-to-one teaching of others, patience, and an orientation to detail are important qualities for these jobs. Being able to accept responsibility, work independently, and direct others is also helpful.

A master's degree in speech-language pathology or audiology is necessary to become a qualified practitioner, and while undergraduate programs are available in the field, they should be viewed as preparatory to entering a graduate program. At the graduate level, in addition to regular course work all students receive supervised clinical training.

In a majority of states, speech pathologists and audiologists in private practice must be licensed.

For advancement, professionals usually have to qualify for the Certificate of Clinical Competence given by the American Speech-Language-Hearing Association. To earn it, you must have a master's degree or the equivalent, complete a one-year internship approved by the association, and pass a national written examination.

For Further Details

American Speech-Language-Hearing Association, 10801 Rockville Pike, Bethesda, MD 20852.

Careers in Health Technology

Health technologists and technicians are those workers who are skilled at operating the latest machinery or performing the latest diagnostic tests. Growth in the health professions as well as the continuing development of new laboratory procedures, diagnostic techniques, and life support systems makes this field one filled with promise.

Both technologists and technicians are discussed in this section, and the distinction between the two positions lies in the complexity of the job. Technologists perform at a higher level of responsibility than technicians and therefore need more training. The exact length of training varies among the different professions. For example, a technologist who uses laboratory techniques to test specimens of body fluids and tissues for evidence of disease needs a bachelor's degree from a four-year college with a specialization in medical technology; medical technicians are generally graduates of two-year programs. Other kinds of technologists may complete their educational requirements in one or two years, while technicians in the same field may be fully trained within six months.

In addition to the jobs mentioned, there are also other specialties that offer career opportunities. CAT (computerized axial tomogra-phy) scan machines, which are used for getting cross-section X rays of the brain and other parts of the body, are operated by *computerized tomographers*. *Mammographers* use X-ray techniques for breast examinations. *Diagnostic medical sonographers* perform sonograms, used to examine internal organs, by viewing pictures produced by sound waves reflected from the body. *Electrocardiograph (EKG) technicians* are just one of the many kinds of cardiology workers. Other *cardiology technicians* perform or assist with phonocardiograms, echocardiograms, stress tests, cardiac catheterizations, and other tests that detect heart problems. *Dialysis technicians* operate kidney machines, and *perfusionists* operate heart-lung machines. All are vitally important in the health field.

Still other occupations will emerge as advances continue to be made in biomedical technology.

Preparation for these careers varies from on-the-job training to formal study. As a rule, the more current the technology the more likely that training will be provided on the job. In most of these jobs, however, workers obtain their training through formal one- or two-year programs offered by hospitals, community colleges, vo-tech schools, and universities.

134

DENTAL ASSISTANTS AND HYGIENISTS

Duties and Responsibilities

Two types of workers can be found assisting the dentist: the *dental assistant*, who serves as the dentist's right hand during certain procedures and who may help make the patient comfortable and assist with some office duties; and the *dental hygienist*, who is licensed to provide direct patient care working under the direction of a dentist.

The *dental assistant* is responsible for such duties as sterilizing and setting up equipment, preparing patients for treatment, handing instruments to the dentist during a procedure, and keeping the patient's mouth clear by using suction or other devices. Some take care of a variety of laboratory, clinical, and office duties. Many develop X rays; some make casts of teeth and mouth from impressions taken by the dentist.

Dental hygienists provide direct patient care. They clean teeth by removing deposits and stains, take and develop X rays, and perform various other preventive and therapeutic services. Many apply topical fluoride to prevent decay, take medical and dental histories, make impressions of teeth, and prepare other diagnostic aids.

A few hygienists assist in research projects, and those who have advanced training may teach in schools of dental hygiene.

Most of these workers are employed in private dental offices. They also work for public health agencies, school systems, industrial plants, clinics, hospitals, dental hygiene schools, and the government.

Dental assistants may acquire qualifications to become hygienists; some become sales representatives for firms that manufacture dental products. There are also teaching and program administration jobs within the dental assisting field. For hygienists, advancement generally consists of gaining more responsibilities and higher pay.

Earnings and Opportunities

Over 140,000 people work as dental assistants, and over 36,000 are employed as hygienists. The outlook for employment is extremely good for both jobs, with employment growth rates of over 40 percent projected in the next decade. Salaries range from $11,200 to $21,000.

Training and Qualifications

Though most dental assistants learn their skills on the job, an increasing number are obtaining training in programs offered by community and junior colleges, trade schools, and technical institutes. Most programs take about a year to complete and lead to a certificate or a diploma.

Competition is keen for admission into dental hygiene schools. Completion of an associate degree program is generally sufficient for the hygienist who wants employment in a private dental practice. To do research, teach, or work in public or school health programs, a bachelor's degree is usually required. Those with a master's degree work as teachers or administrators in dental hygiene and dental assisting training programs, public health agencies, and in research.

For Further Details

American Dental Assistants Association, 666 N. Lake Shore Dr., Suite 1130, Chicago, IL 60611. Commission on Dental Accreditation, 211 E. Chicago Ave., Chicago, IL 60611. Dental Assisting National Board, Inc., 666 N. Lake Shore Dr., Suite 1136, Chicago, IL 60611. Division of Professional Development, American Dental Hygienists Association, Suite 3400, 444 N. Michigan Ave., Chicago, IL 60611. National Board of Dental Examiners, 211 E. Chicago Ave., Chicago, IL 60611.

DENTAL LABORATORY TECHNICIANS

Duties and Responsibilities

If you've ever had dental work, in all likelihood, you are wearing, or have worn, something made by a dental laboratory technician. They are skilled craftspeople who make and repair a wide variety of dental items such as dentures, inlays, crowns, and braces.

After receiving written instructions and usually a mold of the patient's mouth from the dentist, technicians make a model of the teeth out of dental stone or plaster pourings. From there, they use plastics, ceramics, and metals to make the crown, the bridge, or the artificial tooth that is needed.

Most technicians specialize. A *denture contour wire specialist* makes and repairs contoured wire frames and retainers; a *dental ceramist* applies porcelain paste over a metal framework to form dental crowns, bridges, and tooth facings; an *orthodontic technician* makes appliances for straightening teeth; and some technicians make and repair full and partial dentures.

Technicians use small hand instruments such as wax spatulas and wax carvers as well as special electric lathes and drills, high-heat furnaces, metal-melting torches, and other specialized laboratory equipment.

Most technicians work in small, privately owned commercial laboratories that usually have fewer than ten employees. About one-fifth of all technicians are employed by private dental practices.

A dental technician may become a manager or supervisor of other workers in a laboratory, and some decide to start their own business. For others, advancement means moving to a related job such as teaching in a dental technician training program or becoming a sales representative for a dental products company.

Earnings and Opportunities

Over 53,000 people hold jobs as dental laboratory technicians, and the outlook for future employment is very good. The number of these jobs is expected to increase 26 percent by the mid-1990s. An aging population in need of more dental work and the tendency of dentists to hire specialists will contribute to this. Dental technicians working in a laboratory can earn from $8,500 to $26,000. Those who specialize can earn more. For example, technicians specializing in ceramics receive about $35,000—the highest average salary reported by a group of technicians. Earnings of the self-employed are generally more.

Training and Qualifications

Manual dexterity, good vision, and the ability to recognize very fine color shadings are assets in this job. Following instructions and doing careful, accurate work are also important.

A high school diploma is recommended, and training can be acquired on the job, as an apprentice, or through formal programs.

An increasing number of candidates are receiving formal training. It is available in dental laboratory technology programs lasting up to two years that are offered by community colleges, vo-tech institutes, and trade schools. Most of the accredited programs lead to an associate degree, some to a certificate or diploma.

For Further Details

American Dental Association, Council on Dental Education, 211 E. Chicago Ave., Chicago, IL 60611. American Fund for Dental Health, at the above address. National Association of Dental Laboratories, 3801 Mt. Vernon Ave., Alexandria VA 22305.

DISPENSING OPTICIANS

Duties and Responsibilities

The person who fitted your glasses or contact lenses was probably a dispensing optician. He or she took the prescription written for you by your ophthalmologist or optometrist, helped you select appropriate frames, took eye measurements, and wrote the orders for the necessary laboratory work. After the glasses were made by the laboratory, the optician checked the power and surface quality of the lenses. Finally, the frames were adjusted to fit comfortably on your nose and face.

In many states, opticians also fit contact lenses. They measure customers' eyes and write specifications for the lens manufacturer. They are then responsible for telling customers how to insert, remove, and care for the lenses. During the adjustment period, which may last several weeks, the optician examines the patient's eyes, corneas, lids, and the contact lenses with special instruments and microscopes at each visit. Minor adjustments can be made in the store; but when major adjustments are necessary, the lenses are sent back to the factory.

Some opticians specialize in the fitting of cosmetic shells to cover blemished eyes; others fit prostheses (artificial eyes); and in some shops they may do lens grinding and finishing on site.

Most opticians work for optical shops or other retail outlets, though some work for ophthalmologists, hospitals, or eye clinics.

The workweek may consist of forty-five to fifty hours, especially for those who work in retail shops that are open evenings and Saturdays.

Many go into business for themselves. Others may eventually become managers of retail optical stores or sales representatives for wholesalers or manufacturers of frames or lenses.

Earnings and Opportunities

Over 18,000 people are employed as dispensing opticians, and employment is expected to increase by 24 percent over the coming decade. Salaries start at $12,000 to $13,800 and can go to over $18,500. Those who own and operate their own shops can expect to earn from $20,000 to $30,000 a year.

Training and Qualifications

Manual dexterity for working with delicate instruments, attention to detail, and a pleasant manner are important qualities for future opticians.

Candidates must have a high school diploma. Most then learn on the job, though an increasing number are obtaining formal training, which is offered by community colleges, vocational institutes, trade schools, and manufacturers. Some programs last a few weeks, others several years. In addition, apprenticeships are offered by optical dispensing companies and major employers. These can last two to four years.

Many states require dispensing opticians to be licensed. Certification in the field is offered by the American Board of Opticianry and the National Committee of Contact Lens Examiners.

For Further Details

National Academy of Opticianry, P.O. Box 19391, Washington, DC 20036. National Federation of Opticianry Schools, Ophthalmic Dispensing Program, J. Sargeant Reynolds Community College, P.O. Box 12084, Richmond, VA 23241. Opticians Association of America, 1250 Connecticut Ave., N.W., Washington, DC 20036.

ELECTROCARDIOGRAPH TECHNICIANS

Duties and Responsibilities

If you're interested in technology and looking for a health-related job with advancement, then you may want to look into becoming an electrocardiograph (EKG) technician. It's an excellent way of entering the field of cardiovascular technology, and opportunities for advancement are good.

Electrocardiograms (EKG's) are graphic tracings of the heartbeat. These tracings record the electrical changes that occur during and between heartbeats. Physicians order EKG's to diagnose forms of heart disease, including certain irregularities, and any changes in the condition of a patient's heart over a period of time.

After explaining the process to the patient, the EKG technician attaches from three to twelve electrodes to his chest, arms, and legs. These produce tracings of the heart's electrical action. A stylus on the machine records them on a long roll of graph paper. Technicians must know the anatomy of the chest and heart to properly select the exact location for the chest electrodes.

Before presenting the graph to a physician for a reading, the technician must check it for technical errors such as crossed wires or electrical interference that would prevent an accurate reading. He or she must also call to the doctor's attention any significant deviations from the norm.

EKG technicians may also conduct tests such as vectorcardiograms, which are multidimensional traces; stress testing (exercise tests); pulse recordings; and twelve-hour and twenty-four-hour recordings of EKG's on magnetic tape. In addition, some technicians schedule appointments, type doctors' diagnoses, maintain EKG files, and care for the equipment.

Most technicians work in cardiology departments of large hospitals. Others may work part- or full-time in small hospitals, clinics, or cardiologists' offices.

With proper training and experience, technicians can advance to specialized types of cardiovascular techniques. Promotion to supervisory positions is also possible.

Earnings and Opportunities

Over 20,000 people work as EKG technicians, and employment prospects are excellent. Starting salaries range from $12,600 to $14,800, and experienced technicians earn over $20,000. In general, those with formal training or those who perform more sophisticated tests earn higher salaries.

Training and Qualifications

Mechanical aptitude, patience, reliability, the ability to follow detailed instructions, and presence of mind in emergencies are helpful qualities to those aspiring to become technicians.

Most receive their training on the job by learning from a supervisor or a cardiologist. Learning about basic testing may take up to one month, and gaining knowledge about more complex testing may take up to a year. Applicants generally must be high school graduates.

Formal training programs offered by vocational and technical schools and junior and community colleges also provide these skills. The basic EKG test can be learned in courses lasting six weeks.

Certification is available to those who pass two written examinations given by the American Cardiology Technologists Association. This may help technicians obtain better-paying jobs.

For Further Details

American Cardiology Technologists Association, 11800 Sunrise Valley Dr., Suite 808, Reston, VA 22091.

EMERGENCY MEDICAL TECHNICIANS

Duties and Responsibilities

"Emergency!" Just as on television, that word means Go! to emergency medical technicians. There has been an automobile accident, a heart attack, a gunshot wound, or some other medical crisis; and these crucial workers must get to the scene with speed and care.

When a call comes from the dispatcher, EMT's—usually working in teams of two and assigned to a specific emergency vehicle—head for the scene of the call as quickly as possible. Once there, they must determine the nature and extent of the victim's illness or injury and establish priorities for emergency care. They may have to open and maintain an airway, restore breathing, control bleeding, treat a victim for shock, assist in childbirth, immobilize fractures, handle mentally disturbed patients, or give initial care to poison or burn victims.

If a person is trapped, additional aid may have to be summoned, but in the meantime, EMT's must attempt rescue and give any medical treatment possible or necessary.

When patients must be transported to the hospital, the EMT's are responsible for their safe transfer to the assigned hospital or to the one that will offer the best care for that illness or injury.

Maintaining a clean, well-equipped, and fully supplied ambulance is also part of an EMT's duties.

There are two other types of EMT's. *Paramedics* in some states work by radio communication with a physician to administer drugs and use more complex equipment than basic EMT's. *Dispatchers* also play an important role, receiving and processing calls for emergency medical assistance. They also serve as the communications link between the EMT's and the hospital and may consult with medical authorities to help decide the best course of action.

EMT's employed by fire departments often have fifty-six-hour workweeks; but those employed by hospitals, private ambulance firms, and police departments usually work forty hours a week but may be on call at certain times. Night and weekend work is common.

Earnings and Opportunities

Over 120,000 people are employed as emergency medical technicians. The employment outlook is excellent. Earnings begin at $12,000 and go to over $20,000.

Training and Qualifications

Physical stamina and strength (EMT's must be able to lift and carry up to 100 pounds), emotional stability, and good judgment under stress are important qualities for EMT's.

Instruction in emergency medical care techniques is mandatory. A standard training course is the 100-hour program designed by the U.S. Department of Transportation, which is available through hospitals, police, fire, and health departments and as a special course in medical schools, colleges, and universities. Admission requirements vary from state to state, but generally applicants must be at least eighteen years old and have a high school diploma and a valid driver's license.

For Further Details

National Association of Emergency Medical Technicians, P.O. Box 334, Newton Highlands, MA 02161.

MEDICAL LABORATORY WORKERS

Duties and Responsibilities

Many times when we go to the doctor, some sort of test is taken that must later be analyzed at a laboratory to detect or diagnose any health problems. Medical laboratory workers—working under the general direction of pathologists and other physicians or scientists—are responsible for performing the intricate tests that are involved.

Medical technologists perform complicated chemical, biological, hematological, microscopic, and bacteriological tests. They microscopically examine blood and other body fluids, make cultures of fluid or tissue samples, and analyze the samples for chemical content or reaction. In small laboratories, technologists usually perform many types of tests.

Medical laboratory technicians perform tests and laboratory procedures that require a high level of skill but not the in-depth knowledge of highly trained technologists.

Medical laboratory assistants assist medical technologists and technicians in routine tests and related work that can be learned in a short time. They perform some of the less complex tests like identifying blood types and are responsible for tasks such as cleaning and sterilizing equipment, preparing solutions, keeping records of tests, and identifying specimens.

Most laboratory personnel work in hospitals. Some are employed in independent laboratories, clinics, physicians' offices, pharmaceutical firms, and research institutions. A workweek is generally forty hours, and those working in hospitals may work some evenings and weekends. Part-time work is available.

Advancement for a technologist usually involves moving to a supervisory position or eventually to administrative medical technologist in a large hospital. Graduate education can speed advancement.

Earnings and Opportunities

Over 205,000 people are employed as medical laboratory workers, and the outlook for future employment is very good. Salaries range from $15,500 to $26,400 and up.

Training and Qualifications

Accuracy, dependability, and the ability to work under pressure are important traits for laboratory workers. Manual dexterity and normal color vision are also highly desirable.

To become a medical technologist, four years of college, with completion of a specialized medical technology training program, are required. For those who wish to specialize, advanced degrees are necessary, usually requiring an additional year of training.

Laboratory technicians need two years of post–secondary school. Many enroll in accredited programs offered by various junior colleges, colleges, and universities. Others receive training in accredited vocational and technical schools.

Most laboratory assistants are trained on the job, but an increasing number are attending one-year training programs conducted by hospitals, community and junior colleges, or vocational schools. Applicants should be high school graduates.

For Further Details

American Society of Clinical Pathologists, Board of Registry, P.O. Box 12270, Chicago, IL 60612. American Society for Medical Technology, 330 Meadowfern Dr., Houston, TX 77067. American Medical Technologists, 710 Higgins Rd., Park Ridge, IL 60068. Department of Allied Health Education and Accreditation, American Medical Association, 535 N. Dearborn St., Chicago, IL 60610.

OPHTHALMIC LABORATORY TECHNICIANS

Duties and Responsibilities

Prescription eyeglasses are one of those things most of us take for granted. We depend on them daily, but probably never think about the fact that someone had to make them. Yet, they must be made with care and precision by technicians who follow the prescription provided by an ophthalmologist or optometrist.

There are two types of ophthalmic technicians: a *surfacer* (lens grinder) and a *bench technician* (finisher). (In small labs, one person may perform both tasks.) First, standard-size lens blanks are mass-produced by optical firms, and then a surfacer takes this blank and grinds and polishes the lens to specification using precision instruments.

Once a pair of lenses has been worked on and refined, bench technicians insert them into frames. They work with tools such as lens cutters and glass drills, as well as small files, pliers, and other hand tools. They also use automatic edging machines to shape lens edges and precision instruments to detect imperfections. In very large laboratories, there may even be specialized workers within these two specialties.

An almost constant humming, whirring sound from the machinery is a part of a technician's work environment, and sometimes goggles must be worn to protect the eyes.

Technicians are mainly employed in ophthalmic laboratories, though some work for opticians or for other retail firms that have optical departments. Part-time work is available.

Ophthalmic laboratory technicians can become supervisors and managers. A few become dispensing opticians, and some go into business for themselves.

Earnings and Opportunities

More than 27,000 people are employed as ophthalmic laboratory technicians, and employment is expected to grow at an average rate through the 1980s. A greater need for prescription glasses from a larger elderly population will be offset somewhat by technological improvements that will make workers more efficient, but employment opportunities should still be good. Earnings range from $12,000 to $18,200.

Training and Qualifications

A basic interest in math and science, and patience to do careful, precise work are important.

A high school diploma is required prior to receiving training. Most technicians learn their skills on the job, but better job prospects and opportunities for advancement may be had by those who attend a formal training program. Three-to-four-year apprenticeships are offered by optical goods companies; and some community colleges, vocational-technical institutes, and trade schools offer programs in optical technology. Length of these programs varies from six months to two years, and graduates receive certificates or associate degrees, depending on the type of training.

For Further Details

National Academy of Opticianry, P.O. Box 19391, Washington, DC 20036. National Federation of Opticianry Schools, Ophthalmic Dispensing Program, J. Sargeant Reynolds Community College, P.O. Box 12084, Richmond, VA 23241. Opticians Association of America, 1250 Connecticut Ave., N.W., Washington, DC 20036.

OPTOMETRIC ASSISTANTS

Duties and Responsibilities

Just as medical office assistants do for doctors, optometric assistants perform a combination of clerical and patient care tasks in order to free the optometrist to spend more time on professional duties.

Assistants, sometimes known as paraoptometrics, keep patients' records, schedule appointments, and handle bookkeeping, correspondence, and filing. They may take initial case histories of new patients and record the results of all eye exams. In offices where eyeglasses are available for purchase, some assistants are trained to measure patients for correct and comfortable fit. They may help the patient select size and shape of frames and may adjust finished eyeglasses by heating, shaping, and bending the plastic or metal frames. They may also teach patients how to insert, remove, and care for contact lenses.

Optometric assistants may also help patients with vision therapy activities to develop eye coordination, focusing, and other visual abilities.

When working in the laboratory, they insert lenses in frames, repair frames, keep inventory, order supplies, and clean and care for the instruments.

Optometric technicians have more extensive training than optometric assistants. They measure the curvature of the cornea; test the patient's ability to see numbers or letters at a specified distance; and record pressures or tensions within the eye.

Most assistants and technicians are employed by optometrists in private practice. Some, however, work for clinics, health maintenance organizations, and optical companies.

A typical workweek is thirty to forty hours, and some weekend and evening work may be required if offices are open at that time.

Earnings and Opportunities

Over 18,000 people are employed as assistants or technicians, and employment is expected to grow as our elderly population grows. Beginning salaries for optometric assistants are between $8,400 and $10,200, while starting optometric technicians earn between $9,600 and $15,300.

Training and Qualifications

Manual dexterity and accuracy are good qualities for future optometric assistants and technicians. The ability to follow routines and procedures is also needed. A neat appearance and courtesy and tact are helpful in working with patients.

Most assistants and technicians are trained on the job. However, training can be acquired in one- and two-year programs offered by community colleges, technical institutes, and colleges of optometry. Optometric assistant training can be acquired in one year, while technicians undergo more extensive training. In any case, a high school diploma is necessary.

Paraoptometric personnel with the proper combination of training and experience can take an exam to become registered with the National Paraoptometric Registry as registered optometric assistants or registered optometric technicians.

For Further Details

American Optometric Association, Paraoptometric Section, 243 N. Lindbergh Blvd., St. Louis, MO 63141.

PHYSICIAN ASSISTANTS

Duties and Responsibilities

Physician assistants have skills similar to, though less extensive than, those of a physician, and they can handle many of the routine or time-consuming tasks formerly performed only by doctors. It may be the perfect profession for those who want a responsible health-oriented position with a great deal of patient contact.

Always practicing under the supervision of a physician, they can be found doing everything from working as part of a medical team in a large city hospital to aiding a physician in a remote rural community where there aren't enough medical doctors to serve the population. Alternate titles sometimes used are MEDEX, physician associate, and community health medic.

Physician assistants perform tasks such as interviewing patients, taking medical histories, performing physical examinations, ordering laboratory tests, making tentative diagnoses and prescribing appropriate treatments. Studies show they have the training to care for eight out of ten people who visit a family practitioner's office in any one day.

Some PA's assist physicians in such specialty areas as pediatrics or surgery. They perform routine procedures such as doing physical examinations, providing post-operative care or assisting during complicated medical procedures. PA specialists include child health associates, orthopedic physician assistants, urologic physician assistants, surgeon assistants, and emergency room physician assistants.

Most PA's work for physicians who are in private practice. About 25 percent are employed by hospitals. More than 40 percent provide crucial health care services in rural areas and inner cities where physicians do not practice in large numbers. In these areas, some are associated with physicians in private practice, but many others are connected with clinics where a physician might be available for just a day or two each week.

For most PA's, advancement takes the form of added responsibilities and higher earnings that come with experience.

Earnings and Opportunities

Over 9,500 people are employed in this profession, and opportunities are good. A 27 percent increase in employment of physician assistants is projected for the next ten years. Earnings range from $22,500 to $34,000.

Training and Qualifications

Emotional stability, conscientiousness, patience, and the ability to gain the trust of others are important qualities for PA's.

Special training is needed, and training programs generally last two years. Programs are run by medical schools, community colleges, and accredited teaching hospitals.

Admission requirements vary from a high school diploma to a bachelor's degree. However, two years of college work in a science or health professions program is common.

Most PA programs award certificates; some give an associate degree; and a few that require extensive college work prior to admission grant a bachelor's or master's degree.

The MEDEX training program is similar to PA training but designed especially for those who have had extensive direct patient care experience such as medical corpsmen or registered nurses. The program generally lasts about eighteen months.

For Further Details

Association of Physician Assistant Programs, 2341 Jefferson Davis Hwy., Suite 700, Arlington, VA 22202. National Commission on Certification of Physician Assistants, Inc., 3384 Peachtree Rd., N.E., Suite 560, Atlanta, GA 30326.

RADIOLOGIC (X-RAY) TECHNOLOGISTS

Duties and Responsibilities

Imagine how excited the medical community must have been when they discovered a way to take pictures of the inside of the human body. The people responsible for taking these pictures today are called radiologic technologists or radiographers (X-ray technologists).

X-ray technology is used for diagnostic purposes and is a widely known specialty. Bone fractures, ulcers, blood clots, brain tumors, and lung disease are among the disorders that can be spotted through radiography.

Once an order has been received for an X ray, the technologist prepares the patient by properly positioning him or her. Equipment must be prepared and adjusted for exposure time, density, and detail. Afterwards, the X-ray film is developed and given to a radiologist for diagnosis.

If the gastrointestinal workings of a patient are to be observed, the technologist prepares a solution of barium sulfate for the patient to drink. As it passes through the patient's digestive tract, a physician can look for diseases, injuries, or defects by watching the process on a special television monitor.

Another specialty in the field is that of radiation therapy, which is mainly used for treating cancer. Working under the close supervision of a radiologist, the technologist applies radiation to the affected part of the body for the specified length of time. Nuclear medicine is yet another specialty. Here, solutions of radioactive material are prepared and swallowed by or injected into the patient in order to trace the development of a disease. Using scanners and cameras that pick up the radioactivity, the technologist records the results.

Technologists also perform administrative tasks such as maintaining records and scheduling appointments. While there are potential radiation hazards, they have been greatly reduced by improved equipment and the use of safety devices.

In large radiography departments, some experienced technologists may qualify as instructors or advance to supervisory positions.

Earnings and Opportunities

Over 106,000 people are employed as radiologic technologists. Employment is expected to increase by 43 percent by the mid-1990s. Salaries range from $15,000 for beginners to over $24,000 for those with experience. Workers with more specialized skills generally earn more.

Training and Qualifications

A high school education is required to enter a formal training program in radiography. These programs are usually two years in length, but may be part of a four-year degree program. They are offered by hospitals, medical schools, colleges, and universities. Those who go on to get a bachelor's degree stand the best chance of advancement.

Registration with the American Registry of Radiologic Technologists is an asset. Once registered, technologists may be certified in radiation therapy technology or nuclear medicine technology by completing an additional year of study in that specialty.

For Further Details

American Society of Radiologic Technologists, 15000 Central Ave., S.E., Albuquerque, NM 87123. Department of Allied Health Education and Accreditation, American Medical Association, 535 N. Dearborn St., Chicago, IL 60610.

SURGICAL TECHNICIANS

Duties and Responsibilities

If you've ever had surgery, there was a very important person present whom you may not have been aware of—the surgical technician. His or her job is to assist surgeons and anesthesiologists before, during, and after surgery.

Surgical technicians, also called surgical technologists or operating room technicians, help set up the operating room with instruments, equipment, sterile linens, and fluids such as glucose that will be needed during an operation. They may prepare patients for surgery by washing, shaving, and disinfecting body areas where the surgeon will operate. Sometimes they are responsible for transporting patients to the operating room.

During surgery, they pass instruments and

supplies to the surgeons and the surgeons' assistants. They hold retractors, cut sutures, and help count sponges, needles, and instruments used during the operation. When a sample has been taken, surgical technicians help prepare the specimen to be sent to the laboratory. They are also trained to operate sterilizers, lights, suction machines, and some diagnostic equipment. After the operation, surgical technicians help transfer patients to the recovery room and assist nurses in cleaning and stocking the operating room for the next operation.

Most surgical technicians are employed by hospitals and other institutions with operating facilities. A few—often called private scrubs—are employed directly by a surgeon who wants them to assist during all operations.

A forty-hour, five-day workweek is normal, although many are required to be on call, since some emergency surgery units require twenty-four-hour coverage.

Some technicians advance to be assistant operating room supervisors who are responsible for ordering supplies, arranging work schedules, and other administrative details.

Earnings and Opportunities

Over 31,500 people work as surgical technicians, and employment is expected to rise 40 percent through the mid-1990s. Earnings range from $7,200 to $20,000.

Training and Qualifications

Stamina for standing during long operations, manual dexterity for handling the instruments carefully and quickly, and the ability to pay close attention to what is going on are all important qualities for future technicians. They must also be willing to keep up to date on new surgical developments in order to work with new equipment and procedures.

In order to obtain training, a high school diploma is necessary. Most technicians receive training in vocational and technical schools, hospitals, and community and junior colleges. Such programs last from nine months to one year; some community colleges have two-year programs that lead to an associate degree.

Some technicians are trained on the job in programs that vary from six weeks to a year. For this training, hospitals often prefer applicants who have already worked in a hospital-related job.

Certification is available from the Association of Surgical Technologists.

For Further Details

Association of Surgical Technologists, Caller No. E, Littleton, CO 80120.

Careers in Hospitality and Travel

Growth in the hospitality (hotel, motel, restaurant, and food service) and travel industries has been so explosive that a shortage of well-qualified personnel has made this a field filled with opportunity for those with ambition.

Hotels and motels—the foundation of the hospitality trade—employ hundreds of thousands of workers in positions ranging from executive housekeepers and front office workers to sales and banquet managers. All contribute to the overall operation of a hotel or motel—providing lodging and service to paying guests. Career opportunities here are exciting. The demand is great, the supply of well-trained applicants is short, and career advancement is rapid, with on-the-job training serving as the key to upward mobility. In this field, it is entirely possible to go from front office clerk to general manager. For some, training and experience at a major hotel provide the background and impetus to start businesses of their own or to move into areas with greater advancement opportunities.

Food service is another part of the hospitality trade. These jobs range from restaurant chefs to managers, as well as all those involved in preparing and serving meals. While training for positions as chefs and managers is offered at colleges and universities and specialized training schools, many enter the field at the bottom and work their way up to challenging, lucrative jobs within the industry. Mobility between restaurants, hotels, catering firms, and institutional food services (hospitals, schools, companies) is very fluid. Some also move on to begin their own restaurants or catering businesses.

The travel business is also enjoying a surge of good health. Deregulation of the airlines, coupled with stable fuel prices, has sparked attractive travel fares, and more Americans are taking to the skies and roads for vacation and business travel.

Supporting that activity are the pilots, crews, flight attendants, and airline and car reservationists. Many of them enjoy the benefits of extended travel (both on duty and off), flexible work schedules, and the chance to meet new and interesting people.

Travel and hospitality workers all share one characteristic: their businesses continue to operate nights, weekends, and holidays, since people are on the go every day of the year. While that may create unusual work schedules, it also allows for some interesting and exciting benefits. Those pluses, coupled with the extended training and advancement opportunities, make this field a promising one for career growth.

AIRPLANE PILOTS

Duties and Responsibilities

While the thrill of flying may be what lures people to become airplane pilots, responsibility for flight safety and a high degree of skill are the essentials of the job.

Most pilots transport passengers and cargo; others specialize in crop dusting, test-piloting, or taking photographs. Some pilots work as instructors, and a few work as "check pilots" to observe other airline pilots and co-pilots periodically to be sure that they are proficient.

Except on small aircraft, two pilots are usually needed to fly a plane. The captain is the more experienced and is in command and supervises other crew members. The co-pilot assists in communicating with air traffic controllers, monitoring the instruments, and flying the plane. Most large airlines have a third pilot, the flight engineer, who monitors and operates many of the instruments and systems.

Before the flight, the pilot confers with dispatchers and weather forecasters and chooses a route, altitude, and speed that should provide the fastest, safest, and smoothest flight. Next, he checks thoroughly to determine that the plane is functioning properly and that the baggage or cargo has been loaded correctly.

Takeoff and landing are the most difficult parts of the flight and require close coordination between pilot and co-pilot. When visibility is poor, pilots must rely completely on their instruments. By following them carefully they can safely fly above mountains or other obstacles and even land "blind."

Pilot flying hours are limited by law, so airline pilots generally work only sixteen days a month. Layovers are usually away from home, and flight times may be at any time of day or night. Pilots employed outside the airlines also may have irregular schedules, but since they usually have more non-flying duties, they tend not to have the blocks of free time that airline pilots have.

Some pilots start as flying instructors to build up flying hours before advancing to fly charter, commuter, or corporate planes.

Earnings and Opportunities

Over 82,000 people are employed as pilots, and the job outlook is quite good, with an estimated increase in employment of 29 percent expected in the next ten years. Earnings range from $27,500 to over $125,000.

Training and Qualifications

Alertness and the ability to make quick decisions and accurate judgments under pressure are excellent qualities for future pilots.

Most airlines require two years of college and prefer to hire college graduates. All pilots must have a commercial pilot's license from the FAA. They must pass a strict physical examination which requires 20/20 vision with or without glasses, good hearing, and no physical handicaps that could impair performance. Applicants must pass a written test and demonstrate their flying ability to FAA examiners.

Airline pilots must pass FAA written tests and flight examinations to earn a flight engineer's license. Captains must have an airline transport pilot's license.

Flying can be learned in military or civilian flying schools.

For Further Details

For a copy of a *List of Certified Pilot Schools* write U.S. Department of Transportation, Publications Section, M-443.1, Washington, DC 20590.

CATERERS

Duties and Responsibilities

For the person who takes pleasure and pride in providing an enjoyable dining experience for others, a career as a caterer offers a fascinating challenge. The work may vary from preparing an intimate dinner for eight to serving drinks and hors d'oeuvres for 500, and each event must be specially tailored to the needs of the individual client.

Caterers tend to be self-employed, though some may work for large catering businesses. Most serve dishes that represent a variety of cuisines, but some—particularly those in urban areas—develop a specialty such as Tex-Mex or nouvelle cuisine, or become known for their expertise in Italian cooking.

The caterer's job begins with an initial meeting with the client when the menu is discussed and the cost is determined (based on the number of people attending and the items to be served). Frequently, the caterer is expected to provide the necessary table settings, linen, silver, serving dishes, china, and glassware. They may also hire the bartenders and waiters and waitresses who will serve the food, and usually provide workers to clean up afterwards.

Preparation for most affairs usually begins in the caterer's own kitchen several days prior to the event. On the day of the event, the food may be transported to the location fully prepared, or additional work at the site may be necessary.

Caterers generally charge a per-head fee, and knowing how to price an event is an art in itself. Costs for food may vary depending on the season, and knowing how to control expenses in order to always make a profit is an important part of the job.

The caterer is responsible for much of the success of a party, since the quality of the food and how it is served are often a very important part of how people evaluate the day's or evening's experience. Extreme care must be taken in the preparation and transporting of food in order to see that everything stays fresh and uncontaminated. It is a job where the behind-the-scenes work is hectic and fast-paced, and yet the effect must be to make everything seem smooth and effortless.

Caterers work throughout the country, although those who launch specialty businesses are more likely to be found in urban areas.

Earnings and Opportunities

Opportunities for caterers are good, but competition for clients is keen. Earnings range from $18,000 to $50,000 and higher.

Training and Qualifications

An eye for attractive food presentation, a feel for fine cooking, good business sense, and strong organizational skills are important qualities for caterers.

While there are no specific educational requirements, aspiring caterers would be well served by a high school education and some additional courses in food preparation and/or attending a college offering a food specialty. Since many caterers also run their own businesses, courses in business planning, accounting, and marketing can also be of great value.

CHEFS AND COOKS

Duties and Responsibilities

Whatever the menu—from fried chicken and mashed potatoes to chocolate mousse and roast pheasant—the quality of food and its preparation are the most important factors in the reputation a restaurant achieves.

While the terms *cook* and *chef* are sometimes used interchangeably, the title chef generally connotes a more highly skilled supervisory professional. Many fine chefs have earned fame for themselves and their restaurants because of their outstanding culinary abilities.

In a small restaurant featuring a limited number of specialties and ready-made desserts, usually one cook prepares all the food and may be assisted by a short-order cook and one or two kitchen helpers.

In a large establishment with a more varied menu, the kitchen staff may include many kitchen helpers and several cooks, one or two of whom are general assistants and the others of whom have specialties such as pastries or sauces. The work is coordinated by the head cook or executive chef.

Most cooks and chefs work in restaurants and hotels, but many are also employed by schools, colleges, airports, and hospitals. Government agencies, factories, private clubs, and many other organizations also employ cooks and chefs.

Many kitchens today are modern and well equipped, with adequate air conditioning, but others may be less up to date. Cooks must stand a great deal, lift heavy pots and pans, and work near hot ovens and ranges. Work hours in restaurants may include late evenings, holidays, and weekends.

For some, advancement is achieved by moving to different establishments for higher pay. Others rise to chef or supervisory or management jobs within their company. Some eventually go into business as caterers or restaurant owners; others may become cooking instructors.

Earnings and Opportunities

More than 1.1 million people work as chefs or cooks and job opportunities are expected to be excellent, with a 33 percent increase in jobs expected in the next decade. Cooks and assistants earn from $15,000 to $32,000. Chefs' salaries range from $20,000 to $45,000. Chefs with national reputations make more than $40,000 a year. Employers generally provide free meals and uniforms.

Training and Qualifications

A refined sense of taste and smell, physical stamina, and the ability to work as part of a team are important qualities in this profession. Those who rise to executive chef positions also need aptitude for management and good organizational skills.

To achieve the level of skill required of an executive chef in a fine restaurant, training is advisable, and those who have had courses in commercial food preparation will have an advantage when looking for jobs in large restaurants and hotels. High school graduates can qualify for training programs available from trade schools, vocational centers, and junior colleges, as well as on-the-job training.

For Further Details

National Institute for the Foodservice Industry, 20 N. Wacker Dr., Suite 2620, Chicago, IL 60606. American Culinary Federation, P.O. Box 3466, St. Augustine, FL 32084. Council on Hotel, Restaurant and Institutional Education, Human Development Bldg., Room 118, University Park, PA 16802.

FLIGHT ATTENDANTS

Duties and Responsibilities

While most people think of flight attendants as workers who attend to the comfort and needs of airline passengers, their prime responsibility is one of safety. Though their life-saving training is not frequently needed, the fact that

it might be necessary makes the job an extremely important one.

Flight attendants are aboard almost all passenger planes and are responsible for passenger comfort and safety. Before a flight, attendants are briefed on weather conditions and any anticipated special passenger needs.

They also check supplies such as food, beverages, blankets, and reading materials, as well as first-aid kits and other emergency equipment. As passengers arrive, attendants assist them in getting settled.

Prior to takeoff, attendants instruct the passengers in the use of emergency equipment and make sure that all are using their seat belts. Once airborne, they answer questions, distribute magazines and pillows, and serve refreshments. On many flights, they heat and distribute precooked meals. They may also be called on to offer special help to youngsters traveling alone, the elderly or handicapped, or those with small children, and they may give first aid to an ill passenger.

In the event of an emergency, attendants are also trained to reassure passengers and to help them evacuate the airplane if necessary.

While the job offers the glamour of travel, the schedules can be rigorous and the work is often hard. Flight schedules are assigned by seniority, so it may take several years before a worker is flying the routes and times he or she prefers. Attendants may work nights, holidays, and weekends; and they may be away from their home bases overnight at least one-third of the time.

Attendants advance by gaining seniority and having improved opportunities to bid on preferred routes and home bases. Some advance by becoming flight service instructors, customer service directors, instructors, recruiting representatives, or they move on to various other administrative positions.

Earnings and Opportunities

Over 56,000 people are employed as flight attendants and employment opportunities are expected to be quite good as training for new employees resumes at the major airlines following the hiring slowdown of the early 1980s. In fact, jobs for flight attendants are expected to increase 29 percent in the next decade.

Earnings range from approximately $16,800 to $38,000. An added benefit is that attendants and their immediate families are entitled to reduced fares on most airlines.

Training and Qualifications

A neat, clean appearance, tact, poise, patience, physical stamina, and a friendly personality are important qualities for these workers.

Applicants for flight attendant positions should be at least nineteen, be high school graduates, and those having several years of college or experience in dealing with the public are preferred. Those hired for international airlines generally must speak an appropriate foreign language fluently.

Most large airlines require that newly hired flight attendants complete four to six weeks of intensive training.

For Further Details

Air Transport Association of America, 1709 New York Ave., N.W., Washington, DC 20006.

FOOD SERVICE SUPERVISORS

Duties and Responsibilities

Making sure that the kitchen runs smoothly and that the food is served promptly and properly is the work of food service supervisors, who are an important part of the behind-the-scenes operation in school cafeterias, hospitals, restaurants, cafeterias, summer camps, and hotels.

In large establishments, food service supervisors report to administrative dietitians and serve as their right hand, supervising employees, overseeing the preparation and serving of meals, helping train new workers, and keeping tabs on the sanitation and safety of work methods used. They are also responsible for monitoring inventory, which may include ordering the food, supplies, and equipment as needed. In institutions where there is no dietitian, the food service supervisor is the person in charge.

Institutional kitchens are usually active,

busy places, and the problems encountered are numerous. Employees fail to show up for work or are late; deliveries don't arrive as expected; equipment breaks down; the power goes out; orders are changed at the last minute; dishes are broken; and spillage and waste occur. The supervisors are responsible for solving each of these problems, as well as foreseeing and preventing as many of them as possible.

The work involves a great deal of time on one's feet, and hours can be irregular, since food service goes on throughout most of the day, seven days a week, 365 days a year. Employment is readily available throughout the country, and usually provides a great deal of stability.

Advancement generally consists of moving to a larger institution where the job of food service supervisor commands more money. Some supervisors continue their education in order to move up to become a dietitian.

Earnings and Opportunities

Outlook for employment is quite good as we open more homes for the aged, as our medical services grow, as the public's ability to travel and to eat more meals out continues. Earnings range from $14,400 to $23,000.

Training and Qualifications

Managerial ability, an interest in food, and a knowledge of food science and nutrition are helpful in this job. Loyalty, dependability, and a willingness to work hard are necessary.

A high school diploma is advised, and a background in home economics, chemistry, biology, and business courses is helpful. In addition, short-term training schools for food service supervisors are being established by hospitals, vocational schools, public health departments, and state universities. Most programs include classroom instruction as well as some practical supervisory experience.

For Further Details

National Food Service Association, P.O. Box 1932, Columbus, OH 43216.

HOTEL AND MOTEL MANAGERS AND ASSISTANTS

Duties and Responsibilities

Those involved in hotel and motel management are in the business of providing lodging and service. To do this efficiently and profitably, hotel managers must see to myriad details. The rooms must be comfortable and inviting, the food and drinks memorable; staff should be courteous; the security good; and advertising must be effective—all in an effort to build and maintain a successful operation.

At a large hotel, a manager and his or her assistants may feel they are running a small city, so many and varied are the duties involved in this type of round-the-clock operation. Individual managers, who report to a general manager, are in charge of the food and beverage operations, housekeeping, accounting, security, and maintenance departments. The general manager is responsible for overall operations and policy.

While all the same functions must be performed at a small hotel or motel, they are performed by a much smaller staff. The manager may work in the front office and at the reception desk taking reservations, greeting guests, and assigning rooms, while also overseeing operations and setting policy. Management trouble-shooting may mean actually having to help. When a maid calls in sick, the manager may find himself making up a room or two. Hotels are open twenty-four hours a day, seven days a week. Some managers work on shifts. Handling problems and coping with the unexpected are all a part of the job. Jobs may be found throughout the United States, though the majority will be found in metropolitan areas and resort communities. Career advancement may sometimes mean re-locating.

Earnings and Opportunities

Over 84,000 people are employed as hotel or motel managers, and employment prospects are very good. In the next ten years the number of these jobs is expected to increase 23 percent. Salaries range from $21,000 to $80,000 for general managers. Food and beverage managers make from $16,000 to $40,000. Lodging and meals may be part of the package in some cases.

Training and Qualifications

Experience is an important consideration in selecting managers, and some management personnel are employees who have risen through the ranks. However, employers are increasingly looking for applicants with a col-

lege education, preferably with a bachelor's degree in hotel and restaurant administration. Many colleges offer four-year programs in the field, and some junior colleges and technical institutes as well as the Educational Institute of the American Hotel and Motel Association also have courses that provide a good background. Part-time or summer work in hotels and restaurants is also good preparation.

Hotel and motel chains may offer better opportunities for advancement than independently owned establishments, because employees can transfer within the company as openings occur.

For Further Details

American Hotel and Motel Association, 888 Seventh Ave., New York, NY 10019. Council on Hotel, Restaurant, and Institutional Education, Human Development Building, Room 118, University Park, PA 16802.

HOTEL AND MOTEL FRONT OFFICE CLERKS

Duties and Responsibilities

If you aspire to work in hotel management, then a job as a reception desk clerk might be just the entry position for you. It's a visible position, with people contact and responsibility, and many clerks have gone on to make hotel work a career.

Handling room reservations and greeting guests, issuing keys, and collecting payments are among the basic duties of the hotel or motel front office clerk. In a small hotel or motel, the desk clerk may also function as bookkeeper, cashier, or telephone operator. However, in a larger operation several clerks may be assigned to each shift, and their duties may be more specialized.

Room or *desk clerks* assign rooms to guests and answer questions about hotel services, checkout time, or parking facilities. They complete guest registration forms and sometimes collect payments. They are highly visible representatives of the establishment for which

they work, and their appearance and attitude contribute greatly to a guest's feelings about the hotel.

Reservation clerks record written or telephoned requests for rooms, prepare registration forms, and notify room clerks of guest arrival times.

Rack clerks keep records of room assignments to advise housekeepers, telephone operators, and maintenance workers that rooms are occupied. Key clerks, mail clerks, and information clerks are also a part of most large hotel staffs.

Since hotels are open around the clock, night and weekend work is common. Many clerk positions involve a great deal of contact with guests, and while this can be quite pleasant, it can also be very trying, and may require tact at times.

The clerk who wishes to advance may move up within the various clerking positions to become assistant front office manager and then front office manager. While a college background is not necessary for becoming a clerk, it is an asset for advancement into management.

Earnings and Opportunities

Over 80,000 people are employed as hotel clerks, and employment is expected to grow. Seasonal job opportunities will continue to be available in resort areas. Clerks earn from $9,200 to $14,800. Those who work a night shift generally receive additional compensation.

Training and Qualifications

A neat appearance, a warm, polite manner and a desire to help people are important traits for hotel workers. In large cities and certain resort areas, a foreign language can be a real plus as well.

Most clerks receive on-the-job training. New workers usually begin as mail, information, or key clerks. They learn about various duties, about room locations, services offered, and the hotel in general. Some clerks may need additional training in computer terminal or office machine operation because of the increased use of computerized front office systems.

Clerks who have taken home- or group-study courses in hotel management such as those sponsored by the Educational Institute of the American Hotel and Motel Association may improve their opportunities for promotion.

For Further Details

American Hotel and Motel Association, 888 Seventh Ave., New York, NY 10019.

HOTEL AND MOTEL HOUSEKEEPERS AND ASSISTANTS

Duties and Responsibilities

Although some hotels and motels provide economical accommodations, while others offer the most luxurious surroundings, all establishments pay serious attention to one thing: the neatness and cleanliness of rooms, hallways, and public areas. Their reputations depend on it.

Hotel housekeepers are responsible for keeping hotels and motels clean and attractive and providing guests with essential furnishings and supplies. They hire, train, schedule, and supervise the housekeeping staff, including linen and laundry workers, and some also supervise certain areas of maintenance.

Housekeepers who work in small or middle-sized establishments may not only supervise the housekeeping staff but perform some of these duties themselves. By contrast, housekeepers in large or luxury hotels are primarily administrators, and they are usually called executive or head housekeepers.

Besides supervising a staff that may number in the hundreds, an executive housekeeper prepares the budget for the department; submits reports to the general manager on the condition of rooms, needed repairs, and suggested improvements; and purchases supplies and furnishings.

Since hotels are open around the clock, night and weekend work is common. Because they must coordinate a variety of functions, hotel housekeepers often work under pressure. Supervising the preparation of rooms for incoming guests around check-out time can be particularly hectic.

A position as assistant housekeeper or floor housekeeper is a logical step toward a promotion to executive housekeeper. Those who have degrees or have taken courses in institutional housekeeping management and other management courses will have the best opportunity for advancement.

Earnings and Opportunities

Over 18,000 persons work as hotel housekeepers, and employment is expected to grow faster than average throughout the 1980s. Seasonal job opportunities will continue to be available in resort hotels and motels that are open only part of the year. Earnings run from $12,500 to $40,000 or more, plus lodging and meals in some cases.

Training and Qualifications

Executive housekeepers should be good administrators. They should have a sense of how the housekeeping department should be run and the ability to direct others. Planning and organizational ability and a strong sense of responsibility are important. Housekeepers should be able to work independently and must learn to keep records and analyze numbers.

While most housekeeping positions do not require specialized educational training, the greater the education, the better the position that can be obtained. Continuing education can lead to promotion and/or a greater opportunity with a larger or more progressive organization.

Several colleges, junior colleges, and technical institutes offer instruction in hotel administration that includes courses in hotel housekeeping. Many schools have developed courses under the guidance of the National Executive Housekeepers Association; and the Educational Institute of the American Hotel and Motel Association offers courses for either classroom or home study.

For Further Details

National Executive Housekeepers Association, Inc., Business and Professional Building, 414 Second Ave., Gallipolis, OH 45631. American Hotel and Motel Association, 888 Seventh Ave., New York, NY 10019.

RESERVATIONISTS AND AIRLINE TICKET AGENTS

Duties and Responsibilities

Because of computers and the reservationists who operate them your vacation to Florida or London is really no further away than your telephone. One quick call and an airline reservationist will be able to tell you flight schedules and seat availability. He or she can then book your seat, reserve a special meal, and arrange for you to have a boarding pass when you pick up your ticket. One more quick phone call to an auto rental company, and another reservationist has arranged for your car; a final call to a hotel reservationist, and you get complete details on what kind of room will be waiting you and at what price.

Each reservationist has access to a computer terminal, and by typing instructions on the keyboard, he or she can quickly obtain information about availability, book your reservation, and give you any other information you may need. Most reservationists work in large central offices. Those who work for the airlines may also answer customer telephone inquiries on late arrivals and departures, fares, schedules, and cities serviced by the airline. Train and bus companies have similar positions, as do cruise lines.

Airline ticket agents work at airports or in downtown ticket offices. The people you see staffing the boarding gates at airports are ticket agents. In addition to booking space for customers, agents also prepare tickets and accept payments. They keep records of passengers on each plane and assist customers with problems such as lost or damaged baggage.

At the boarding gate, agents announce departure times, collect tickets, sometimes assign seats, and check to make sure flight attendants have all the food needed for the flight. At small airports, ticket agents may also load and unload baggage and freight.

Reservationists and agents normally work a forty-hour week, though schedules may be somewhat irregular. Most companies try to provide telephone reservation service late into the night, and workers who are employed by the airlines—a twenty-four-hour-a-day business—may work at any time.

Reservationists and ticket agents may be promoted to supervisory positions.

Earnings and Opportunities

About 49,000 people are employed as airline reservationists, and 37,000 work as ticket agents. Outlook for employment is fair. Earnings range from $18,200 to $31,000. As an added benefit, most airline employees and their immediate families are entitled to reduced fares on their own and other airlines.

Training and Qualifications

In these jobs, workers deal directly with the public by phone and sometimes in person, so a neat appearance, a friendly personality, and a good speaking voice are helpful.

A high school diploma is generally required, and some college training is preferred. Reservationists must also be able to type.

Airline reservationists receive about a month of classroom training in which they learn about company policy and government regulations that cover ticketing procedures. Ticket agents also receive classroom instruction, and on-the-job training follows for both.

For Further Details

Air Line Employees Association, 5600 S. Central Ave., Chicago, IL 60638.

TRAVEL AGENTS

Duties and Responsibilities

Planning a trip to Disneyland for a family on a budget is quite different from arranging for air travel, limousine service, and a first-class hotel suite for a business executive; and it's just that kind of variety that makes the travel agent's job interesting.

Some travel agents work in storefront businesses and have a great deal of personal contact with clients. Other agents specialize in making travel plans for corporate executives, and most of their work is done over the phone, coordinating and confirming arrangements with executive secretaries.

Travel agents also do considerable promotional work on behalf of their companies. They may give special group presentations, arrange advertising displays, and meet with business managers to suggest company-sponsored trips. Some work as tour guides, actually taking groups on trips through foreign countries.

Agents can usually travel at substantially reduced rates, and sometimes hotels or resorts offer them free vacations to give them firsthand knowledge of a new locale. Except for those who head tours, most travel agents do not spend an exceptional amount of time traveling. Most days are spent in the office conferring with clients, completing paperwork,

contacting airlines and hotels for reservations, and promoting group tours. Approximately one-quarter of all travel agents are self-employed. Most agents, but especially those who are self-employed, work long hours.

Advancement for travel agents generally means launching their own company or rising within the agency where they work, taking on additional clients and increasing salary, responsibilities, and status.

Earnings and Opportunities

Over 52,000 people work as travel agents, and the employment outlook is quite promising, with a 43 percent increase in the number of jobs projected over the next ten years. Salaries range from $9,600 to $18,500.

Training and Qualifications

Selling is a key to success in this industry, so the best person for the job is one who can generate excitement about a particular trip or location. He or she must be organized, patient, and good with details, and should feel comfortable working with the public. Having traveled is an advantage, since a first-hand knowledge of a city or foreign country can be quite valuable.

Employers prefer to hire college graduates. Courses in geography, foreign languages, history, and computer science are most helpful; and a few colleges offer a bachelor's degree in travel, service marketing, and tourism. Travel courses are also offered in vocational schools and adult education programs as well as through home-study courses.

First-hand experience in an agency, sometimes starting out as a receptionist or clerk, helps potential agents learn the business. Sometimes formal or informal training programs are available.

For Further Details

American Society of Travel Agents, 4400 MacArthur Blvd., N.W., Washington, DC 20007.

Careers in Law

The legal profession is changing, and those who enter the field are going to benefit from the new opportunities that are coming about.

Perhaps the most significant has been the development of the legal clinic, which features walk-in access and quick and inexpensive response on simple legal matters for the public and lower overhead, higher-volume business for those storefront attorneys. This new concept will provide more opportunities for those entering the profession, including those who want to use the experience as a stepping-stone to jobs in government and private industry.

Traditionally, the field of law has always attracted bright minds because the work is fascinating and varied. It runs the gamut from defending accused murderers to filing patents; from handling maritime accident claims to writing franchise agreements; from handling the numerous details of divorces and wills to working on multimillion-dollar business deals.

Our nation's freedoms are based on a system of law. Indeed, it has prospered as the most successful nation—and democracy—on earth because of the way those laws were written, used, and upheld. As interpreters of the law, lawyers play an integral part in the process of maintaining the practice and principles of our system of justice. And as the legal system becomes more varied and more complex, the need for lawyers increases.

The importance of legal training itself has come to extend beyond the legal profession. Major government job holders and elected officials, top industry leaders, and those in the nonprofit field have legal degrees or some level of legal training and experience.

Those with paralegal training are also facing a promising future. As the legal field grows, so too will the demand for well-trained, knowledgeable workers who can perform in-depth legal research and provide important assistance.

LAWYERS

Duties and Responsibilities

One of our country's unique institutions, what makes America the great country it is, is its legal system. It affects almost every aspect of our lives, from basic law and order to establishing protective regulations in areas such as consumer products, transportation, communications, and conservation. The experts who interpret our laws, rulings and regulations and, in turn, advise us about them are, of course, lawyers (also known as attorneys).

Lawyers generally work in one of two capacities: as advocates or as advisers. As advocates, they represent opposing parties in criminal and civil trials by presenting arguments that support their side in a court of law. As advisers, they counsel their clients as to their legal rights and obligations and suggest particular courses of action.

Their work involves several types of activities. First and foremost is the interpretation of the law and its application to a specific situation, which may call for extensive research. For example, an attorney may first research other cases and precedents that have been set by those rulings before offering advice to a client.

Almost all lawyers spend a good deal of time with clients, often discussing confidential matters. (They are bound to secrecy in these matters by a strict professional code of ethics.) Attorneys also spend time preparing reports and briefs that communicate their research and their feelings on a subject clearly and concisely.

Certain attorneys spend time in court. Speaking well, thinking quickly, and having a good understanding of courtroom protocol and tactics are important here.

While there will always be attorneys who are generalists and will help people with anything from a home mortgage to a simple business contract, more and more are specializing. Just a few of the specialties include the following: *Family law* attorneys generally handle divorces and child custody cases; those who specialize in *wills* and *trusts* are knowledgeable about not only the legal but also the tax aspects of these documents. So specialized is this line of work, *patent* attorneys often have an engineering background in order to be knowledgeable enough to help inventors obtain patents on their creations. *Communications* lawyers usually represent radio and television stations in their dealings with the Federal Communications Commission. Attorneys specializing in *corporate law* may be on

staff with corporations or are retained by them on a regular basis to advise and help solve the legal problems that arise in business. Those who know about *franchising* specialize in setting up these business arrangements. *Tax* attorneys may also have a background in accounting and work with clients in setting up advantageous business structures to incur a minimum amount of tax expense. *Trial* or *litigation* lawyers may have their own practices or are employed by the government as prosecutors or public defenders, and they are expert at courtroom strategy. *Maritime* lawyers are well versed in the laws of shipping and sea transport, and *trade name* attorneys specialize in the registering of trade names, usually for corporations.

About three-fourths of all attorneys are in private practice, either in law firms or in solo practices. Some are employed by corporations, and are known as house counsel; a good number are employed throughout the government. Some work for legal aid societies; others teach in law schools. In addition, legal services are increasingly being offered as an employee benefit for union workers, so attorneys are needed for this as well.

While house counsel and government attorneys may work close to a forty-hour week, those in private practice frequently put in very long hours. Law school graduates who are hired by some of the prestigious major law firms particularly find that they work very demanding schedules in their attempt to become partners.

For advancement, some attorneys are made partners in the firms where they practice; some go into business for themselves; some become judges. Still others use their legal background to pursue careers as politicians, journalists, management consultants, financial analysts, and in many other fields.

Earnings and Opportunities

Over 425,000 people are employed as lawyers, and the outlook for employment is quite good, with a projected increase in employment over the next ten years of 34 percent. Earnings: $17,500 to $200,000.

Training and Qualifications

Integrity, objectivity, and the ability to think logically and analyze situations thoroughly are key qualities for future attorneys. Good communications skills are very helpful.

All lawyers must pass the bar examination of the state where they intend to practice; and to qualify for the test, an applicant must graduate from a law school approved by the American Bar Association or the state authorities. Graduates receive the degree of *juris doctor* (J.D.) or bachelor of law (LL.B.). Advanced law degrees are recommended for those planning to specialize, do research, or teach. Some students enroll in joint degree programs, which generally require an additional year or more and give graduates a law degree as well as an advanced degree in a specialty such as business, public administration, or city planning.

For Further Details

Information Services, American Bar Association, 1155 E. 60th St., Chicago, IL 60637. National Association for Law Placement, Boston University School of Law, 207 Bay State Rd., Boston, MA 02215. Association of American Law Schools, 1 Dupont Circle, N.W., Suite 370, Washington, DC 20036.

LEGAL ASSISTANTS

Duties and Responsibilities

For those who are fascinated by the legal profession but have no particular desire to attend law school, the position of legal assistant may be a perfect one. These workers become involved in some complex issues, and most jobs carry a fair amount of responsibility—enough to keep the position interesting without becoming burdensome.

Legal assistants, sometimes called paralegals or legal technicians, generally perform background work for lawyers. For example, for a case about to go to trial, an assistant may investigate the facts of the case and then research the appropriate laws, recorded judicial decisions, and other pertinent records in order to prepare a written opinion on the subject. The attorney then decides how the case should be handled. In preparation for the court date, the assistant may then prepare legal arguments, file pleadings with the court, obtain affidavits, and assist the attorney during the trial.

Legal assistants may also help draft documents such as contracts, mortgages, separation agreements, and trust instruments. Some help prepare tax returns and do some basic estate planning.

Those who work for corporations help attorneys handle such matters as employee contracts, shareholder agreements, stock options and employee benefit plans. They may help prepare and file annual financial reports and secure loans for the corporation.

The majority of legal assistants are employed in private law firms. Others are employed throughout the government and in many corporations.

Those in small and medium-sized law firms may be involved in trial work one day and spend the next day on a child custody case. However, most legal assistants work for large law firms, where they usually specialize in areas like real estate, estate planning, family law, labor law, litigation, or corporate law. In large firms, some become supervisors of other legal assistants. A few are promoted to managerial positions.

Earnings and Opportunities

Over 36,000 people are employed as legal assistants, and the outlook for employment is excellent, with a whopping 94 percent increase in the number of jobs projected over the next decade. Earnings are $12,500 to $26,000.

Training and Qualifications

The skills to do exacting research and think logically are key qualities for legal assistants. Good communications and investigative skills are also helpful.

Educational requirements vary greatly, but most employers prefer candidates who have graduated from formal legal assistant training programs, which are available at some colleges and universities, law schools, community and junior colleges, and business schools. Depending on the program, graduates may receive a certificate, an associate degree, or in some cases a bachelor's degree in legal assistance.

For Further Details

American Bar Association, Standing Committee on Legal Assistants, 1155 E. 60th St., Chicago, IL 60637. National Association of Legal Assistants, Inc., 3005 E. Skelly Dr., Suite 120, Tulsa, OK 74105. National Federation of Paralegal Associations, P.O. Box 1410, Ben Franklin Station, Washington, DC 20044.

Careers in Management and Office Administration

American business is supported by millions of administrative personnel who literally form the foundation for the efficient, effective, and consistent operation of all companies. From administrative managers who run the office, and personnel and benefits managers who see to the employees' needs, to telecommunications specialists who provide the latest information on handling voice and data communications, these workers provide the necessary assistance and support to keep business moving.

Workers in the clerical support area will have to meet the technological revolution head-on. We are only beginning to witness the work-style changes coming about because of word processors, computers, and new types of electronic communications systems. Those who are eager to learn to work with the new equipment will be justly rewarded with higher pay and greater advancement opportunities. In addition, computer and word processing operators will increasingly have the option of working from home.

There are hundreds of different jobs and titles in this rapidly expanding area. Especially as America moves to a service-based economy, there will be an increasing need for more effective support personnel to keep new and growing businesses running better than ever.

ACQUISITION SPECIALISTS, BUSINESS BROKERS, AND FRANCHISE SALES WORKERS

Duties and Responsibilities

Buying and selling companies is a big business, and those who succeed at it have developed it into an art that requires a sharp business sense, negotiating skills, and a finely honed sense of timing.

Businesses are sold for a variety of reasons: the death or retirement of the owner, lack of capital to operate, or simply in order to make a profit.

When a small business such as a motel, card shop, machine shop, or restaurant needs to be sold, the owner will generally hire a *business broker*. The broker will then seek out potential buyers and try to get the best price possible for the business. Sales may run from $50,000 to $2 million or more. Occasionally, brokers will conduct a search for a person or a firm looking to buy a particular type of business. Brokers are usually self-employed or employed by small local firms, although there are some nationally franchised business brokers.

Acquisition specialists usually represent a large firm seeking to buy one or more smaller firms. After consulting with company management as to what kinds of businesses they wish to buy, the acquisition specialist researches all companies of that type, approaches those companies (whether they are for sale or not), and proposes that they consider selling. Prices of companies bought in this way may range from $250,000 to $50 million or more.

Merger and acquisition specialists work to merge two companies in order to create one stronger company. They may also be hired to sell off divisions of companies that a corporation wishes to sell in a confidential manner.

Franchise sales workers usually market the concept of their company (motels, fast food, business services, retail stores) to individuals who wish to go into business for themselves but are limited in both capital and know-how. When a sale is made, the larger firm then helps arrange for additional capital for the purchaser and the use of the company name, and it provides training in the operation of the business.

Earnings and Opportunities

Outlook for employment is excellent. Earnings range from $30,000 to $60,000 and usually include sales bonuses. Total annual earnings can exceed $100,000.

Training and Qualifications

Business acumen, an eye for opportunity, and the ability to work well with all types of people are the qualities needed.

The vast majority of those who enter this field are college graduates, and many have advanced degrees in various fields ranging from business or accounting to engineering.

Virtually all come to these jobs with business experience; they may be former CEO's, financial vice presidents, or marketing executives. Some come from the accounting field. Most of the Big Eight accounting firms as well as major investment firms have acquisition departments.

Business brokers usually come from the commercial real estate field or a background similar to that of the acquisition specialist.

Franchise sales workers generally have a background in sales and marketing.

ADMINISTRATIVE MANAGERS

Duties and Responsibilities

Administrative managers are indispensable for keeping large businesses and government offices running smoothly at every level of organization. By taking over what are essentially administrative functions, they free top management to concentrate on policy decisions, and sales management to continue contributing to the company's bottom line.

Office managers, sometimes called *clerical pool managers*, are employed by companies who use a great many clerical workers or support staff, and they handle administrative details such as employee absence, vacation scheduling, and very often some personnel paperwork. If a secretary in a large law firm calls in sick, for example, it doesn't make sense for an attorney whose time may be billable at $100 per hour to find a substitute. An office manager can solve the problem more efficiently and at less cost to the company. In many cases, employees must report to an executive or supervisor for work assignments, but they report to the office manager for matters such as sick days, maternity leave, vacations, or scheduling difficulties. Overall, the office manager is responsible for seeing that personnel policies are not abused and that there are qualified workers in support positions at all times. In some companies, these duties are combined with another department responsibility, such as purchasing. Most office managers are promoted to these positions through the ranks, so that they have a thorough understanding of how the office works and what the employees need.

A *department manager* generally has broader responsibilities, and might have an office manager reporting to him or her. The department manager must handle the administrative paperwork, scheduling, and overall coordination for a special department, such as a group of inside salespeople or insurance workers whose job it is to handle policy inquiries by phone. Similar departments can be found in banks (where customer service telephone numbers are becoming common), brokerage firms, mail order houses, and industrial firms.

Division managers are responsible for the administrative management of an entire division and may have office managers and department managers reporting to them. It is their job to see that the paperwork and the internal services within the company function smoothly.

Working conditions depend on the industry and the company, but most administrative managers work a standard forty-hour week. The jobs may carry considerable responsibility, and the pace can be quite hectic at times.

Earnings and Opportunities

Opportunities for employment are excellent. Salaries for office managers range from $21,000 to $35,000; department and division managers may make up to $53,000.

Training and Qualifications

Excellent organizational skills and the ability to motivate others are necessary. Since managers often rise to these positions from the clerical work force, educational backgrounds vary from high school diplomas to some college education or even a bachelor's degree. Many have pursued business training or a college degree in evening programs or correspondence courses, and those who aspire to advancement would do well to follow this course.

ADMINISTRATIVE ASSISTANTS

Duties and Responsibilities

At one time men found their way into the business world by starting as secretaries and moving up to become administrative assistants, and ultimately to become busy executives. Today administrative assistant jobs are being filled both from the secretarial ranks and by people hired directly for such responsibilities, and the job of an administrative assistant can still lead to an excellent position in management.

Practicing the management philosophy of finding out what a person does well and then encouraging him or her to do it, many companies use these slots to find talented people and expose them to a wide variety of responsibilities. Eventually their strengths emerge and

they can select the area that appeals to them. Both the company and the employee benefit from this arrangement.

In general, assistants handle all the routine organizational and administrative work for their bosses, as well as any special projects that may be assigned, and their duties can be as varied as those of the executives they work for. An assistant may coordinate all the details of a boss's business trips, for example, which may include itinerary; air, hotel, and limousine reservations; appointment scheduling; and meeting-room preparations. An assistant may be given complex assignments involving research, such as gathering facts and statistics for sales reports. Administrative assistants are often called upon to read reports and condense them for quick consumption by their superiors. Of course, the specific tasks that make up an administrative assistant's day depend upon the industry and area of management he or she works in.

In order to do their jobs, assistants in large companies are constantly communicating with their counterparts in other departments. These information networks make them extremely knowledgeable about the inner workings of the corporation and the business world, and this in turn gives them the inside track on promotions to more responsible decision-making positions throughout the company.

Typing is usually a fact of life in these jobs. Assistants may also be expected to use transcribing equipment or word processors. Others use minicomputers for retrieving information. They may be asked to do personal tasks such as getting coffee, parking the boss's car, lugging his or her golf clubs, or relaying a message to a spouse.

Earnings and Opportunities

There is a great need for administrative assistants, and job opportunities are expected to increase dramatically. Earnings range from $14,800 to $30,000.

Training and Qualifications

Good organizational skills, the ability to work well with people, a strong desire to succeed in the business world, and the willingness to start at the bottom are paramount to becoming an administrative assistant.

Those who are promoted from a secretarial job can be high school, business school, or junior college graduates, although the greatest opportunities will go to those with a college degree. Those who are hired expressly to be administrative assistants will usually have a business degree or a degree related to the specific industry they are joining.

CORPORATE BENEFITS MANAGERS

Duties and Responsibilities

A significant development in American business has been the added importance and the increase in the range of employee benefits. From the traditional offering of pension, medical, and life insurance coverage, benefits have expanded to include dental and eye care, family medical and life insurance, stock ownership plans and employee investment funds, financial counseling, and still more. In addition, more companies are moving to "flexible benefits" plans that offer a selection of such benefits from which to choose. All this requires effective and well-organized management, and a good corporate benefits manager is of key importance to most companies.

Generally a part of the human resources department, benefits managers are responsible for understanding, explaining, and administering these plans. They must be thoroughly familiar with the benefits packages available to the company's staff, how they may differ under certain situations, what the eligibility

requirements are, and how more information can be obtained. They are often responsible for advising on claims as well as on the types of protection offered.

Benefits managers keep current in the employee benefits field through attending seminars given by specialists in certain areas, reading voluminously, and meeting with representatives of firms offering benefits products and services. Such activity updates their knowledge of existing plans and of the newest offerings and the latest packages as well as future industry trends. Running seminars for employees to introduce new benefits and sometimes doing one-to-one counseling are all a part of the job.

As benefits become more and more important to employees and factor in as a vital part of their overall compensation packages (running from 20 to 40 percent above their salary), the need to be competitive and aggressive in this area also grows. The corporate benefits manager who helps his or her company excel in this area in order to attract and keep good employees is well positioned to move up within the department and may occasionally move into senior management.

Earnings and Opportunities

Outlook for this field is quite good. Earnings range from $18,200 for trainees to $48,000 and up for experienced managers, depending on the size of the company.

Training and Qualifications

The ability to work well with people, some mathematical aptitude, and excellent communication skills, both oral and written, are important qualities for this job.

Employers look for candidates with college degrees and some experience in the benefits field or in the personnel or human resources areas. Knowledge of the benefits field is essential, and helpful courses on benefits and personnel administration are offered at many colleges and universities and as part of extension programs.

For Further Details

American Society for Personnel Administration, 30 Park Dr., Berea, OH 40017.

CREDIT MANAGERS

Duties and Responsibilities

As anyone who has filled out an application for a loan or a credit card knows, someone has to evaluate whether or not one's financial history merits the credit requested. This is the job of a credit manager, who may be employed by retail stores or financial institutions that grant credit to individuals, as well as by manufacturing companies, wholesalers, and large financial institutions that extend credit to businesses.

In extending credit to individuals (consumer credit), a credit manager makes decisions about applicants based on personal interviews and credit bureau and bank reports.

In extending credit to businesses (commercial credit), a credit manager or assistant analyzes financial statements, reviews credit agency reports, previous loan history, and interviews company representatives to determine a firm's record in repaying debts.

Loan policy is very important in organizations that extend credit, and credit managers work with the rest of management to formulate a policy that allows sales to grow while still denying credit to questionable customers.

In small companies, credit managers may do much of the interviewing, analyzing, and deciding final approval themselves. They are often responsible for collection of delinquent accounts.

In large offices, credit managers establish office procedures and supervise other workers who perform these duties.

Generally these workers put in the standard thirty-five-to-forty-hour week. However, seasonal increases in wholesale and retail businesses can also produce greater work volume and longer hours for the credit department.

Newly hired workers normally begin as trainees in order to learn the company's credit procedures. They may analyze previous transactions to learn how to recognize creditworthiness. They also learn how to deal with credit bureaus, banks, and other businesses that may have information on the credit histories of their customers.

Within a large organization, a trainee would hope to advance to management, where he or she would help set policy and supervise all procedures.

Earnings and Opportunities

About 55,000 people are currently employed as credit managers. The job outlook is fair. Salaries range from $16,500 to $52,000 for credit managers and to over $90,000 for executives.

Training and Qualifications

Credit managers should feel comfortable working with numbers and should have a good grasp of finance. They should be able to analyze detailed information and draw valid conclusions. Some credit positions feature a good deal of customer contact, so a pleasant manner can be an asset. Other positions require the ability to plan and oversee the work of others.

More and more employers are seeking entry-level applicants who have college degrees. Courses in accounting, economics, finance, computer programming, statistics, and psychology are all valuable in preparing for a career in credit management.

For Further Details

National Retail Merchants Association, 100 W. 31st St., New York, NY 10001. National Association of Credit Management, 475 Park Ave. S., New York, NY 10016.

DISTRIBUTION MANAGERS

Duties and Responsibilities

By the time you take home a new suit, a toaster, a mattress, or a car, that item has already traveled a long way in order to be sold to you. Raw goods to make the item have been shipped to the manufacturer, and in turn the manufacturer has shipped the finished product to the retailer's warehouse, from which it is then sent out to your local store.

Overseeing the logistics of getting items where they need to be for the least amount of money is a challenge taken on by distribution managers. Their primary job is to develop internal and external distribution systems in order to assure prompt and efficient arrival and delivery of goods. In a manufacturing company this could mean handling an influx of raw materials and seeing to the shipment of finished or semi-finished products. In retailing or wholesaling it may involve the receipt of finished goods, their warehousing, and their ultimate distribution to different stores.

Depending on the company, the distribution manager may also be involved in warehousing and materials management as well as transportation.

Sometimes called traffic managers, distribution managers handle all corporate traffic functions and continually strive to lower freight costs, negotiate contracts with the various carriers, and look for cost-saving traffic systems for their companies. They must be familiar with all methods of transportation, including air, rail, truck, barge, and ship. They are also expert at freight classification and shipping procedures and are responsible for handling loss and damage claims. They must be completely familiar with all transportation laws, both federal and state, and all ICC (Interstate Commerce Commission) regulations.

In cases where a company has its own fleet of trucks, distribution managers must get maximum utilization from the equipment by improving routing procedures and dispatching methods. They also supervise the testing and hiring of fleet drivers. Depending on the company, they may also oversee the testing and hiring of forklift operators and may be responsible for the purchase and maintenance of such equipment.

In a small company, they may work as part of a one- or two-person staff, but in larger firms, their duties include the recruiting, employment, training, supervision, and motivation of many people. Often distribution managers are directly involved with customers and must work hard to avoid problems with damaged materials and/or late deliveries.

When warehousing is part of their job, managers are responsible for inventory control, material handling equipment, stock location planning, security, and in some cases purchasing.

Computers are becoming an increasingly important part of the job, since they offer an accurate, efficient way to keep track of the exact location of inbound and outbound goods, details concerning management of a company fleet, as well as comparison rates on the various transportation methods available.

Earnings and Opportunities

Opportunities for employment are excellent, since there will be a continuing need for these workers throughout the 1980s. Salaries range from $14,000 to over $60,000 a year.

Training and Qualifications

Management ability, a talent for handling logistics, and the ability to keep track of many details are important qualifications for this work.

In smaller companies, high school graduates who have been administrative assistants or secretaries sometimes rise through the ranks to become distribution managers after working in the warehousing, purchasing, or transportation department. However, in larger companies, distribution managers need college degrees, usually in economics, accounting, business administration, or computer science.

Like any other position that may lead to upper management, the more advanced courses you have taken in traffic, materials handling, transportation, and labor relations the better the chance of advancement.

GOODS MANAGERS

Duties and Responsibilities

As the cost of living stays high and business continues to be extremely competitive, companies are finding it vitally important to avoid unnecessary losses by watching their inventories carefully and shipping in the most economical way possible. Money saved here can make the difference between failure and success in some companies, making goods management an important field.

Whether a company makes automobiles or cereal, or a store sells dresses or soap, someone must keep track of all the raw materials and finished goods that are shipped and received. In a small company, one person may be capable of handling all the details, but in a large company, a number of specialists, often heading entire departments, are needed:

Shipping and receiving managers are in charge of all the goods that come into or go out of a plant, warehouse, or store. It is their responsibility to establish a control and record-keeping system that can be easily overseen by themselves or their staffs.

Once they arrive, goods may be turned over to a *warehouse manager,* who sees that they are safely and properly stored and rotated.

When items are needed, oldest materials are brought out and used first.

Expeditors keep things moving. They usually work directly on the plant or production floor checking to see that orders are at the proper stage of production or shipping. They report to management regularly, and if plans are not proceeding according to schedule, management can evaluate the situation and decide on a course of action.

Inventory control managers are responsible for keeping company inventory at the desired level. Too much inventory can needlessly tie up hundreds of thousands or millions of dollars; too little inventory can lead to costly shortages. To manage the inventory, workers are constantly studying old production and customer order records and comparing them with incoming figures. Cyclical business must be planned for, and unexpected business anticipated.

Firms who do a tremendous amount of shipping sometimes employ a *traffic manager* who makes shipping arrangements, weighing the pros and cons of air, rail, truck, and boat. They negotiate rates and then advise the shipping and receiving manager as to the arrangements that have been made.

While goods managers have the opportunity to move up within their own ranks, these jobs can also be stepping-stones to other management jobs. The expeditor, with his frequent contact with management, is in a particularly good position for this.

Earnings and Opportunities

Opportunities for employment are excellent. Earnings range from $17,200 to $58,000 a year.

Training and Qualifications

Workers come to these jobs from all walks of life. Some are college graduates who are trained in these particular fields; others have worked their way up from the bottom, where they pushed a dolly or operated a forklift truck while taking evening courses in order to better themselves.

MANAGEMENT CONSULTANTS

Duties and Responsibilities

While the expression "You can't see the forest for the trees" was not intended to describe a business problem, it does explain why corporations call in outside management consultants. Their role is to provide an independent, detached expert's opinion on various aspects of a business's operation and make recommendations as to how the organizational structure and various business systems can be improved for greater efficiency and a tighter organization.

Management consulting is a large field. In the early 1980s it was a $32 billion a year industry and growing. It came into being partly because of business's practice of rapid expansion during favorable economic times. Companies add staff to handle increased loads, and layer upon layer of procedures grow up around the developing business. Then once faced with a glitch in the economy, a sales lag, or a product failure, the company has an immediate need to reduce costs and improve operating efficiency. That's when the management consultant is needed.

Management consultants must become thoroughly acquainted with a business in order to correctly identify the necessary and the unnecessary. They generally perform their investigation through observation and personal interviews with employees. For the business that is operating inefficiently, they might do studies on organizational structure, considering such questions as these: Are there too many layers of management? Is work being duplicated? Are there better ways to perform the tasks? Are all the tasks really necessary? Once an evaluation has been made, it is generally put into written form, and solutions are recommended. Sometimes the consultant will be asked to stay on to implement the suggested program.

Management consultants generally have an area of special expertise such as accounting, management systems, personnel, executive search, communications, computers, engineering, office design, employee benefits, or marketing.

About half of all management consultants are employees of a management consulting firm—some of which employ fifty consultants or more. These consultants may work in teams, each bringing a certain expertise to the work being done for the client company. A great deal of travel may be involved. The remainder of management consultants are self-employed and have usually gained expertise in some area before striking out on their own.

Earnings and Opportunities

Approximately 50,000 people are employed as management consultants, and opportunities are expected to grow as business and government continue to look for more efficient and effective management methods.

Average income for the full-time consultant is $50,000, but earnings can range from about $35,000 to $120,000 and up.

Training and Qualifications

Communication skills, analytical ability, decisiveness, and a talent for selling one's ideas to others are important qualities to bring to this field.

Minimum educational requirement is a college degree, and many potential candidates obtain a master's degree in administration.

While some enter the consulting field directly from college, others obtain expertise in another field before turning to consulting.

For Further Details

Institute of Management Consultants, 19 West 44th St., Room 810, New York, NY 10036.

PERSONNEL AND LABOR RELATIONS SPECIALISTS

Duties and Responsibilities

Whether hiring a new person for a job, conducting training seminars, planning new employee benefits, or negotiating with the firm's unions, personnel and labor relations specialists are an important element in almost every large American company.

They fall into two basic categories. *Personnel specialists* interview and help select applicants to fill job openings. They handle matters such as equal employment opportunity (EEO) compliance, personnel policy, wage and salary administration, employee benefits, and training and career development. *Labor relations specialists* work for unionized companies. They help company officials prepare for collective bargaining sessions, participate in contract negotiations, and handle ongoing labor relations matters.

In large personnel departments there will be many specialists.

Recruiters are constantly searching for and trying to attract promising candidates. They may travel extensively, most frequently to college campuses.

EEO representatives or *affirmative action coordinators* handle a complex and sensitive area. They maintain contact with women and minority employees and investigate and resolve EEO grievances.

Job analysts, sometimes called compensation analysts, collect and examine detailed information about job duties in order to prepare job descriptions. The *compensation manager* establishes and maintains a firm's pay system.

Training specialists are involved in human development. They may conduct orientation sessions for new employees, instruct workers in the impact of new procedures, or teach supervisory skills to newly promoted managers.

Employee-welfare managers handle the benefits programs. *Labor relations specialists* advise management on all aspects of union-management relations.

Most personnel and labor relations specialists work in private industry for companies of every description. They may advance to better personnel jobs within their own company or transfer to another employer. Usually a personnel specialist's goal is to manage a major element of the personnel program such as compensation, training, or the EEO area.

Earnings and Opportunities

Over 178,000 people work as personnel and labor relations specialists, and the outlook for employment is quite good, with a 23 percent increase in the number of personnel jobs expected in the next decade. Earnings run from $17,500 to $56,000 and up.

Training and Qualifications

A sense of fairness, the ability to communicate well orally and in writing, and a talent for getting along well with all types of people are the basic qualities needed.

A college degree is required for most beginning positions. A major in business, personnel administration, or industrial and labor relations is helpful, though many have backgrounds in psychology, counseling, or education.

Most companies are realizing that their greatest assets are their employees. As one moves into total human resource utilization many skills come into play—among them, sales and marketing, management, administration, finance and budgeting, and forecasting and modeling. In these areas a master's degree in business administration can be helpful.

For work in labor relations, graduate study in industrial or labor relations may be required. A law degree is seldom needed for entry-level jobs, but most of the people responsible for contract negotiations are lawyers, and a combination of industrial relations courses and a law degree is highly advisable for those who wish to advance.

For Further Details

American Society for Personnel Administration, 30 Park Dr., Berea, OH 44017. American Society for Training and Development, 600 Maryland Ave., S.W., Suite 305, Washington, DC 20024.

PURCHASING AGENTS

Duties and Responsibilities

Getting the best price on goods and services is vital to the bottom line of every organization, and purchasing agents are the ones who see to it that top quality goods are bought at the lowest possible cost. Depending on the nature of the business or the division of government, agents may purchase anything from nuts and bolts, finished machinery and raw materials, to cars and trucks, office supplies, or bed sheets and towels. Contracting for services may also be part of the job.

Agents may buy supplies when stock on hand reaches a predetermined reorder point, when a department in the organization requisitions items it needs, or when market conditions are especially favorable. They are often responsible for spending large sums of money and must feel comfortable with the decisions they make.

They make their choices after comparing catalog listings, directories, and trade journals; and they often meet with sales representatives to discuss items and examine samples. Frequently agents invite suppliers to bid on large orders, and then they select the lowest bidder from among those who meet the requirements for quality and delivery date. Negotiation is often a part of the process.

The agent who maintains good business relationships with suppliers can help his or her organization save money, and get favorable payment terms and quick delivery on emergency orders.

In large companies, agents usually specialize in a commodity or group of commodities, like steel, lumber, cotton, or petroleum products. These agents are supervised by purchasing managers, each of whom oversees agents who buy related commodities. In smaller organizations, purchasing agents generally buy a wider variety of goods ranging from raw materials to pencils and erasers.

A purchasing agent may be promoted to assistant purchasing manager in charge of a group of purchasing agents, and then advance to purchasing manager, director, or vice president of materials management.

Earnings and Opportunities

Over 172,000 people are employed as purchasing agents, and job prospects remain very good for this decade, with a 27 percent increase in employment projected. This can be attributed in part to the fact that more and more service organizations, such as hospitals and schools, are recognizing the importance of professional purchasers in reducing costs. Salaries range from $19,300 to $38,500 depending on the complexity of purchased goods and services. Directors of purchasing can earn $50,000 and more.

Training and Qualifications

Those interested in a career as a purchasing agent should be able to work independently and feel comfortable in a decision-making role. Getting along well with people will help in working with suppliers. Negotiation skills should also be developed.

Most large organizations require a college degree. Companies that manufacture machinery or chemicals may look for applicants with sales or management backgrounds in those fields.

Graduates of associate (two-year) degree programs in purchasing often are hired by small companies, who also may promote clerical workers into the purchasing department.

For Further Details

National Association of Purchasing Management, Inc., 11 Park Place, New York, NY 10007.

SECURITY MANAGERS

Duties and Responsibilities

Private security management is a growing field and is as important in our society as the police protection we take for granted. And while we generally think of security as involving the guarding of people and premises, the protection of information by means of computer security is one of the fastest-growing branches of the field.

The specific responsibilities of the security manager depend upon the size, type, and location of the employer. In office buildings, banks, hospitals, and department stores, security managers supervise guards who watch over records, merchandise, money, and equipment both day and night. In stores, undercover detectives are frequently part of the guard force watching for theft by customers or store employees. At ports and railroads, security managers are in charge of seeing that nothing is stolen during loading or unloading. Their staffs patrol these areas frequently, always on the lookout for fires or prowlers. In public buildings such as museums, managers station guards in most rooms or assign them specific routes for patrolling the building. Factories, laboratories, and military bases station security managers and staffs at desks or booths to check the credentials of people and vehicles entering and leaving the premises. University, park, and recreation staffs perform similar duties. At social affairs, sports events, conventions, and other large public gatherings, security management consists of maintaining order and watching for potential troublemakers.

Computer security as a field is in its infancy. There is an urgent need to develop ways to prevent theft of information while still making the data reasonably accessible to legitimate users. Computer security experts must have complete technical command of computers.

In a large organization, a security officer may oversee the entire guard force; in a small organization, he or she may work alone. Jobs can involve nights or weekends, since security is usually needed twenty-four hours a day. Some guards patrol on foot, by car, or motor scooter, sometimes accompanied by a guard dog. Others are stationed at security desks, checking traffic and often monitoring electronic security and surveillance devices.

About one-half of all security workers are employed by industrial security firms and guard agencies.

Some security managers advance to higher level supervisory positions.

Earnings and Opportunities

Employment opportunities for security managers are expected to be quite good in the coming years, and the demand for security guards, a position which can be the equivalent of an entry-level spot, will increase by almost half by 1995. Earnings: $15,800 to $46,000.

Training and Qualifications

Excellent character references, good health, including good hearing and vision, and the ability to manage and direct the work of others are important qualities for security managers.

Most rise from the ranks of guard, a job for which a high school diploma is preferred. Employers also seek people who have had experience in the military police or in state and local police departments. Some who are entering the field of computer security come from security management, but most come from the computer field. Some legal training is also helpful.

TELECOMMUNICATIONS SPECIALISTS

Duties and Responsibilities

Skyrocketing telephone costs for businesses as well as the breakup of AT&T have virtually established a new career—that of the telecommunications specialist. With all the telephone and data communications systems now available from different manufacturers and the many ways one can now lease transmission lines, companies have a crying need for expert advice on how to put together the best system of equipment and line use as well as how to control costs. Some have telecommunications specialists on staff, while smaller companies bring them in as consultants.

In a communications marketplace that continues to explode with technology, the specialist must continually stay up-to-date in the field and be prepared to advise on the most efficient, effective, and economical system for the company involved. Specialists must be knowledgeable about everything, from computerized telephone systems to the use of data communications systems, computerized mail (electronic mailboxes), videoconferencing, teletext (written messages transmitted to video terminals), telegrams, telex, and facsimile (paper copies of documents transmitted over phone lines).

An analysis of the current system and the company's needs is the first step in developing and installing a new or improved system. The number and types of telephone instruments needed, the volume of calls (and whether they're local or long distance), and how much information must go out via data communications (information communicated by computer) must be examined. Next, the right systems must be selected and designed to suit specific needs. Installation must be carefully supervised, and a framework for efficient and economical operation must be established. For example, many systems are now computer-assisted and designed so that the system can decide on the cheapest long distance service to choose from based on the number of calls and the time of day.

Telecommunications specialists are employed by large companies, particularly insurance, banking, investment, communications, and sales and manufacturing organizations, as well as the government. Others work for private firms that specialize in telecommunications consulting. Still others are freelance specialists, working for client corporations. And, of course, the phone companies and their competitors all have such specialists on staff.

Earnings and Opportunities

With the continued emphasis on telecommunications and the growing options available in both equipment, voice, video, and data transmission services, opportunities in this field should increase dramatically. Earnings range from $26,500 to $65,000 and up.

Training and Qualifications

The ability to communicate well orally and in writing, an understanding of technology, basic sales ability, and problem-solving skills are important qualities to bring to this field.

Most employers look for a bachelor's degree, preferably in business (or telecommunications, which is a field of study only recently available). For a full understanding of the complex systems available, computer courses of all kinds are most helpful.

For Further Details

International Communications Association, 9550 Forest Lane, Suite 319, Dallas, TX 76243. Society of Telecommunications Consultants, 1 Rockefeller Plaza, Suite 1912, New York, NY 10020.

TRAINING AND DEVELOPMENT SPECIALISTS

Duties and Responsibilities

In the last ten years there has been a significant growth in the field of training and development, and currently corporations and government are spending more than $30 billion a year in this area. This means that there is an ever-increasing need for training specialists who can help organizations improve employee productivity and retention by teaching a wide variety of skills.

Areas where trainees are needed range from organizational development to stress management, conflict resolution, management development, supervisory skills training, sales and sales management, and the operation of technical equipment, to name a few. Trainers also work with employees in improving writing and presentation skills as well as time management.

Training specialists generally work with two types of employees: those who need to be trained in order to do a specific job (e.g., how to do strategic planning or operate a word processor), and those whose skills can be improved to help them do a better job (e.g., the sales staff of a company will benefit from a session on how to successfully close a sale). They also work in some cases with customers, franchisees, dealers, and/or other representatives of their firms. This usually necessitates travel, which can be extensive.

To most companies, training programs that produce tangible results are very important, so trainers are under great pressure to send attendees away with new or measurably improved skills. For that reason, they function much more as facilitators than as lecturers. Instruction is geared to providing hands-on experience for employees in order to help them fully benefit from what is being taught. Most training includes give and take with the instructor.

Development of training materials is very important to the success or failure of a training program. Sometimes trainers work with materials prepared by others, and in some cases they develop their own. These range from simple typewritten handouts to sophisticated videotapes, and may also include slides, skits, overhead projections, and tests to check the validity of the training. Training manuals and training tapes play an ever increasing role in training and motivation.

Roughly 75 percent of all training specialists are employed by business or government. Others work as outside consultants. Advancement in the field may mean becoming a director of training or venturing out to set up one's own consultancy.

Earnings and Opportunities

Outlook for employment is very good, and an increasing number of jobs are surviving economic downturns as companies are realizing that effective employee training and development contributes positively to the bottom line. The American Management Association says that attendance at their 1983 spring management training classes in New York City was up 30 percent from the previous year. Earnings range from $20,000 to $50,000 and up.

Training and Qualifications

Working well with people, and good writing and presentation skills are helpful qualities for this job.

Trainers must have a bachelor's degree; many have masters' degrees and a few have Ph.D.'s. While it is possible to enter the training field right out of college, most of those currently employed as trainers have a background in other fields. Many are former teachers, and others bring a special expertise (knowledge of data processing, expert business writing skills, sales and marketing, career counseling experience) to the field.

For Further Details

American Society for Training and Development, 600 Maryland Ave., S.W., Washington, DC 20024. American Society for Personnel Administration, 30 Park Dr., Berea, OH 44017. International Association of Personnel Women, 150 W. 52nd St., New York, NY 10019.

BUSINESS MACHINE REPAIRERS

Duties and Responsibilities

To the business executive with a deadline to meet, there is nothing more frustrating than a machine breakdown, and no more welcome sight than the arrival of the business machine repairer who will be able to put the equipment back into operation again.

These workers maintain and repair machines ranging from typewriters, adding and calculating machines, cash registers, dictating machines, and postage meters to duplicating and copy equipment. Most specialize in one type of machine, although those who work for small independent repair shops usually must be able to work on many different types of equipment.

Repairers, often called field engineers or customer service engineers, usually make office calls. Depending on the type of equipment and the arrangement with the company, some offices are visited only when a machine malfunctions. Other offices are visited regularly for preventive maintenance. On these visits, repairers inspect the machine for unusual wear and replace any worn or broken parts. Then the machine is cleaned, oiled, and adjusted to ensure peak operating efficiency and to prevent future breakdowns. The repairer may also advise machine operators how to use the equipment more efficiently and how to spot trouble in the early stages.

If a visit is made because of a machine malfunction, the repairer must examine the machine to determine the cause of the problem. Minor repairs are generally made immediately. However, more serious repairs may require that part or all of the machine be taken into the shop.

About eight out of every ten repairers work for business machine manufacturers, for firms that provide maintenance service to businesses, or for repair shops. The remainder work for organizations large enough to employ their own staff of full-time repairers.

Because of their knowledge of the machinery, repairers are particularly well suited to advance to sales jobs. Those with management ability sometimes become service managers or supervisors or have their own shops. Those who work in manufacturers' branch offices may become independent dealers or buy sales franchises from the company.

Earnings and Opportunities

More than 55,000 people work as business machine repairers, and employment opportunities are expected to increase 72 percent in the next ten years. Salaries range from $11,500 to $44,000 and up.

Training and Qualifications

Mechanical aptitude, good eyesight (including color vision) for working on small parts, good hearing for detecting problems by ear, and a pleasant cooperative manner for dealing with customers are key qualities for repairers. The ability to manage one's own time and work without supervision is also an asset.

The amount of education required varies.

Some employers hire applicants with a high school education, while others look for at least one year of technical training in basic electricity or electronics.

Trainees with manufacturing companies may attend company-sponsored courses lasting from several weeks to several months. Independent repair shops usually offer less formal training consisting of self-study and on-the-job instruction given by a more experienced repairer.

For Further Details

Computer and Business Equipment Manufacturers Association, 1828 L St., N.W., Washington, DC 20036.

CUSTOMER SERVICE REPRESENTATIVES

Duties and Responsibilities

Anyone who has ever had a complaint with a department store, an incorrect billing on a credit card, or needed information from the telephone company knows the vital role in business played by the customer service representative. It is his or her responsibility to provide customer support by answering questions or listening to and taking action on customer complaints.

In general, representatives take phone calls from customers, provide information on prices and service, field complaints, and, in some cases, try to sell additional company services.

Usually working via phone calls or customer contact by mail, good representatives are a mixture of public relations workers (they demonstrate company goodwill) and expeditors (they often have to trace through complicated billing or shipping problems or investigate service difficulties and then provide solutions). Well-trained ones also serve as sales representatives by not only solving a customer's problems but also informing him or her of other products or services that might be of interest.

When dealing with irate customers, discretion and sound judgment are important. Representatives must know when to kindly but firmly defend the company as well as when to pull out all stops (such as lowering the price or providing the service gratis) in order to re-establish customer goodwill.

In the computer product industry, highly skilled customer service representatives are so thoroughly trained on the various machines that they can often diagnose and solve problems by phone, calling for a service technician only when absolutely necessary.

In some companies, representatives may have additional duties such as actually assigning the necessary workers to correct certain problems, invoicing customers, and performing the duties of a work order control clerk.

In addition to working for companies selling consumer goods, customer service representatives can also be found working for manufacturers, dealing with the companies who buy and use the manufacturers' products. In some instances this calls for visits to the customers' places of business and may call for extensive travel.

Advancement may mean becoming head of customer service or, in a small-to-medium-sized firm, becoming office manager.

Earnings and Opportunities

The outlook for employment is very good, and salaries range from $10,500 to $42,000.

Training and Qualifications

A friendly manner, patience, organizational ability, and a get-it-done attitude are very helpful for customer service representatives.

A high school diploma is generally necessary, and a college degree can be an advantage in getting ahead.

Most companies train such reps, some with extensive classroom and fieldwork; others use OJT (on-the-job training) for individuals who have worked for the company in another capacity.

For Further Details

A directory of private business schools located throughout the country can be obtained at no charge from: Association of Independent Colleges and Schools, 1730 M Street N.W., Suite 600, Washington, DC 20036.

FILE CLERKS

Duties and Responsibilities

"Mary Smith is on the phone. Why isn't her information on file?" Questions such as this have plagued American business for years, and even as we move into the age of computer technology for the automated filing and retrieval of outgoing documents there will be a continuing need for top-notch file clerks who can manage the incoming paper flow.

Responsibilities of the file clerk include classifying, storing, and retrieving office information. Incoming material must be evaluated, and if it is to be filed, folders may need to be prepared. All information must be properly processed in order to incorporate it into the system.

When information is needed from the files, clerks must locate it for the borrower, and the item's whereabouts must be noted in case it is needed while out of file. If it is likely to be passed on to another department, most companies try to establish a system for tracking its progress. That way when "Mary Smith" phones there is a way of locating the information from her file.

Most of a file clerk's day involves a set routine within a structured environment. It may involve collecting information from around the office that needs to be returned to the files, evaluating new material as to where and how it should be saved, and finally doing the actual filing. Pickup of materials may occur throughout the day in businesses such as insurance companies in order to see that as much material as possible is kept where it can be found easily.

Approximately one-half of all file clerks work in banking, insurance, and real estate, or for lawyers, doctors, or other professionals. However, almost every kind of organization employs file clerks.

Working as a file clerk provides the opportunity to observe the workings of a business, and it can be a good position from which to move into other support service jobs within the office. Further education and specialized training can lead to management positions over large staffs of clerks.

Earnings and Opportunities

The outlook for employment is excellent, and salaries range from $8,600 to $26,000.

Training and Qualifications

Attention to detail, organizational skills, the ability to read quickly and accurately and spell well are important qualities for file clerks.

A high school diploma is generally necessary for employment. Courses in typing and bookkeeping and some knowledge of office practices can be helpful to the person who wants to advance.

For Further Details

A directory of private business schools located throughout the country can be obtained at no charge from: Association of Independent Colleges and Schools, 1730 M Street N.W., Suite 600, Washington, DC 20036.

OFFICE SERVICE WORKERS

Duties and Responsibilities

Routine detail work—filing, copying, sorting, mailing—is never-ending in business and government, and a good office staff can make all the difference. The largest proportion of workers in this category are mail room operators, copy machine operators, or clerks.

Mail room operators have a great deal of responsibility. Their job is to see that items are delivered on time in the most economical way possible. In the biggest companies, they oversee large budgets and staffs in the performance of sometimes very complex tasks. When a company has a message to send to thousands of stockholders and employees, for example, the mail room operator may need to coordinate with the printing department. Occasionally shipping responsibilities are included in this job.

Today's copying machines have become an essential tool in business. Not only have they made carbon copies virtually obsolete, but they provide a number of amazing additional functions—some print in color; some enlarge or reduce copy size; still others print on both sides; and almost all now collate. As these machines are relied upon more and more, maintenance is needed to keep them producing at peak efficiency. The position of *copy machine operator* was created in response to this need and to companies' needs to control copying costs. Generally a copying machine is placed under the supervision of the operator, who keeps it locked when not in use, and who is responsible for preventing unauthorized or wasteful use of the machine. The operator or an assigned substitute also takes primary responsibility for operating the machine in order to avoid costly breakdowns due to improper use.

Clerks have worked on office staffs for as long as business has operated out of offices. They are in charge of establishing a workable filing system, doing the day-to-day filing, answering phones, and generally taking care of any office task that's needed. By performing these duties, they free typists and secretaries to do the work they are trained to do.

Most office service workers put in a standard forty-hour week, though working conditions depend on the industry and company.

Promotion opportunities do exist in these jobs, and they can be a great way to get a foot in the door of the company or industry you're interested in. The television industry, for example, is filled with true stories of top executives who started out in the mail room.

Earnings and Opportunities

Opportunities are excellent for these workers, because big companies always need someone to take care of the detail work. Earnings: $7,800 to $26,000.

Training and Qualifications

Organizational skills, the ability to follow instructions and a sense of responsibility are important qualifications for office service workers. Employers prefer high school diplomas and look favorably on those who are pursuing additional training and education.

For Further Details

A directory of private business schools located throughout the country can be obtained at no charge from: Association of Independent Colleges and Schools, 1730 M Street N.W., Suite 600, Washington, DC 20036.

RECEPTIONISTS

Duties and Responsibilities

Receptionists are very important to their companies because as front line representatives they give customers and clients their first impression of a firm. They are also in a position to get an excellent overview of the workings of their company.

The basic job entails greeting customers and other visitors, determining their needs, and referring them to the appropriate staff member. Many receptionists are also responsible for answering incoming telephone calls and switching them to the correct person or department. Their other duties may vary depending on where they work. In hospitals and doctors' offices receptionists may take personal and financial information before directing the patient to the waiting room; in factories or large businesses they may provide visitors with identification cards and then arrange for escorts to take them to the right office; those in beauty salons may greet customers and arrange appointments.

Sometimes duties include keeping a detailed log of who called, when, and to whom they were referred. When receptionists are not busy with callers, they may accept payments, do typing or filing, open and sort mail, and take and distribute messages. Others do simple bookkeeping.

Receptionists are employed in almost every type of organization. Almost one-third work for doctors, dentists, hospitals, nursing homes, and other health service providers. Large numbers also work in factories, wholesale and retail stores, real estate offices, and business and personal service firms.

Because their work is highly visible, receptionists tend to be positioned in carefully designed and pleasantly furnished surroundings. Most work regular hours, though those employed by hospitals or certain professional offices may work evenings or weekends.

Promotion possibilities depend to some extent on personal background. Some see the job as an opportunity to observe an industry and select a job for which they then gain special training. Those with excellent clerical or bookkeeping skills may rise to be a secretary, administrative assistant, office supervisor, or clerical supervisor. In industries like publishing and broadcasting, college graduates may take a receptionist position to make contacts, in order to move into managerial or talent areas.

Earnings and Opportunities

Over 635,000 people work as receptionists, and the job outlook for the coming years is very favorable, as the number of receptionist jobs is expected to increase 45 percent in the next ten years. Salaries range from $7,200 to $17,500.

Training and Qualifications

Good grooming, a pleasant manner, and the desire to help strangers feel comfortable are important qualities for receptionists. Good clerical skills are an asset.

The position of receptionist is a good occupation for people without previous work experience, but most employers do prefer high school graduates.

English, typing, shorthand, business arithmetic, basic accounting, bookkeeping, and office procedures are useful courses to have taken. College or business school training can be helpful in advancing to better paying office jobs.

For Further Details

A directory of private business schools located throughout the country can be obtained at no charge from: Association of Independent Colleges and Schools, 1730 M Street N.W., Suite 600, Washington, DC 20036.

SECRETARIES AND STENOGRAPHERS

Duties and Responsibilities

Any business person will tell you that good secretaries and stenographers are worth their weight in gold. Without them, communication within business and government would come to an absolute standstill.

This field, once dominated by men, has been the domain of women since 1940. As salaries continue to rise, however, a greater balance between the sexes should occur, since these jobs are excellent stepping-stones into management.

Though some secretaries perform a few specialized duties, most are generalists who take care of a variety of tasks such as scheduling appointments, answering telephones, maintaining files, filling out forms, and taking dictation—which may be done manually but is increasingly being done on electronic dictating equipment—and transcribing it. In offices with word processing centers, *administrative secretaries* handle everything except dictation and typing. In addition to regular secretarial duties, they may answer letters, do research, or prepare statistical reports. Skill in using word processing equipment can only enhance secretaries' value, allowing them, in part, to quickly prepare perfect documents, to electronically file and retrieve large quantities of documents, and to query the computer for additional information.

Some secretaries do highly specialized work for which training is necessary. *Legal secretaries* prepare legal papers and correspondence such as summonses and complaints, motions, and subpoenas. They may also assist with legal research. *Medical secretaries* must know medical terminology as they transcribe dictation, prepare correspondence, and assist physicians or medical scientists with reports, speeches, articles, and conference proceedings. *Technical secretaries* assist engineers or scientists and need to be knowledgeable in their chosen field or specialty.

Secretaries who work for membership or small nonprofit organizations may take care of all office responsibilities including maintaining membership lists, receiving dues and contributions, and disseminating information about the organization.

Stenographers and *stenotype operators* take dictation in shorthand or using a stenotype machine that prints symbols as keys are pressed. They then transcribe their notes on a typewriter. Stenographers may also perform other general office duties. *Technical stenographers* must know the terms used within their special area. Some take dictation in foreign languages.

Shorthand reporters are specialized stenographers who record all statements made in a given proceeding, and accuracy is vital. Many work as court reporters, taking down everything said at legal proceedings and presenting their record as the official transcript. Some work as *freelance reporters* who record out-of-court testimony for attorneys or whenever exact transcriptions are needed. Some are now using computer aided transcription, which lets a computer directly translate the reporter's shorthand notes into English.

Most workers put in a thirty-seven-to-forty-hour week, though many others are taking advantage of the new availability of flexible work situations. Some work part-time or hold temporary jobs. Others split duties with another worker in a job-sharing arrangement; still others are experimenting with home-based offices where a secretary works at home on a computer that transmits the work to the main office.

Secretaries and stenographers are employed in virtually every type of business and in all parts of government. Two out of five stenographers work for government agencies, reflecting the large proportion of shorthand reporters working in courts, legislatures, and agencies.

For secretaries, advancement may mean being promoted to administrative assistant, supervisor of their area, or office manager. Those who continue their education may progress into entry-level management positions. Those with word processing skills may become trainers, supervisors, or managers of word processing departments or get a job with a manufacturer of word processing equipment as an instructor or as a sales representative. Stenographers may become secretaries, and those who acquire the necessary speed can become shorthand reporters.

Earnings and Opportunities

About 2.5 million people are employed as secretaries, and approximately 280,000 work as stenographers. The job outlook for secretaries is excellent, with a projected increase in employment of 29 percent over the next ten years. The demand for stenographers is declining except in court reporting, where demand should continue to be strong. Earnings range from $11,500 to $38,000.

Training and Qualifications

Organizational ability, excellent typing skills, good judgment, and initiative are good qualities to bring to these jobs. Adaptability and versatility are also going to be important as office technology continues to change.

A high school diploma is generally necessary, and most employers prefer applicants who have had some secretarial training at a college or a business school. Shorthand reporters must complete a two-year course in shorthand reporting, including stenotype if possible, since high-speed computer transcription of stenotype notes is becoming more and more common.

Exact requirements vary from company to company, but in general, many firms look for a typing speed of sixty-five to eighty words a minute, and an increasing number are seeking applicants with word processing skills as well.

For Further Details

Professional Secretaries International, 2440 Pershing Rd., Suite G10, Kansas City, MO 64108. Association of Independent Colleges and Schools, 1730 M St., N.W., Suite 600, Washington, DC 20036. National Association of Legal Secretaries, 3005 E. Skelly Dr., Tulsa, OK 74105. National Shorthand Reporters Association, 118 Park St., S.E., Vienna, VA 22180.

TELEPHONE OPERATORS

Duties and Responsibilities

When you pick up the phone and dial "O," the person who answers no longer sits before a switchboard ready to hand-connect your call with a plug. In just about every part of the country, telephone operators have entered the computer age.

At telephone companies, operators known as *central office operators* help customers with calls that require assistance such as person-to-person and collect calls. They obtain the information needed to complete the call, and in noncomputerized offices they may record the details for billing. Those who make long distance connections are called *long distance operators*. *Directory assistance operators* look up and provide telephone numbers.

Many large businesses and organizations re-

ceive so many calls that they employ operators to run their highly sophisticated yet easy-to-learn switchboards. They connect interoffice or house calls, answer and relay outside calls, assist company employees in making long distance calls, supply information to callers, and record charges. In small establishments, these operators may do other office work such as typing or sorting mail. Many act as receptionists or information clerks.

Other types of operators include *police district switchboard operators* who receive and transmit calls for the police; *communications center operators* who handle airport authority communications systems and monitor electronic equipment alarms; and *answering-service operators* who take messages for clients.

The majority of telephone systems are now operated by push button, and more and more systems are becoming computerized. Directory assistance operators no longer have to leaf through paper directories—they now read the information on a computer screen.

Jobs can be found throughout the country, and roughly one-fourth of all operators work part-time. In hotels, hospitals, and other places where telephone service is needed twenty-four hours a day, operators work on shifts, and holiday and weekend work is common. Operators usually work in pleasant surroundings, but the pace of the switchboard may be hectic and demanding during peak calling periods.

Some operators are promoted to service advisors who conduct switchboard training classes for major telephone company customers; others become service observers, assisting the supervisor by monitoring telephone calls to observe operator behavior, technical accuracy, and adherence to company policy. Other operators advance to clerical jobs or to telephone craft jobs such as installer or repairer. Large businesses may advance their operators to clerical or management positions with more responsibility.

Earnings and Opportunities

Over 340,000 people are employed as telephone operators, and employment is expected to grow more slowly than the average because of increasing use of automated equipment. Salaries range from $8,600 to $16,000.

Training and Qualifications

Persons interested in becoming telephone operators should enjoy serving the public and have a courteous, patient manner and a pleasing voice. Good hearing and being able to listen well are also important. New operators learn through special instruction and on-the-job training.

For Further Details

Contact your local telephone company, or write for "Independent Phonefacts" and "Is it for You? A Career in the Independent Telephone Industry," available from: United States Independent Telephone Association, 1801 K Street N.W., Suite 1201, Washington, DC 20006.

TEMPORARY OFFICE WORKERS

Duties and Responsibilities

Temporary work is an interesting phenomenon of our times, and it has supplied millions with jobs when they needed them the most.

The type of temporary work available runs the gamut and includes positions as varied as file clerk, welder, machinist, sales clerk, accountant, Santa Claus, draftsman, secretary, engineer, dishwasher, nurse and truck driver, to name just a few. The majority, however, work in offices. Secretaries, receptionists, and typists are all in great demand, with the highest wages of this group going to those with word processing skills. Data processing workers and medical technicians are also highly sought after right now.

While some employers do hire temporary help directly, most employ them through a temporary help agency, and hundreds of these companies have sprung up recently with at least several in virtually every city. Some are national and even international in scope, and some are part of a permanent employment service. Employers use temporary services for a variety of good business reasons: fluctuating or seasonal work load, illness, special projects, budget and personnel constraints, vacations, or unavailability of permanent staff.

The temporary worker is actually employed and paid by the agency, which is, in turn, paid by the client who uses the temporary help. Sometimes the job will last a day, other times a year or longer.

Temporary work can be the ideal situation for people arriving in a strange city with little or no funds who need money to tide them over until they find permanent employment; for students who need to tailor their work schedules around classes; for those returning to the job market, who use it as a way to brush up their skills before moving ahead. Still others may use it as a way to explore companies and/or industries for career possibilities.

Some workers seek temporary employment because of its great flexibility. They can work when they want, where they want, and for as long as they want. If they need time off to be with family or friends or to take a trip, they are free to take it without fear of losing their jobs. Another benefit is that skills are transferable from one company to another and from one area of the country to another.

Earnings and Opportunities

The demand for temporary help is increasing, and jobs will continue to be in great supply throughout the 1980s. Earnings depend on the work, but are usually comparable to similar permanent jobs in the same field, and according to temporary agencies nationwide, pay for "highly skilled" jobs rose 15 percent in 1983. Fringe benefits vary but are usually less than those available to permanent employees. This is the trade-off for instant and/or flexible employment.

Training and Qualifications

Flexibility, a pleasant manner, taking pleasure in meeting new people and enjoying new experiences are good qualities for temporary workers. The ability to take direction well is also an asset. Except for manual labor or unskilled jobs, competence in the particular field in which temporary work is desired is important. In anticipation of the soaring demand for word processing workers, some temp personnel agencies are running major programs to train people in these skills.

For Further Details

A directory of private business schools located throughout the country can be obtained at no charge from: Association of Independent Colleges and Schools, 1730 M Street N.W., Suite 600, Washington, DC 20036.

TYPISTS AND WORD-PROCESSOR OPERATORS

Duties and Responsibilities

Typewriters have gone from manual to electric and are now entering the electronic age, but until the voice-activated typewriter is perfected, fast, accurate typists will be essential in the business world. What's more, good typing skills can be the key to many other job opportunities.

Beginning typists usually do simple tasks like addressing form letters and typing up handwritten drafts of memos, letters, and documents. They may perform other office duties as well, such as answering telephones, filing, and operating copiers, calculators, and other office machines.

More experienced typists do work that requires a high degree of accuracy and independent judgment. Senior typists may take information directly from dictating equipment; or they may work from complicated rough drafts or those containing technical information. In addition, they may plan and type statistical tables, combine and rearrange materials from different sources, or prepare master copies for reproduction. Many specialize. There are medical, legal, and statistical typists as well as computer input typists, and these enhanced skills increase the value of the typist.

Every day, word processing equipment is becoming more commonplace in the office environment. By the end of the decade, most people who type will be using word processing equipment of some kind. Secretaries, stenographers, transcription typists, and general typists will be able to greatly increase productivity by using word processing equipment not only to handle routine correspondence and reports but also to replace their voluminous paper files with speedy electronic storage of all written materials. Additionally, they will be using this equipment to query the computer for information.

The use of such equipment will certainly enhance a secretary's value to the company and will free her up to handle additional administrative and decision-making tasks. Other typists who do nothing but type all day long will find this equipment a blessing, since it completely eliminates the problem and worry of making mistakes and the time taken for erasures and corrections. While straight word processors are paid more than normal typists, they could find themselves in a dead end job unless they make a specific point of applying the skills learned to move into broader secretarial and administrative assistant jobs.

Word processors enter their work directly into a minicomputer while viewing it on a display screen. Others spend much of their time making corrections of the work of other typists who have entered their material through an optical scanner. This saves countless hours of retyping.

Other typist positions include *varitype operators*, who produce material in different typefaces for printing purposes; *cryptographic-machine operators*, who operate cryptographic equipment to code, transmit, and decode secret messages; *braille typists*, who prepare reading material for the blind.

Many typists hold part-time or temporary jobs and some are freelance typists who are self-employed. Increasingly, workers who use word processing equipment are able to work at home with the new integrated office systems that allow managers to supervise and communicate with workers who are not on site.

Typing skills can lead to many other opportunities, such as secretary, administrative assistant, or office manager.

Earnings and Opportunities

Over 1.1 million people are employed as typists, and good job prospects are expected in the years ahead. Earnings start at $8,300 to $12,800 and can go to over $24,000. Word processing operators start at $12,400 to $14,500 and up. Both men and women are needed for these positions, and retraining is quick and inexpensive for those who have held other positions or who have been out of the work force for some time.

Training and Qualifications

A good vocabulary plus above average spelling, punctuation, and grammar are important skills for typists. Attention to detail and neatness and accuracy are important work habits to develop, and good concentration is also a big help.

Typists should have a high school diploma, and as much typing experience and training as possible.

Additional courses in typing, word processing, transcribing, and specialties such as legal, medical, and general business practices are available in high schools, community colleges, business schools, and through home study courses.

For Further Details

A directory of private business schools may be obtained from Association of Independent Colleges and Schools, 1730 M St., N.W., Suite 600, Washington, DC 20036.

Careers in Marketing

Don't ask what the seller wants, ask what the buyer wants—that's the key to marketing, and it's a philosophy that has succeeded in American business. Companies that have invested time and resources to "get close to their customers" have been rewarded with profits and growth.

Marketing has evolved from simply "selling" to the more calculated, sophisticated science of defining customer needs and fulfilling them. Along the way, research, testing, product sampling, advertising, and promotion are all involved. The need for marketing expertise exists on every level of business and is growing all the time.

Market research is just one area with enormous potential. Here, research and statistics are used to gather information about a product or service and its degree of public acceptance. Jobs range from entry-level data collectors to highly trained statisticians and research specialists. People from a variety of backgrounds are finding jobs here—engineers, mathematicians, psychologists, social and political scientists, as well as media experts and behavioral specialists, to name a few. They are all being put to work to help determine what consumers want and need, how much they will pay for it, and how to reach them in the most economical way.

The current high demand for marketing executives is expected to continue. As America's consumer economy becomes more competitive, companies will depend on marketing strategies to gain the best position they can for their products and services, and they'll need top-notch people.

Marketing is a stepping-stone to top management and is one of the most mentally stimulating, challenging, and rewarding careers you can have.

ADVERTISING ACCOUNT EXECUTIVES

Duties and Responsibilities

The advertising account executive functions primarily as a liaison between client and agency. Ever mindful of the client's budget, the AE is involved from the concept of the advertising program right through to its completion, including the placement of ads in print or on radio or television. Selling for the ad agency is important too. Bringing in new

184

clients and continuing to satisfy the old ones is very much a part of the job.

If a potential client agrees to a meeting, an account executive will take charge of making a presentation about his agency's talents and track record for other clients. In some cases this includes displaying ads specifically designed for the prospective client.

Once the client signs on with the agency, the account executive becomes the go-between for agency and client. Market research must usually be done prior to planning an ad campaign, and the AE works with the research department to decide how to go about obtaining the needed information.

Once the market for the client's products or services has been clearly identified, the AE calls in the creative department to design and write ads, commercials, billboards, or brochures. The client's approval is generally needed many times throughout the process, and frequently the account executive must do a good bit of selling here.

Once a campaign has been approved, the AE is still involved with placement of the ads and works closely with the media buyers within the agency to be sure that the ads are placed in media where they will best reach their markets. Some account executives are assigned certain companies because of their expertise or track record in a certain area.

The work of account executives is very demanding, and the pressure is great. Lose one or two accounts, and they're likely to be fired.

Hours can be hectic, and deadlines must always be met. Travel is often a part of the job.

Account executives usually come from the sales field. Others start out in advertising departments of companies and then move into ad agencies. They may assume a junior position working under an experienced AE before rising to be an account executive.

Advancement may come through handling more accounts or fewer but larger accounts; some account executives work only for one major client. In large agencies, some AE's rise to supervise the work of other account executives; some will leave and start their own agencies.

Earnings and Opportunities

The outlook for employment is quite good. Earnings: $30,000 to $65,000, with some over $100,000.

Training and Qualifications

Good communication skills, organizational ability, and the power to persuade are important qualities in this job.

Most account executives are college graduates, although areas of specialty vary from liberal arts and business administration to marketing. Some also have a master's degree in business administration, although it is not a prerequisite.

ADVERTISING COPYWRITERS

Duties and Responsibilities

"Where's the beef?" . . . "It's the real thing!" . . . Writing words that sell—that's the job of advertising copywriters, who produce everything from short slogans to entire texts for sales material.

Writing selling copy is like no other type of writing, because the operative word is "sell." While it may not look difficult to come up with a phrase like "We are driven," chances are the copywriter tried a number of variations before settling on that line. And long hours meeting with the account executive and client were probably also spent debating the merits of one slogan over another.

In addition to writing slogans and sales materials, copywriters also produce print ads and brochures and prepare scripts for radio and TV commercials. Sometimes a concept is given to them, and sometimes they must develop it on their own or as part of a creative team.

While there are proven methods for writing certain types of ads or sales material, the good copywriter has a feel for when those rules should be broken in order to shock, surprise, or otherwise interest the readers. Correct grammar and punctuation and logical flow may be abandoned in an effort to grab and keep consumers' attention. This is also an area where length of copy is usually immaterial. A terrific print ad may consist of one short sentence, or the writer may feel that a strong headline must be followed by several paragraphs of text. The copywriter's decisions are based on the product being sold, the place where the ad will appear, and a strong sense of what he or she feels will work.

For radio and TV advertising, copywriters often must write a mini-drama that makes the sale in ten, thirty, or sixty seconds—not an easy thing to do.

Copywriters frequently become known for a certain specialty. Among the better-paid freelancers are those who specialize in direct mail that sells. The success or failure of a direct mail campaign depends heavily upon the written copy.

Some copywriters start out as junior copywriters in order to learn the profession. Others enter with writing experience gained in other fields.

Many copywriters are employed by advertising agencies, public relations firms, or within the marketing departments of major companies. A good number work freelance.

Those on staff are generally scheduled to work a normal forty-hour workweek. However, late hours are common when deadlines must be met. Advancement generally consists of increased pay and better assignments.

Earnings and Opportunities

The outlook for employment is very good. Beginning copywriters earn from $16,400 to $19,600. Those with experience can earn up to $46,000 and beyond.

Training and Qualifications

Creativity, self-discipline, and a feeling for the marketplace are helpful qualities to bring to this field.

A bachelor's degree with a liberal arts major is recommended. A portfolio of one's work is helpful in gaining employment.

For Further Details

Send a self-addressed stamped envelope to American Advertising Federation, 1225 Connecticut Ave., N.W., Washington DC 20036. American Association of Advertising Agencies, 666 Third Ave., New York, NY 10017.

COMMUNICATIONS CONSULTANTS

Duties and Responsibilities

Companies communicate with many key audiences every day—consumers, stockholders, government officials, special interest groups, employees, and clients, to name a few. And the messages they communicate often need to be expressed differently to different groups, depending on their interests. The work of communications consultants involves deciding how to communicate these messages and anticipating how they will be received. The job requires that they be knowledgeable in

areas ranging from public relations and press information to advertising and personal contact.

Communications consultants work closely with companies and organizations (government, educational institutions, nonprofit organizations, special interest groups) to provide strategies that will meet their communications goals. This involves working with the media, developing relationships, handling personal contact, and creating and writing materials such as speeches, letters, articles, releases, booklets, and reports. Usually this work is done in conjunction with the company's communications department or with the top executive.

Sometimes their work focuses internally. For example, consultants may be assigned to analyze and recommend ways to improve employee communications that will lead to more productivity. Other times the focus is external, and they may be working to improve the organization's image in Washington or with the press.

Crisis management has become a new area of specialization for communications consultants. Knowing how to effectively handle a crisis (plant closing, strike, tragedy, product recall) is critical to business survival. The management of stories such as nuclear plant problems or consumer product tampering calls for smart thinking on the part of communications consultants in order to give the public the information it needs while helping to salvage company credibility.

Communications consultants may be employed by major companies or public relations firms. Their jobs range from account executive to senior management positions. Others are self-employed and work with clients on a daily, monthly, or assignment basis.

Earnings and Opportunities

The outlook for jobs appears to be quite good because of American businesses' growing need to improve their methods of communication. Earnings range from $32,000 to $85,000, depending on the size of the firm and the consultant's role in that organization.

Training and Qualifications

The ability to communicate well (orally and in writing), think quickly, and analyze accurately is necessary for working in this field. Contacts are helpful, especially in the media.

Most communications consultants come to the field with college degrees ranging from liberal arts and business to engineering, though a specialty in communications is a plus. Many have obtained work experience in public relations, advertising, journalism, or management prior to moving into the field.

For Further Details

International Association of Business Communicators, 870 Market Street, San Francisco, CA 94102.

FUND RAISERS

Duties and Responsibilities

Professional fund raisers play a vital role in the world of nonprofit organizations. They are responsible for raising money for everything from cancer research to sending an inner city child to summer camp.

Planning, organizing, and directing fundraising campaigns are done for a variety of organizations, including colleges, hospitals, charities, religious institutions, health agencies, museums, research laboratories, social service agencies, civic groups, and community organizations such as theaters, opera companies, symphony orchestras, and recreational facilities.

It takes money to raise more money, and fund raisers administer their own budgets,

which can be quite substantial. Depending on the size and type of organization, fund raisers may work on their own, oversee staff, or have access to volunteers who will aid in the campaign. In a large organization, fund raisers usually take on management responsibilities and train and supervise others, both paid and volunteer. They may also work with an advisory board to determine the nature of the appeal. Awards dinners, sales of merchandise, telethons, and paying personal visits to companies or wealthy individuals to ask for donations are just some of the methods used to raise money.

Vast sums of money are also brought in by direct mail campaigns, which either solicit donations or seek new members. A direct mail campaign can be extremely expensive, so pressure is great to hire or enlist the best help available in assuring that the campaign will be a successful one.

Publicity can be a vital part of this work. Whether it's a direct pitch for donations in an alumni magazine or an article in the town newspaper about the struggles of the local museum, fund raisers use various ways to increase the organization's visibility. They may work with public relations professionals on stories, or in a small organization they may do some or all of the press contact work themselves.

Though most fund raisers are employed by the organizations themselves, some work for firms that specialize in fund raising for others. Some are self-employed and work as consultants.

Earnings and Opportunities

Opportunities for fund raisers are excellent, and earnings range from $15,500 to $75,000 and up.

Training and Qualifications

Organizational ability, a sense of purpose, a talent for persuasion, and the ability to work well with others are important qualities for fund raisers.

Most people who work in the profession have college educations and come into the job with some work experience. A background in marketing or public relations can be an asset, as can experience working in the field for which money is to be raised (e.g., the experience of a hospital administrator might provide him or her with excellent ideas for raising money for any type of health-related organization).

For Further Details

The American Association of Fund-Raising Council, Inc., 500 Fifth Ave., New York, NY 10021.

BUSINESS HOME ECONOMISTS

Duties and Responsibilities

When many of us think of home economists, we tend to remember our seventh-grade teacher who taught us cooking. While she may still be there teaching, times are changing, and the home economist has become an important part of the business world. That delicious-looking dessert you saw in the magazine ad, the recipe you tried from the back of the cereal box, and the instructions you followed in operating your new food processor all had the input of a home economist. They are found in many businesses advising on matters relating to food and products for the home.

Many home economists are employed by companies that produce goods and services for homemakers. Some are employed by marketing companies and advertising agencies that specialize in home products and services. Their basic responsibilities usually include advising companies on product use and development, promoting goods via department store or civic group demonstrations, and offering advice to homemakers as to the best use of the company product. Home economists also organize consumer education programs, perform research, and test recipes.

Often involved in all stages of product development and marketing, these workers might help a company consider the following: Will the product, say, frozen fish filets, cook well consistently? How long should they be cooked in the oven? The broiler? The microwave? What kind of packaged sauce could be enclosed with the fish? When it's time to design the package, home economists will be consulted not only on what packaging might appeal most to consumers, but they will be closely involved in helping photograph the product in the most appetizing way possible. This may involve selecting side dishes and preparing several versions of the entire meal in order to get a shot that is right.

Some home economists are employed by women's magazines, and one of their prime responsibilities is to test recipes that are scheduled to be printed. Many still work as teachers in both public and private institutions.

A growing number of home economists are starting their own businesses and are working on a consulting basis with manufacturers and marketing companies, and providing such services as cooking demonstrations for stores or advising on cookbook preparation.

Earnings and Opportunities

Employment opportunities are quite good, and earnings range from $15,700 to $42,000.

LOBBYISTS

Duties and Responsibilities

Oil companies want the government to open more offshore drilling areas; business advocates the passage of special tax incentives to provide more jobs; citizens' groups campaign for stronger consumer protection laws such as no smoking on airplanes or safety in toys. Representing different groups on a variety of issues is the work of lobbyists, whose job is to follow legislative issues and to gain support for the interests of their clients.

Working in all fifty state capitals as well as in Washington, D.C., lobbyists introduce new ideas to legislators and their staffs and follow current legislative activity in order to take stands on the passage or defeat of certain laws.

Lobbyists help design and implement plans to bring forth advocates for their particular needs. These may include employees of unions, the government, corporations, members of trade associations, religious groups, and other groups who would not only approve their view but would also be likely to look for reciprocal help when lobbying for their cause.

Since it is virtually impossible for legislators and their staffs to be knowledgeable on all subjects, the lobbyist's role in educating them is a vital one.

Training and Qualifications

A sense of what will sell, an interest in cooking and homemaking, and good business sense are helpful qualities for these workers.

While a bachelor's degree in home economics has usually been sufficient, more and more are entering this field with masters' degrees, which many employers now look for.

For Further Details

Executive Director, Home Economists in Business, Tower Suite 505, 301 Maple Ave. West, Vienna, VA 22180.

Visibility for their causes is very important, and some lobbyists promote their views by writing and publishing articles, submitting news releases, and participating in radio and television broadcasts. Getting to know the legislators who are particularly interested in the same issues is also an important part of the job.

Because our legislators, for the most part, want to be responsive to the needs of all people, they want to be sure that introducing or backing certain legislation will not adversely affect their chances for re-election. For that reason, presenting the issues in a way that is not one-sided is one of the challenges faced by lobbyists. Compromise and the acceptance of workable alternatives are often necessary in order to make gains on certain issues. For example, through lobbying, citizens' groups effectively campaigned for and got "denied boarding compensation" for passengers. However, since airlines do need to overbook to protect themselves from inevitable passenger cancellations, they are given a certain period of time within which they must get passengers to their destination. If they can't accomplish that goal within the time frame given, then passengers receive payment for the inconvenience.

Lobbyists are employed by unions; trade associations; government bureaucracies; large businesses; industrial, financial, and political organizations; as well as public interest and other nonprofit groups. Currently, lobbyists at the state level are expanding in numbers and status as corporations realize the importance of lobbying state legislatures as well as Congress on issues such as taxes and the environment. A recent conference board study found that 60 percent of 196 big companies now employ staff lobbyists to work at the state level. Though most lobbyists are employed directly by the organizations they represent, some work for firms who lobby for many clients; still others are self-employed and function as consultants. Workweeks may be long during peak legislative periods.

Earnings and Opportunities

Opportunities for employment are excellent, and earnings vary from $18,500 to $75,000 and up.

Training and Qualifications

An interest in political issues, a persuasive personality, and problem-solving ability are helpful qualities for lobbyists.

Minimum educational requirement is a college degree, and many lobbyists find law degrees useful, since interpretation of complex legal issues is very much a part of the job. Experience working for a congressman or for the government or political work done on a volunteer basis is an asset.

MARKET RESEARCH ANALYSTS

Duties and Responsibilities

Who buys what and why, when, where, and how they do it are the questions that market research analysts try to answer. They work for companies with products and services ranging from shampoo to life insurance.

Market research analysts plan, design, implement, and analyze the results of surveys. First, information is collected about the product or service and the people who are likely to use it. Analysts study everything from product availability and store placement to price of product and income level of purchasers. Results are then reported back to management. Based on this information, they may decide to alter such things as price, packaging, product attributes, marketing strategy, slant of advertising, or image.

Of course, the consumer's likes and dislikes are paramount in this business, and for that reason, much of the research involves telephone, personal, or mail surveys as well as "focus group" discussions with consumers to find out more about their preferences and buying habits.

Specialists are important in this field. Statisticians may help select consumer groups to be surveyed, and motivational research specialists design the survey questions to produce reliable results. Trained interviewers then conduct the survey, and office workers tabulate the results under the direction of market research analysts.

Most analysts are employed by manufacturing companies, advertising agencies, and independent research organizations. Many are employed by stores, radio and television firms, and newspapers; others work for university research centers and government agencies. Organizations may vary from one-person operations to firms with a hundred employees or more.

Analysts sometimes work as part of a team, but there is still a great deal of work to be done alone planning surveys and going over the results. Computers are used extensively in analyzing data. Travel may be involved, and long hours may be required in order to meet deadlines.

Analysts frequently start out in junior or assistant positions, and as they gain experience they may assume responsibility for a specific research project or advance to a supervisory position. Some rise to become market research director or vice president for marketing or sales.

Earnings and Opportunities

Over 30,000 people are employed as marketing research analysts, and the employment outlook is excellent. Starting salaries range from $18,500 to $32,400. Those with experience or in management slots can earn from $40,000 to $60,000 and more.

Training and Qualifications

Objective problem analysis and the creative ability to solve research problems or to formulate new ways for obtaining needed information are important in this job. Patience, perseverance, and the ability to communicate well orally and in writing are also important.

For trainees, a bachelor's degree is usually sufficient. However, graduate work—such as a master's in business administration (MBA)—is necessary for many specialized jobs.

For Further Details

A pamphlet, *Careers in Marketing,* may be obtained from American Marketing Association, 250 S. Wacker Dr., Chicago, IL 60606.

POLLSTERS

Duties and Responsibilities

You benefit from their efforts almost daily as companies alter their products and services to be more responsive to the feedback they get from consumers. And you hear about the results of their work on the news all the time: "According to the CBS News/New York *Times* poll . . ." Who are they? Pollsters—the people responsible for doing one-on-one interviews for market research companies and/or conducting news polls.

In market research, pollsters work with survey material prepared by marketing research analysts in order to help companies better understand public response to their products, and how they can improve their position in the marketplace. Trying to elicit specific information about a product, pollsters may work with a yes/no questionnaire or a broad-ranging one that asks questions such as these: Does a particular household buy a certain cleanser? If so, why was it picked above others? Does it do the job? Is it used in other ways? What was the motivating factor in making the purchase?

Surveys and interviews are usually conducted by phone, but some are conducted in person on a one-on-one basis. Many market research companies also rely on the "focus group," where the most experienced interviewers lead a discussion about the product with several people brought in for that purpose. The discussion may range from the best way to advertise a particular toy (for example, why would *you* buy it?) to selecting a name for a new type of cologne.

Polls are used by news organizations to get a feel for national or regional sentiment on such topics as presidential candidates and the economy. Here, too, pollsters generally conduct surveys by telephone, working with very detailed, specific questions prepared by the polling organization.

Pollsters are generally employed by market research companies, polling organizations, advertising agencies, and companies large enough to have a substantial market research department.

Some pollsters hold positions as junior market research analysts and eventually move up to become senior analysts. Others are employed on a part-time or freelance basis.

Earnings and Opportunities

The outlook for employment is good. Earnings range from $8,700 to $19,200 for supervisors.

Training and Qualifications

The ability to put others at ease and a knack for drawing out information are good qualities for interviewers.

A bachelor's degree is required for those hoping to be hired as junior analysts who specialize in interviewing. Some candidates also have obtained a master's degree in business administration in order to move ahead more quickly. Pollsters working freelance or part-time may be hired with only a high school diploma.

PRODUCT MANAGERS

Duties and Responsibilities

Every product—from an automobile or a cake mix to an insurance policy—needs to be marketed, and introducing it to the marketplace (or reintroducing an item that has faded from public notice) is the job of a product manager.

His responsibility is to take whatever steps are necessary to build or increase sales for a particular product. With their staffs, product managers will do everything from identifying appropriate advertising, promotion, or marketing campaigns to consulting on product design and packaging. They may also advise and sometimes work on the creation of print and broadcast ads as well as direct mail solicitations. It is not unusual for work on a single product to take a year or more to complete.

Because market research is such an important tool in this work, the product manager is often also involved in the design and implementation of test-marketing procedures. For example, sometimes market research will reveal that a product concept or an existing product should be revamped before being marketed. Market research also shows product managers to whom an item should be sold and how best to appeal to that market. Because the stakes are so high in launching or reintroducing a product, often an item is test-marketed in just a few communities before all details are agreed upon for a nationwide campaign. If test results are not successful, companies often choose to cancel a product rather than go ahead with it.

Because the success or failure of a product rides on the shoulders of the product manager, the responsibility is enormous. Depending on the size of the firm or the division they are representing, their budgets may run anywhere from a quarter of a million dollars to $25 million or more. In addition to their staffs, product managers work closely with other support services such as market research, public relations, and advertising. Ultimately, of course, they also work closely with the sales department.

Hours are long; and while the salaries paid are high, the burnout because of pressure is high, too. Those who succeed find that the skills and abilities they gain serve them well as they move into other positions in marketing, sales, or management. Some product managers find that their skills and abilities are useful in an entrepreneurial pursuit, and they start their own businesses.

Earnings and Opportunities

The outlook for employment is excellent. Earnings start at $28,000 to $35,000 for trainees and range to $60,000 to $80,000 and above for those with experience.

Training and Qualifications

Managerial and analytical skills, creativity, and the ability to handle pressure are important qualifications for product managers.

A bachelor of science degree in business administration or marketing is the minimum educational requirement for this field, and many go on to get a master's degree in business administration. Those who have only a bachelor's degree must usually gain marketing or sales experience prior to moving into a product management slot.

PUBLIC RELATIONS WORKERS

Duties and Responsibilities

Most of us are completely unaware of how often we receive information via public relations sources. The presidential spokesperson, the company representative, sometimes even the "high level source" quoted in newspapers, magazines, and on radio and TV—these are all public relations people. In addition, media stories like self-help financial advice or a report on the latest model car may actually originate with the public relations department of a bank or large corporation.

Public relations workers help businesses, governments, universities, and other organizations build and maintain a positive public image. They disseminate information that keeps the public aware of their organization's policies, activities, and accomplishments. PR workers also do studies to help management understand the attitudes and concerns of customers, employees, and other "publics."

For a particular PR campaign, written material is prepared and sent out, and then workers personally contact people in the media who they think would be especially interested in doing the story. Arranging for public appearances, writing speeches for company representatives, and preparing films or slide shows are often a part of the work.

At a large public relations firm there may be 200 PR workers or more, most of whom specialize. Some may concentrate on press writing releases or speeches, while others mainly work with the media.

Within a large company, staffs may also be big, and the department head is usually a vice president who is part of top management. Workers who handle publicity for an individual or direct public relations for a university, small business, or nonprofit organization may work alone and handle all aspects of the job: planning the campaign, writing the releases, and doing the follow-up work.

Press stories know no schedule, and, depending on the industry, middle-of-the-night phone calls from members of the media are not unheard of.

PR workers may move to surpervisory positions, become part of top management, or choose to start their own businesses.

Earnings and Opportunities

Over 87,000 people are employed as public relations workers, and this number is expected to increase by 29 percent by 1995. Starting salaries range from $14,000 to $21,000. Experienced PR people earn from $35,000 to over $100,000, and those in business for themselves can earn $180,000.

Training and Qualifications

Strong writing ability, initiative, good research skills, and fresh ideas are important in public relations work. Those who wish to do public contact work also need an outgoing personality, self-confidence, and the ability and enthusiasm to motivate people in a pleasant manner.

Experience working for the media can be helpful. Even writing for a school publication or television or radio station can help.

A portfolio of published articles, slide presentations, television or radio programs, or other work samples is usually an asset in landing the better jobs.

For Further Details

P.R. Reporter, Dudley House, P.O. Box 600, Exeter, NH 03833. For career information and a list of schools, send one dollar to Career Information, Public Relations Society of America, Inc., 845 Third Ave., New York, NY 10022.

Careers in Media and Communications

No question about it, America's shift to an information-oriented society has fueled the communications and media industries. The job opportunities here are interesting and varied. From writing and reporting news and information to producing movies, television, and theater, those who work in media and communications are part of a fast-paced, exciting field.

The public's growing thirst for information and entertainment bodes well for radio and television broadcasting. Today there are more listening and viewing choices than ever before. Advances in technology have created a new video marketplace with such services as cable television, direct-to-home satellite transmission, videotext and teletext home information services. All are contributing to growth. This trend should continue, as should the demand for more workers.

Positions here include roles in front of and behind the scenes: reporters, hosts, news anchors, weathercasters, sales and managerial jobs, as well as technical personnel like studio technicians and transmission specialists. Especially good opportunities await those technical professionals who can operate and maintain the sophisticated recording, editing, and transmitting equipment.

The entertainment field is enjoying a great period of development. Creative and technical opportunities in motion pictures and theater are on the increase. New techniques in production are enhancing the type of work being done in the field.

Being able to communicate well via the written word is taking on a special new significance. Americans receive so many forms of communications every day—television, radio, newspapers and magazines, telephone calls, office memos and reports, and the mail—that good writing often makes the difference in what gets read and what doesn't. Positions in news, entertainment, business, training, and government should keep expanding as the need for clear, direct communication continues to grow.

BROADCAST TECHNICIANS

Duties and Responsibilities

Broadcast technicians (or engineers) operate and maintain the electronic equipment used to produce and transmit radio and television programs. Along with production people and performers, they are important members of the team that is responsible for getting shows on the air.

Technicians work with cameras, microphones, lighting, videotape machines (as operators and editors), transmitters, and other equipment. In small stations, broadcast technicians generally perform a variety of duties, handling several technical assignments, which vary from day to day. In large stations, cable companies, and networks, they are more specialized and become expert at camera work, audio, editing, or special effects.

Technicians usually take their moment-to-moment instructions from the program's director or producer, while the overall activities and scheduling of technical personnel are handled by the chief engineer or technical supervisor.

Broadcast technicians usually work in studios, though some are assigned to cover news and sports events that involve fieldwork. Since broadcasting is a twenty-four-hour-a-day, seven-day-a-week business, technicians may have to work long hours and nights, weekends, and holidays. The pace of the job varies, and can become hectic when technicians and program staff are under great pressure to meet broadcast deadlines.

Entry-level workers generally begin their careers in small stations where they can learn to operate various types of equipment and are supervised by the chief engineer or other experienced technicians.

Good technicians can move up to larger stations where the pay is likely to be better, and those who demonstrate above average ability may move into top-level technical positions like chief engineer.

Earnings and Opportunities

About 17,000 are employed as broadcast technicians, and opportunities are expected to be quite good, with the number of jobs expected to increase 27 percent in the next ten years. Technicians in radio earn $12,600 to $34,000 and in television $14,200 to $48,000 and higher.

Training and Qualifications

Mechanical aptitude, an understanding of electronic equipment, and manual dexterity are necessary. The ability to work well as a member of a team, to take direction, and to react quickly to changing instructions are also important qualifications.

Federal law requires that those who operate broadcast transmitters have a permit from the Federal Communications Commission. Those who work with microwave or other internal radio communication equipment must have a general radiotelephone operator's license, issued after the applicant passes a series of written examinations. Many schools give courses especially designed to prepare the student for the FCC license test.

For those who hope to move up, advanced courses at a technical school or community college or a college degree in engineering offer an advantage. And with the growth of computer-controlled broadcast equipment, knowledge of computers provides an extra edge.

For Further Details

Federal Communications Commission, 1919 M St., N.W., Washington, DC 20554. National Association of Broadcasters, 1771 N St., N.W., Washington, DC 20036.

CINEMATOGRAPHERS

Duties and Responsibilities

How often we've marveled over the beauty of a filmed sunset scene or the exciting action coverage of a dangerous chase sequence, thinking little of the enormous amount of work and talent it takes to put these scenes on film.

Cinematographers are responsible for capturing the combined work of the writers, actors, producers, designers, and directors—everyone connected with a movie or commercial—on the film itself. Their work combines artistic talent with the technical knowledge needed to utilize the camera in the most effective way possible. They are thoroughly knowledgeable about the technical aspects of filmmaking and are expert at knowing how colors will look and how lighting affects certain scenes. And they fully understand the flexibilities and limits of the camera.

The cinematographer (also called director of photography) works closely with the director. Together they discuss the interpretation of the story and the scene to be shot, and then the director relies on the cinematographer to suggest camera angles, light quality, camera movement, and other factors that are part of the filming process. The cinematographer then directs the crew in setting up the shot and checks the scene before shooting.

The director of photography on a big feature film generally supervises a support staff, which may include one or more additional cinematographers, camera operator(s), first and second assistant cameramen, gaffers (who set up lights) and grips (who move the scenery around). Cinematographers involved in smaller setups often operate the cameras themselves.

By definition, cinematographers work in film, which includes theatrical feature films, documentaries, TV movies and series, and commercials. The majority of cinematographers work in New York (commercials) and Hollywood (television and film). Most are not associated on a full-time basis with any studio or program; they are hired, by reputation and experience, on a per-film or a per-project basis. Therefore, their track records, talents, and skills are their main selling points.

Earnings and Opportunities

Opportunities for employment vary on a year-by-year basis, depending on the output of the movie and television and commercial industries. Earnings range from $35,000 to $65,000 and up.

Training and Qualifications

A good eye, technical aptitude, and the ability to work well with others are good qualifications for this field.

The art of cinematography is one that must be learned through a process of apprenticeships and on-the-job training. Film schools offer courses in cinematography, and while the technical skills involved in camera work can be taught, the creative aspects of the work depend on individual talent and ability. Becoming an assistant on a film crew is the best way to begin to learn. Commercial work is great training for those who aspire to work on feature films, and many have made their entry through that aspect of the business.

COMMERCIAL ARTISTS, ILLUSTRATORS, AND GRAPHIC DESIGNERS

Duties and Responsibilities

Most people dream of being gainfully employed doing something they love. Those with artistic talent need look only as far as the field of commercial art (also called graphic design) to find that there are numerous rewarding careers to be had.

Workers in this field usually fall into the category of illustrators or designers. Illustrators are those artists who paint or draw pictures. *Fashion illustrators* specialize in usually stylized drawings of the latest fashions in women's and men's clothing. They may work for department stores, ad agencies, or designers. *Technical illustrators* make drawings of technical products for instruction manuals, sales brochures, and advertisements. They often work closely with engineers and technicians and must understand the workings of what they draw. Accuracy is vital. *Medical illustrators* combine art ability with a basic knowledge of biology and specialize in drawings of parts of the human body. Their work is used in medical textbooks and other publications, for research purposes, and in lectures and presentations.

Cartoonists draw comic strips, comic books, or political or humorous cartoons. Some cartoonists are supplied with ideas by someone else on staff or a regular partner. A freelance cartoonist sometimes buys ideas from writers. However, most have the ability to make biting political comments or write their own humorous thoughts.

Animators draw the series of pictures that, when transferred to film, form the animated cartoons seen in movies. They are employed almost exclusively by the motion picture industry. Some draw background or continuity pictures, while others may work on the characters.

Story board illustrators work for ad agencies drawing story boards for TV commercials. (A story board presents a commercial in a series of scenes similar to a comic strip.) This enables the ad agency and client to look at and evaluate the commercial while it is still in the idea stage.

Illustrators also draw for children's books, specialize in book or record jacket illustrations, or create greeting cards.

Designers are responsible for planning newspaper and TV advertisements as well as catalogs, books, brochures, instructional manuals, and any other items requiring visual appeal.

Graphic designers tend to be generalists, and the term may describe anyone from a designer specializing in corporate symbols or business letterheads to a person who designs magazine covers or menus. *Package designers* use their knowledge of art and a keen marketing sense to create designs that appeal to the consumer. *Book designers* design book jackets, select type for text, and prepare layouts of photographs and art. *Textile designers* plan the prints and designs woven into or printed on textiles. They need a knowledge of textile production as well as a good sense of design.

Letterers specialize in type styles and are responsible for choosing appropriate ones or hand-lettering headlines and text.

Entry-level workers such as those responsible for layout or pasteup take the photographs, illustrations, and text for an advertisement or a magazine or book page and position them according to the art director's or designer's exact instructions. What they create is known as a mechanical, which is then photographed and made into a plate for printing purposes.

Art directors hold what is the top commercial art-related job and are responsible for the visual appearance of whatever is being produced, including arrangement on the page (or object), its type style, and how photographs and illustrations are used. Directors often supervise photographers, layout workers, illustrators, and designers, and in large companies may oversee other art directors as well. They are usually well paid and have commensurate responsibility.

Most artists and designers work in advertising or publishing, either directly or indirectly as freelancers. Many companies have their own artists or art departments to service their advertising, public relations, and internal communications departments.

Many artists work as salaried employees with relatively regular office hours. To some extent, they must be able to create "on demand," which is challenging but not easy, and they must frequently work under pressure to meet tight deadlines.

Artists hired in advertising agencies or graphic design studios often start with work on pasteups or mechanicals. They may advance to assistant art director and then to art director.

Others may choose to freelance. Advancement for the freelancer consists of developing a reputation and a set of clients who produce a steady income. Some develop recognition in a field such as children's book illustration or high fashion; and in addition to earning high incomes, they can pick and choose the type of work they do.

Earnings and Opportunities

Over 120,000 people work as commercial and graphic artists and designers, and the employment outlook is excellent. Jobs for graphic artists are expected to increase 26 percent in the next decade. Earnings range from $12,500 to $75,000 and above.

Training and Qualifications

Artistic talent, a strong color sense, an eye for detail, and a sense of balance and proportion are important qualities to bring to this field. In addition, problem-solving skills and the ability to work independently are important. Those who aspire to be self-employed need self-discipline, business acumen, and sales ability.

In this field, a good portfolio—a collection of samples of a person's best work—is essential. And though some who have no specialized training do well, the majority need to acquire skills in a post-secondary art school in order to build a professional-quality portfolio. Usually a four-year program is best. Some students freelance part-time, which is an excellent way to build a portfolio while still in school.

For Further Details

The Graphic Artists Guild, 30 E. 20th St., Room 405, New York, NY 10003. The National Art Education Association, 1916 Association Dr., Reston, VA 22091. Motion Picture Screen Cartoonists Guild, 12441 Ventura Blvd., Studio City, CA 91604.

COPY EDITORS AND PROOFREADERS

Duties and Responsibilities

Editorial details are the concern of copy editors and proofreaders, whose efforts assure that printed matter is factually and grammatically accurate.

Copy editors in the book publishing industry are employed to check for factual accuracy, syntax, grammar, and punctuation. They correct mistakes and query authors when the meaning of a sentence is unclear. They ready the manuscript for the typesetter by labeling headings and writing special instructions in the margins. They also check spelling, especially highly technical terms, names, and unusual or coined words. Some of the work in this area is being done through use of word processing dictionaries with capacities of 70,000 to 100,000 words. At times, proofreaders may be responsible for reading the mechanicals (the final boards from which printing plates are made) to see that the typesetters and pasteup artists have followed the copy editor's and designer's instructions. Copy editors may work on staff or as freelancers, and sometimes specialize in particular kinds of books, such as cookbooks or scientific or business books.

Copy editors are also employed by magazines and newspapers, where they have similar responsibilities. On a newspaper, the copy editor usually receives a story just prior to its being forwarded to the composing room. Often working under a very tight deadline, the copy editor gives directions for setting it in type, writes the headline, and may shorten the story when necessary.

The proofreader is the person of last resort for checking and double-checking that no typos or grammatical or punctuation errors have slipped through the editorial process. Proofing galleys (the typeset copy) against the manuscript, these workers check for errors and correct them on the galleys. They must know standard proofreader symbols so that their instructions are clear to the typesetter who will make the indicated changes. Proofreaders generally hope to become copy editors.

Most are employed in magazine and book publishing, but there are also jobs wherever much printed matter is produced. Many workers are employed by law firms and in the insurance industry, proofreading the highly detailed copy used on insurance policies. Many proofreaders are freelancers.

Earnings and Opportunities

Outlook for employment is good, and earnings for copy editors range from $16,500 to $32,000.

Salaries for full-time proofreaders go from $14,000 to $23,000.

Training and Qualifications

Organizational skills, attention to detail, a large vocabulary, an above average grasp of the English language, and the ability to spot grammatical errors are good qualities to bring to these jobs.

Employers look for candidates with bachelors' degrees; and majors in English, history, or the liberal arts are preferred. There are specialized courses on copy editing available, though most learn the business by working as proofreaders or as editorial assistants.

EDITORS, BOOK AND MAGAZINE

Duties and Responsibilities

Editors are responsible for delivering magazine and newspaper articles or book manuscripts containing well-written information to a wide and interested reading public. They must be experts at working with the written word, but surprisingly their jobs also involve more managerial responsibility and marketing savvy than most people would think.

Staff editors at magazines and newspapers are planners; the newspaper editor must constantly be thinking of stories for the following days and weeks; while magazine editors plan ahead weeks or months in advance. They have to know what is news and what their particular audience wants. Readers of *The Wall Street Journal* are looking for something different from what is of interest to readers of *Family Circle*, for example. Addressing these interests is vital, because if the publication fails to interest its readers, circulation will drop and sales of advertising will go down.

Basic duties include assigning stories to writers, reviewing and editing material, and deciding what to use. Some editors are also responsible for overseeing some aspects of production.

Typically, future editors start out as *editorial assistants*, where the duties are primarily secretarial. *Assistant editors* or *associate editors* may assign and edit some stories, and they usually do some writing as well. *Senior editors* generally supervise a major editorial department and may have a title indicating their specialty, such as *sports* or *fashion* or *financial* or *business* or *automotive* editor. *Bureau chief* is usually the title of those who assign stories from a base in the field. The *managing editor* coordinates editorial and art production schedules, keeps expenses under budget, and is generally responsible for getting each issue to press on time. The *editor* or *editor-in-chief* has ultimate responsibility for the magazine's or newspaper's entire editorial content. However, some become more involved in the overall direction of the publication, leaving the day-to-day editing to others.

At book publishing houses, editors cultivate authors, develop ideas, negotiate with literary agents, and ultimately commission writers to deliver books that the editors believe will sell. They too must have a feel for what the public wants, but it is based less on the day-to-day news than on broad cultural trends, although timely books are sought after and fought for.

When an author submits a manuscript, the editor must then read and edit it and make suggestions. With works of fiction, the comments tend to indicate ways in which the author might make improvements. With nonfiction, however, an editor normally line-edits (actually changes) the manuscript and may even rewrite certain sections.

After the manuscript is put into production, the editor must keep tabs on it at every stage to make sure deadlines are met and all goes according to plan. The editor also works closely with various other departments such as promotion, publicity, subsidiary rights, and sales in order to see that the book has every opportunity to succeed in the marketplace.

In book publishing, the entry-level spot is that of *editorial assistant,* a job that combines the duties of secretary with the role of apprentice editor. The next step is *assistant editor,* followed by *associate editor, editor,* and *senior editor.*

Earnings and Opportunities

Opportunities for editors are good, and salaries range from $18,000 to $40,000 and above.

Training and Qualifications

Excellent writing skills, managerial ability, and creativity are good qualities to bring to this field.

A college degree is required. Some employers look for a broad liberal arts background; others seek applicants who have a degree in communications or a master's degree in journalism.

For Further Details

Women in Communications, Inc., P.O. Box 9561, Austin, TX 78766. The Newspaper Fund, Inc., P.O. Box 300, Princeton, NJ 08540. American Society of Magazine Editors, 575 Lexington Ave., New York, NY 10022.

PHOTOGRAPHERS

Duties and Responsibilities

Using a combination of technical expertise and aesthetic judgment, photographers use visual means to inform, instruct, and sometimes even inspire us. Most professionals use sophisticated cameras and a variety of lenses, filters, lighting systems, and reflectors; and they are employed in a number of different fields.

Portrait and *fashion photographers* take pictures of people, individually or in groups, and may work in a studio or on location. (For a portrait photographer, this may mean a church wedding or a backyard party; the fashion photographer may find himself at a clothing store or at an ocean-side shooting.) They are frequently self-employed and therefore handle much of the office work, billing, and bookkeeping themselves.

Industrial-commercial photographers are employed by businesses to take pictures of everything from livestock and consumer goods to buildings and people. Companies use their photographs in publications for stockholders, employee magazines, or to advertise company products or services. They may also make movies or videotapes of company activities for promotional or training purposes.

Scientific photographers and *biological photographers* provide illustrations and documentation for scientific publications, research reports, and teaching materials. These photographers usually specialize in a particular field such as engineering, aerodynamics, medicine, biology, or chemistry. In these fields, photographers often rely on special techniques such as time-lapse photography (where a normally slow action appears to be accelerated) and photomicrography (where a subject is magnified fifty to seventy-five times or more).

Photojournalists shoot newsworthy events and people for newspapers, magazines, or television. They may also prepare slides, filmstrips, videotapes, and movies.

Some photographers develop and print their own photographs. Others send their work to labs for processing. In the past, photographers tended to specialize in either still photography, motion picture, or video photography; but today the demand is growing for those who have training in all areas.

Working conditions vary. Freelance press and industrial photographers may travel frequently and may work long hours in uncomfortable surroundings. Photojournalists assigned to cover stories on natural disasters or military conflicts may find some assignments to be dangerous. Like journalists, many work under the pressure of regular deadlines.

Magazine and news photographers who start at small publications may move to staff positions on national news magazines. They may eventually become heads of graphic arts departments or photography editors. Photographers with exceptional ability may gain national recognition for their work and exhibit their photographs in art and photographic galleries or publish them in books.

Earnings and Opportunities

Over 91,000 people work as photographers, and employment is expected to grow by about 18 percent through the mid-1990s. Earnings vary widely. Experienced staffers average from $23,000 to over $35,000. Those who are self-employed may make much more.

Training and Qualifications

Photographers must have good eyesight and color vision, artistic ability, and manual dexterity. They should be patient, accurate, and enjoy working with detail. Commercial photographers must be imaginative and original; news photographers must recognize potential photographs and be able to react quickly; portrait photographers need the ability to help people relax.

A high school education is the minimum, and those who want to make a career out of photography should acquire training in colleges, universities, junior colleges, or art schools.

For Further Details

Professional Photographers of America, Inc., 1090 Executive Way, Des Plaines, IL 60018.

RECORDING ENGINEERS

Duties and Responsibilities

While there is little doubt about the talent and appeal of many musical artists, the quality of their sound on records and tapes depends in great measure on the ability of the recording engineer in the studio. Using sophisticated technical equipment, the recording engineer must skillfully mix and balance various instruments and voices, knowing exactly where to place the sensitive microphones, and must regulate the sound levels of each element of an ensemble.

Music (as opposed to the spoken word) makes up the bulk of the work in the recording industry. Go into any large record store and it's obvious that the industry encompasses every popular and classical style, and the possibilities for sound run the gamut—including both vocal and instrumental music, acoustic, amplified, or synthesized sound production, with ensembles ranging from a solo player to a full symphony orchestra. Knowing how to get the full value of a given sound for its presentation on records and tapes is a very specialized skill, and recording engineers must be familiar with the operation and setup of ever more sophisticated recording equipment, most of which is now computer enhanced. Understanding the basic elements of sound is an integral part of the job, especially when it comes to balance, mixing, and placement of microphones.

In some cases the engineer's job entails meticulous planning sessions with record producers (and sometimes with the performers themselves), followed by often lengthy rehearsals and recording sessions. Other jobs call for recording improvisation on the spot, placing the engineer under great pressure. This is usually the case when taping live performances, with audience participation and unusual acoustics testing the engineer's skill and ability.

Recording engineers usually work for studios. Most are located in the major production centers of New York, Los Angeles, and Nashville. Some work freelance, and others work for independent production companies that record concerts and special events. Some work exclusively for individual performers or groups, becoming very familiar with their style and their requirements, needing only to adapt to the place in which they are performing.

Most engineers learn through on-the-job training. Many studios hire talented people as assistants who train and learn while helping out with some of the recording duties.

Earnings and Opportunities

The employment outlook in this very specialized field is brighter now that the recording industry has recovered from the poor health it experienced in the late 1970s and early '80s. New groups and popular songs have given the business a lift, and record production is again on the increase. This trend is expected to continue over the next few years, which bodes well for job opportunities. Engineers with major recording houses can make from $18,500 to $44,000. Freelancers and those with smaller independent operations average somewhat less.

Training and Qualifications

A keen ear, an appreciation of music, stamina for lengthy recording sessions, and the ability to work well with the creative and sometimes temperamental personalities of producers and performers are important qualifications for this job.

Knowledge of and experience with electronic recording equipment and a complete understanding of the principles of sound recording are essential. Some specialized courses are available, and naturally, prior experience is a valuable asset in getting hired.

REPORTERS AND CORRESPONDENTS (PRINT)

Duties and Responsibilities

Some call them "our eyes and ears on the world," and it's easy to see why. Reporters and correspondents perform the vital role of keeping our society informed about events and issues, whether they happen across the street or around the world.

When covering a story, reporters collect facts and information through various forms of research, personal interviews, and on-scene observation. In a sense, the reporter's job is part investigator and part writer.

Reporters are assigned by editors to specific stories, and may work in teams when covering major issues like politics, economics, or defense. Others have specific "beats," like city hall, the police station, or the courts. Some are specialists and write only about one specific area like health, business, foreign affairs, sports, theater, or travel.

Depending on the size of the paper or magazine, reporters may cover all aspects of a story, including investigation of the facts, writing, and even taking the pictures. At some major publications reporters gather the facts while other staff members are responsible for writing them up.

Newspapers, magazines, and wire services frequently station reporters, known as correspondents, in large cities as well as in other countries to prepare stories on major news events occurring in those locations.

The work is often hectic. They are under pressure to meet deadlines and must work under trying conditions both in the newsroom and out in the field. The nature of the work demands long hours, irregular schedules, and some travel.

As reporters gain knowledge and experience, they can move up to larger papers and publications or press services. Some top reporters become columnists, editorial writers, editors, or top executives. Others find satisfying careers in related fields such as public relations or writing news copy for radio or television.

Earnings and Opportunities

Over 57,000 people work as reporters and correspondents at salaries ranging from $9,000 to $13,000 for trainees to $30,000 to $100,000 for top columnists. Employment opportunities are expected to increase 29 percent in the next decade.

Training and Qualifications

News reporting involves a great deal of responsibility, since what a reporter writes frequently influences public opinion. Reporters should be dedicated to serving the public's need for accurate and important news.

Important personal characteristics include a nose for news, curiosity, persistence, initiative, poise, resourcefulness, an accurate memory, and the physical and mental ability to deal with the pressure of deadlines, irregular hours, and sometimes dangerous assignments.

A background in journalism and liberal arts is preferred by most editors. Overall, graduates who have majored in news-editorial journalism, have a master's degree in journalism, and/or have completed an internship while in school should have the best prospects. The ability to read and speak a foreign language can help in some cases.

Typing skill is essential. The typewriter and now the computer keyboard are the primary tools of the trade. The ability to take shorthand or fast, accurate notes is also a must.

For Further Details

American Newspaper Publishers Association Foundation, The Newspaper Center, Box 17407, Dulles International Airport, Washington, DC 20041. The Newspaper Fund, Inc., P.O. Box 300, Princeton, NJ 08540. Association for Education in Journalism, University of South Carolina School of Journalism, Columbia, SC 29208. Women in Communications, Inc., P.O. Box 9561, Austin, TX 78766.

RESEARCHERS

Duties and Responsibilities

How many albums has a rock star sold? What percentage of children live in single-parent households? What is the background of the person being appointed to an ambassadorship? What questions should a book author be asked when she appears on a morning news program? These are the types of questions that concern researchers in the broadcasting and publishing industries, where they are a vital part of the editorial process.

Their basic duties are to provide documented information needed by writers, reporters, and management. Possible places of employment include the news department of a radio or television station, the local newspaper, a documentary unit at a television network, or at magazines ranging from *Time* and *People* to *The New Yorker*.

In large organizations, where staffing al-

lows for a great deal of specialization, the researcher is more likely to conduct work from a base in the company's library. Material is gathered from reference books and computer data bases. Telephone and face-to-face interviews are also used to track down facts for a story. Researchers for radio and television may also be expected to find audio- or videotape from past stories in order to provide background for certain segments.

In a smaller organization, researchers may have to fill more gaps in staffing, and for that reason they sometimes have added responsibilities. On occasion, they may have the opportunity to initiate stories, pre-interview key people for background material, and in some cases, prepare the skeleton of the story before passing it on to the writer or newscaster for the major interviews and final preparation of the story.

At magazines (and at the other media when

time permits), fact checking is very important. Researchers often must track down each fact mentioned in a story in order to verify it. Usually working from the writer's notes, they may have to re-interview sources and basically retrace the steps taken in preparing the story. It is painstaking, detailed work.

The job of researcher carries a lot of responsibility, since publications and programs must be very sure of their facts. One slip-up may require a simple retraction, while another can lead to a costly lawsuit.

Weekend deadlines of news magazines, round-the-clock radio and TV programming, and the daily preparation of stories for newspapers mean that hours can be irregular. Travel is sometimes involved.

While some people spend many years working in this career, others use it as a stepping-stone to other jobs. In broadcasting, a researcher may become an associate producer and eventually a producer. In print, a move to writer or reporter is logical.

Earnings and Opportunities

The outlook for researchers is good. Earnings: $10,000 to $35,000 and above.

Training and Qualifications

Attention to detail, intellectual curiosity, and the ability to analyze and interpret information are important qualities for researchers.

Employers look for candidates with a bachelor's degree, and many who are hired have also earned graduate degrees in journalism.

TECHNICAL WRITERS

Duties and Responsibilities

Have you ever read an article or book on some aspect of technology or science and marveled at how simply and directly the information was presented? If so, you were probably admiring the skills of a technical writer, whose job is to put technical information into readily understandable language.

There is a growing need for clear, direct communication of technical and complex information, for businesses, the government, and the public, as well as at the in-house company level. Technical writers combine their knowledge of a field with verbal skills to provide this service. They explain complicated material to audiences ranging from the average reader with a specific technical interest, to managers and sales representatives, to mechanics, technicians, engineers, and even scientists. Some writers work at jobs where they prepare manuals, catalogs, or instructional materials. For example, a technical writer might write a training manual for medical technicians who monitor diagnostic equipment in a coronary care unit. Others prepare training or instructional materials for organizations ranging from the military to the computer industry.

Many technical writers prepare reports on research that communicate scientific advances in one field to scientists and engineers in other fields. Others write detailed reports for government regulatory agencies. Some write grant proposals requesting money or facilities; others write speeches and news releases; still others edit and write technical books and journals and prepare articles for popular magazines.

Many technical writers are employed by large firms in the electronics, aircraft, energy, chemical, pharamaceutical, computer, and communications industries. Hospitals, drug firms, and laboratories also employ technical writers. Other technical writers work for publishing houses, magazines, public relations firms, and advertising agencies, as well as the federal government.

Experienced writers in companies with large staffs can advance to editorial positions or shift to administrative jobs in the publications or technical information departments. Some rise to be a publication manager, the person in the company who oversees the production of all technical documents. For some, advancement means having enough contacts and expertise to freelance or start their own business.

Earnings and Opportunities

Over 25,000 people work as technical writers and editors, and job opportunities are excellent. Earnings range from $18,500 to $28,000 and higher for editors and supervisors.

Training and Qualifications

Intellectual curiosity, the ability to organize large amounts of material logically, and being persistent and patient are key qualities for technical writers. Self-discipline and the ability to work as part of a team are also important.

Most employers expect applicants to be college graduates. Some prefer that the degree be in the appropriate scientific or technical area, while others prefer that the degree be in English, journalism, or technical communications.

Often technical writers do not enter the field directly from college. Some may have worked as technicians, scientists, engineers, or as research or editorial assistants before taking on writing responsibilities.

For Further Details

Society for Technical Communication, Inc., 815 15th St., N.W., Suite 506, Washington, DC 20005. American Business Communication Association, c/o University of Illinois, 100 English Building, 608 S. Wright St., Urbana, IL 61801.

TELEVISION DIRECTORS

Duties and Responsibilities

"Calling the shots" is the phrase that aptly describes the work of television directors, who have overall responsibility for both the creative and the technical decisions needed for every television broadcast.

There are basically two types of directors: entertainment (filmed or taped drama, comedy series, movies) and live events (news, sports, specials).

In entertainment, the director's job begins long before the performance or program is shot. Working with the script and consulting with the show's producers, the director will be involved in the preproduction aspects of planning the action, arranging the camera positions to get the best shots, and selecting background music when appropriate. He or she will also work with the actors on their interpretation of the script. After the shooting, the director may also be involved in the postproduction editing process on shows that are taped. Shows that are done on film are generally handled by the film director.

Directors of live specials and sports and news broadcasts have different responsibilities. Their planning is done a lot closer to the time of the actual broadcast, and their events are less "scripted," since their work will be dictated by the action that unfolds live. For the length of the broadcast, these directors will be in the hot seat, selecting which camera to put on the air and switching from camera to camera as the action happens, often changing shots every few seconds. While there is a great deal of stress during this time, those who do the work find that it is a thrilling challenge that tests creativity, organization, and the ability to tell a story all at once.

The job immediately under that of director is *associate/assistant director,* whose responsibilities are more technical in nature. These workers assist the director and oversee timing, script progression, camera position, special effects, sound effects, music, and all the odds and ends involved in production.

The phenomenal growth in programming for cable and other new technologies is providing an increasing number of jobs. Many corporations are also using television to communicate with their employees, their clients, and various other audiences.

Earnings and Opportunities

The outlook for employment is good. Network and studio directors command from $50,000 to $150,000 and up, while in local TV the range is $20,000 to $50,000.

Training and Qualifications

Creativity, organizational and communication skills, and the ability to work well with many people from different branches of the business —from producers and performers to set designers, camera operators, and production assistants—are important qualities for directors.

While there are no specific educational requirements, most people who become directors will have received at least some college education. Any kind of production experience in college or local theater and television is a help.

Work experience is a must, and most directors start as production assistants, work up to associate director (or assistant director), and eventually, with experience and expertise, to director.

For Further Details

Directors Guild of America, 110 W. 57th St., New York, NY 10019.

TELEVISION NEWS ASSISTANTS

Duties and Responsibilities

Behind every Dan Rather, Barbara Walters, Tom Brokaw, and their counterparts in hundreds of TV studios around the nation are scores of behind-the-scenes support personnel performing various essential functions. Needed in every newsroom is the news (or desk) assistant, a job that is very much at the center of activity and which provides one of the best ways to learn about how TV gathers the news.

Primarily an entry-level slot, this position involves all types of tasks (some mundane and some rather exciting) that support newsroom activities. One of these is gathering copy from the news wires. The assignment may be to collect all information that came in during the past twelve hours on the Mideast, on a particular country, or a certain political figure. Then in some cases collate, subgroup, and even condense it for easy review by the newscaster. Some news assistants specialize, but most must be able to tackle all assignments from hard news to sports. Calls may have to be made for more up-to-date information or for background material. The station's film and tape libraries may be utilized to provide additional data. The question always arises: "What did we say about this last month or last year?"

There are also the daily routine (and some not so routine) tasks: answering phones, logging stories or assignments, typing crew lists, figuring out logistics and itineraries for travel of crews and shipping of tapes, making calls for information, gathering material for correspondents and crews, and sometimes getting coffee and sandwiches. The range of duties varies at different locations, but the total effort is the same: general support and assistance to news personnel.

Because news is a twenty-four-hour-a-day business, news assistants frequently work nights and weekends.

News assistant jobs are excellent paths to careers in broadcasting and broadcast journalism. Turnover is high, since the jobs are used as stepping-stones to other positions. With exposure to almost every aspect of the business and the chance to make important personal contacts, there's plenty of opportunity for upward mobility. However, the positions are highly sought after, so leads must be carefully and persistently pursued. Career progress can involve starting at smaller stations and moving to progressively larger ones as experience is gained.

Earnings and Opportunities

While the outlook for employment is good, salaries are not high, because of supply and demand. They vary according to the station's size and location, and range from $15,000 to $26,000.

Training and Qualifications

An interest in broadcasting journalism, the ability to work well with people, communication and organizational skills as well as flexibility are important qualities for this job.

Because the jobs are highly competitive, employers usually hire only college graduates, and many who are hired have graduate degrees in journalism. Any direct experience in the field or work at a college newspaper or radio/TV station is also helpful in gaining employment.

TELEVISION PRODUCERS

Duties and Responsibilities

All the elements of a television production, from initial idea to the finished product, are the responsibility of the producer. Whether it is entertainment, news, sports, or a special event, the producer is in charge of gathering and coordinating all the creative and technical elements of the program as well as sometimes securing the financial backing and seeing to the ultimate sale of the package in order to get it on the air.

On entertainment programming, producers work closely with writers to develop the scripted material for production. They're often involved in casting the talent, choosing the director, and arranging for the facilities that will be used for production. One of the producer's main responsibilities is to administer the production budget.

Specific responsibilities vary depending on the type of production. While there will be a producer with overall responsibility for an entertainment program, many shows also have associate or assistant producers (or producers whose titles reflect their responsibilities) who take over certain duties. Some spend most of their time in offices, reading and reviewing scripts, working on budgets, and meeting with talent. Others, often called *line producers,* work on location or in the studio and oversee the day-to-day work as it progresses.

News and sports producers are involved with the flow and schedule of events. They choose the types of material to be covered and decide on the specific content of the broadcast. Here too there will be one producer with overall responsibility, as well as *field producers* who actually shoot the stories on location and take care of the budget, and supervise the interpretive coverage of specific show segments. Field producers may travel extensively in preparation of news reports, interviews, or sports features. In news, time spent on a foreign assignment is not unusual.

While networks, studios, and local stations provide many of the jobs for producers, growth in programming for cable, direct satellite transmission, home video, and other new technologies are providing an increasing number of opportunities.

Earnings and Opportunities

The employment outlook is good. Network and studio producers of weekly series and specials earn $100,000 and above. News and sports producers generally earn between $25,000 and $250,000. Local producers earn $20,000 to $50,000.

Training and Qualifications

Organizational skills, an interest in the financial aspects of programming, creativity, and the ability to manage others are important qualities for producers.

While there are no specific educational requirements, most who become producers will have some college education, generally in the communications field or in business. Amateur theater or television experience is a help.

Producing skills are learned through on-the-job training. Entry-level jobs that might lead to producing include news or production assistant, researcher, general office assistant, and production coordinator.

TELEVISION AND RADIO ANNOUNCERS, REPORTERS, AND NEWSCASTERS

Duties and Responsibilities

Announcers, reporters, and newscasters hold the most visible and glamorous jobs in broadcasting and are the link between the station, cable company, or network and the listening and viewing audience.

At radio stations, many announcers function as disc jockeys, playing music, reading news and weather, perhaps conducting phone and personal interviews, and reporting on items of local interest. At small stations, they may operate the technical equipment, sell commercial time, and write news as well.

At television stations and large radio stations, announcers usually specialize in a particular field like sports or weather.

Jobs in news broadcasting on television and radio range from reporter to anchorperson. The anchors, sometimes called newscasters, are the hosts of the broadcast and introduce film clips and interview segments. Reporters generally cover news in the field.

At a small local radio or television station, the newscaster may write and deliver his own reports. At a large station, he may be part of a news team, gathering and reporting stories from the wire services or out in the field. He or she may be aided by producers and writers in preparing material for the program.

Because they are visible figures in the community, broadcasters frequently participate in local activities—everything from serving as master of ceremonies at a community dinner to participating in a special charity function or school activity. Because broadcasting is a seven-day-a-week, twenty-four-hour-a-day business, night, weekend, and holiday work is common, as are last-minute calls for special assignments.

College graduates and others hired by television stations usually start out as production assistants, researchers, or reporters and are given a chance to move up if they show an aptitude for the business. After gaining experience at a small station, an ambitious and talented person may move to a better-paying job with more exposure in a larger city. Advancement may be easier for those who specialize in a particular field, like sports or consumerism, and gain a reputation for their expertise.

Earnings and Opportunities

Over 51,000 people hold such positions, and this number is expected to increase to 70,000 by the mid-1990s. Since television is a glamour profession, competition for jobs is stiff. Salaries range from $12,000 to $500,000 and more.

Training and Qualifications

Poise, an appealing personality, good judgment, and the ability to react quickly in emergencies are important, as is the ability to ad-lib on the air. A well-controlled voice and good speaking manner will enhance chances of success. For newscasters and reporters, knowledge of current events, research techniques, and writing are important background skills.

A liberal arts education provides a good background, and many universities offer specific courses in broadcasting. A number of private broadcasting schools offer training as well.

For Further Details

Broadcast Education Association, 1771 N St., N.W., Washington, DC 20036.

THEATER, FILM, AND TELEVISION SUPPORT PERSONNEL

Duties and Responsibilities

Whether it's a movie, a play, a ballet, or a television news show, all media presentations rely heavily on the efforts of behind-the-scenes support personnel. Their work ranges from applying makeup to designing lighting and those who hold these jobs play a vital role in bringing a production to life.

Lighting directors are responsible for pre-planning the lighting to be used and establishing a cue system or a computerized system for when and how lights are to be changed. They try to create an effect that will enhance the action, create a mood, and add to the meaning of the presentation. For a ballet without scenery, a lighting director may be totally responsible for creating the onstage mood for the dancers. In film, when night must sometimes be turned into day for the purposes of a shoot, the lighting director is the person who must meet this challenge. In television, the lighting director is also responsible for the lighting during taped and live broadcasts. Elsewhere that responsibility usually falls to *lighting technicians*.

Set designers are responsible for creating a mood that will blend in with the acting or the newscast without upstaging it. Their work ranges from deciding on the appropriate backdrop to working with the *property person* to select indoor furnishings, outdoor surroundings, and all props. They may be called upon to create a 1940s look, a futuristic set, or an exciting background for a special television news program announcing election results. They oversee construction of the set and then decide on exact placement of all props. In theater, designing sets that can be changed easily is very much a part of the art. Some Broadway shows have such elaborate set changes that the audience comes away talking as much about them as about the show itself.

Costume designers help create characters by selecting the appropriate clothing for the performers to wear. Knowing the clothing styles of different periods is often necessary. Prior to starting their work, designers must often do special research on the history and geography of the setting. Sketches must be prepared and approved by the director, and finally the designer will oversee construction of the clothing.

Understanding the medium for which they are designing is very important. Those who work for television and film must consider how the outfits will photograph; those who design for stage must be aware of how they will look from a distance. All must be conscious of how comfortable costumes will be. Can the dancer move easily in the special shoes? How will the star's dress look after she is pushed in the pool? These are important considerations for the costume designer.

Casting directors are responsible for finding the perfect people for specific parts. Being able to spot talent and the right look takes intuition and experience. Their work may involve extensive travel, and they may audition all types of people, ranging from schoolchildren who have never acted before to aspiring actors and actresses who show up at casting "cattle calls." For casting major roles, they usually work closely with the director of the film, play, or program.

Makeup artists do everything from enhancing the looks of a star to adding bruises and lumps to an "accident victim" in a movie or working on talk show guests to give them a look that will not be washed out by the harsh lights of the television studio. Knowledge of cosmetics and an understanding of one's medium are very important.

Stage managers carry overall responsibility for much of the behind-the-scenes work. They are part of the director's staff and act as a go-between for cast and director. They also plan and organize the activities of the stage crew. During a theater performance, stage managers give cues for curtains, lights, and sound effects, and they prompt actors when necessary. They may also supervise set changes.

Support personnel who work in television frequently are on staff, and their work schedules can be erratic. Those who work in theater or in film are generally hired freelance. They may face long periods of unemployment between assignments, and when they do work, hours are often long and irregular.

This is a highly competitive field where the path to becoming steadily employed can be a difficult one. For those who succeed, however, it can offer rewarding, lucrative careers.

Earnings and Opportunities

Outlook for employment is good, though employment in films and theater is highly dependent upon whether the public has money to spend on tickets. Employment in television is less volatile, since there is a need to produce programming regardless of the economy. Earnings are difficult to estimate. Many who go into these professions start out by working for free on amateur productions. Once they gain experience and move into the professional world, pay can be excellent (e.g., makeup artists can command a day rate of $138 and above; stage managers can make from $285 to over $800 per week). However, except in television, year-round employment is unusual. Those in theater and film who gain a name for themselves may sometimes also be able to command a percentage of the profits.

Training and Qualifications

A love of the arts, special talent in one's field, and the ability to work as part of a team are helpful qualities in these professions.

Educational requirements vary. A makeup artist must have a high school diploma and some vocational training in order to qualify for the necessary state certification. Otherwise, a bachelor's degree with a major in theater is recommended, though a costume designer will also be well served studying fashion design.

TRANSLATORS AND INTERPRETERS

Duties and Responsibilities

Making the knowledge and thoughts of people who speak different languages accessible to others is the work of translators and interpreters.

Absolute fluency in two or more languages is a must, and a perfect knowledge of the subtleties of both languages is required, since certain words, expressions, and idioms often cannot be translated word for word.

Translators work with the written word, and they may specialize in news and legal documents, scientific papers, or literature. Because they usually work on their own, they can take time to achieve the closest possible meaning or develop a more literary style. They are employed by government agencies, publishers, companies doing overseas business, lawyers who specialize in international legal affairs, transportation companies, travel agencies, and import/export firms.

Interpreters work with the spoken word rather than the written one. They translate speeches, meetings, and conversations from one language to another in the presence of the speaker. Not only is a complete understanding of the foreign language important, but interpreters must be able to think quickly on their feet, since they must frequently be translating one thought while listening to the next one and organizing how that should be translated. Interpreters often work as intermediaries between government officials who do not speak the same language. Some are employed by business people who work with foreign clients and a few are employed at colleges and universities. Others are employed at places like the United Nations, where all meetings must be interpreted in a wide variety of languages.

In most cases the responsibility placed on the translator or interpreter is enormous, since the success or failure of foreign relationships may ride on it. If one phrase in a legal document is in error, or if part of a speech is muddled, the misunderstanding could be quite difficult to straighten out.

Some workers are on staff with certain institutions, while others work freelance and set their own schedules. Traveling with business people or foreign dignitaries is sometimes part of the job.

Earnings and Opportunities

Opportunities are limited, and earnings vary from $11,000 to $17,000 and up.

Training and Qualifications

A facility for language, the ability to think quickly, writing ability, and honesty are important qualifications for these jobs.

Some individuals learn one or more languages through family situations and/or living in bilingual or trilingual areas. In any case, to be able to translate and/or interpret, they need further schooling in such languages, especially to broaden their vocabulary and sharpen their skills. Some schools have specialized programs that focus on building these skills. Potential candidates must develop a perfect understanding of the languages in which they intend to specialize.

For Further Details

American Translators Association, Box 401, Camden, NJ 08101.

WRITERS, FICTION AND NONFICTION

Duties and Responsibilities

Professional writers are paid to do highly creative work communicating information and ideas by means of the written word. They may work on staff or as freelancers, and are employed by magazines, newspapers, book publishers, and businesses of all kinds.

On magazines and newspapers, writers are normally assigned stories by their editors, though sometimes the idea originates with the writer. They gather information through interviews, research, and personal observation prior to beginning to write. Sometimes on a big story, or at a magazine or newspaper with a large staff, the writer composes the piece based on someone else's research. Writers often specialize in a topic like health or sports, or in a type of article like feature writing.

Book publishing companies do not "employ" the writers of fiction and nonfiction in the usual sense of the word, but they do pay them to write by sharing a percentage of book sale profits (known as royalties) with them. Writers who want to be published must submit their material to an editor. Nonfiction can often be sold on the basis of a proposal and sample chapters, but fiction writers must gen-

erally submit a completed manuscript. This may mean months of work with no real assurance that the book will sell. Once a contract is signed, the nonfiction author must research, write, and deliver the manuscript. The fiction writer may only need to do some revisions.

Ghostwriters are also important to the book publishing industry, where it is common for a professional writer to be hired to rewrite material already provided in rough form by an expert in a specific field, or to collaborate with a celebrity on writing a book from scratch.

Since effective communication is vital to the corporate organization at every level, writers are needed here too. Business writers prepare reports, speeches, business plans, and presentations, or write copy for brochures, catalogs, sales pieces, and other business materials. In training and development departments, capable writers can find steady work writing manuals, pamphlets, and instruction or training guides.

Most staff writers in business work a standard forty-hour week. Magazine and newspaper staff writers work at least that long, and may work evenings and weekends when under deadline. A writer's work environment may be a corporate office, a hectic newsroom, or the kitchen table; and while research may begin in the library, it can take the writer almost anywhere.

Earnings and Opportunities

Employment opportunities are good and should increase by about 35 percent in the next decade. Earnings range from $100 for freelance work to $34,000 and above.

Training and Qualifications

A college degree is usually required. Some employers look for a broad liberal arts back-ground, others for a degree in communications or journalism.

All prospective writers need practical writing experience. High school and college newspapers, magazines, and small community papers all provide valuable (but sometimes unpaid) experience.

For Further Details

The Newspaper Fund, Inc., P.O. Box 300, Princeton, NJ 08540.

Careers in Medicine

There are two words to keep in mind when one considers a career in the field of medicine: *growth* and *change*.

Growth refers to good news for job seekers. Employment in the medical profession, in health services, and in hospitals and laboratories is expected to grow quickly during the coming decade because of the expanding health care needs of a growing and aging population. The increasing availability of public and private health insurance, the broader access to health care, and an increased interest in preventive medicine and rehabilitation all lead to an increase in the number of jobs available.

Change refers to the fact that those interested in medicine and health should be avid students, regardless of the area of employment. Medical advances are occurring so rapidly that regardless of what you may learn during initial preparation for a position, things are sure to change, and change again. The doctor must keep up on all the latest information on cancer as well as the common cold; today's dental student may see the time when cavities become almost nonexistent; and the pharmacist will encounter amazing progress in the types of drugs being used to treat various diseases.

One final note for those who hope to become physicians. Doctors are perhaps one of the most misunderstood groups of professionals in the country today. When they save our lives or those of our loved ones, we can't thank them enough. When we get their bills we're staggered by the fees. While an income of $150,000 to $200,000 may sound extraordinarily generous, keep in mind that business people making the same amount of money are getting a better return on their investment. Why? Because of the time and money involved in becoming a doctor. Most physicians invest seven to twelve years of their lives gaining the necessary education and training, at costs ranging from $70,000 to $150,000.

While the value of work done by physicians is undisputed, those who choose the profession must possess zealous dedication. If they are totally committed to their career choice, the profession holds unlimited opportunities to do important work in this field.

ANATOMISTS, EMBRYOLOGISTS, MEDICAL MICROBIOLOGISTS, PHARMACOLOGISTS, AND PHYSIOLOGISTS

Duties and Responsibilities

These are life scientists who contribute to medicine through their in-depth study of living organisms and life processes—reproduction, growth, and development. Those who do basic research may discover the cause of a disease. Others, working in applied research, may develop new medicines to cure that disease. Scientists engaged in research and development usually work in laboratories, and a familiarity with research techniques and the use of laboratory equipment and computers is essential.

Not everyone in this field works in a laboratory, however. Some work in management or administration, planning and administering programs for testing medicines or certain treatments. Some teach in colleges or universities; others work as consultants to business firms or to government. Still others write for technical publications or test and inspect food, drugs, and other products.

Biological scientists are usually classified by the type of organism they study or by the activity they perform:

Anatomists study and examine the structure of organisms, from cell structure to the formation of tissues and organs. Many specialize in human anatomy. Research methods may entail dissections or the use of electron microscopes.

Embryologists study the development of an animal from a fertilized egg through the hatching process or birth, and the causes of healthy and abnormal development.

Medical microbiologists study the relationship between bacteria and disease or the effect of antibiotics on bacteria. Other microbiologists study virology (viruses) or immunology (mechanisms that fight infections).

Pharmacologists and *toxicologists* conduct tests on animals such as rats, guinea pigs, and monkeys to determine the effects of drugs, gases, poisons, dusts, and other substances on the functioning of tissues and organs. Pharmacologists may develop new or improved drugs or medicines.

Physiologists study life functions of plants and animals under normal and abnormal conditions. Physiologists may specialize in functions such as growth, reproduction, or respiration.

Most scientists work regular hours in offices, laboratories, or classrooms.

Earnings and Opportunities

Over 90,000 people are employed as biological scientists, and the employment outlook for those with advanced degrees is very good. Salaries range from $14,700 to $78,000 and up.

Training and Qualifications

A fascination with living things, curiosity, an analytical mind, and the ability to work independently or as part of a team are important qualities for future scientists. Being able to communicate well orally and in writing is also important.

A master's degree is sufficient for some jobs in applied research, and the Ph.D. is generally required for college teaching, independent research, and for advancement to administrative research positions and other management jobs.

For Further Details

American Institute of Biological Sciences, 1401 Wilson Blvd., Arlington, VA 22209. American Physiological Society, Education Officer, 9650 Rockville Pike, Bethesda, MD 20014.

CHIROPRACTORS

Duties and Responsibilities

Some people swear by the relief they get from going to a chiropractor. They may be dancers looking for help with a recurring muscle pain, people suffering from backache, or other patients who simply find that their general health is improved by chiropractic treatment.

Chiropractic is a system of treatment based on the principle that a person's health is determined largely by the nervous system, and that interference with this sytem impairs normal functions and lowers resistance to disease. Chiropractors treat patients primarily by manual manipulation (adjustment) of parts of the body, with special emphasis on the spinal column.

Most chiropractors use X rays to help locate the source of a problem, and then they recommend treatment and set up a schedule for performing the adjustments. Patients then may come for brief visits regularly for a period of time until the condition is corrected.

Chiropractors also use water, light, massage, ultrasound, and electric and heat therapy; and they prescribe diet, supports, exercise, and rest. Most state laws specify the types of supplementary treatment permitted to be used by chiropractors, and they are not licensed to dispense prescription drugs or perform surgery.

About half of all chiropractors work in small communities of 50,000 people or less. Most are in private practice, a few work as salaried assistants of established practitioners or work for chiropractic clinics, and a small number teach or conduct research at chiropractic colleges.

Chiropractors usually work in comfortable private offices. A typical workweek is four and a half or five days. Because most are self-employed, they enjoy both freedom and the responsibility that it entails. While they must work hard to build a successful practice, they may also set their own schedules and can practice well beyond normal retirement age.

Earnings and Opportunities

Over 23,000 people work as chiropractors, and employment prospects are very good, as this number is expected to increase by 27 percent in the next ten years. Income ranges from $24,000 to $52,000, with some earning in excess of $100,000.

Training and Qualifications

Chiropractic therapy requires a keen sense of observation to detect physical abnormalities and considerable hand dexterity, since adjustments consist of physically manipulating the patient's body. Sympathy, understanding, and the ability to listen carefully are also important qualities.

All chiropractic colleges require applicants to have a minimum of two years of undergraduate study. In the first two years of chiropractic study, the emphasis is on classroom and laboratory work in subjects such as anatomy, physiology, and biochemistry. The last two years stress clinical experience. Courses include study of manipulation and spinal adjustments as well as subjects such as physiotherapy and nutrition. Students completing the training earn the degree of doctor of chiropractic (D.C.).

Chiropractors are licensed throughout the United States.

For Further Details

American Chiropractic Association, 1916 Wilson Blvd., Arlington, VA 22201. International Chiropractors Association, 1901 L St., N.W., Suite 800, Washington, DC 20036. Council on Chiropractic Education, 3209 Ingersoll Ave., Des Moines, IA 50312.

DENTISTS

Duties and Responsibilities

From the child who has an overbite to the adult with a bad toothache, everyone needs to see a dentist at least once in a while, and dentistry can be a fascinating, lucrative profession.

Dentists spend most of their time with patients, examining teeth and tissues of the mouth to diagnose diseases or abnormalities. They take X rays, fill cavities, straighten teeth, and treat gum diseases. Badly decayed teeth may be extracted and artificial dentures, designed for a particular individual, may be substituted. Dentists may also perform corrective surgery of the gums and supporting bones.

Dentists with small practices may clean teeth themselves and do their own laboratory work such as making dentures and inlays. In larger practices, dentists usually send their laboratory work to outside firms. They also employ dental hygienists to clean teeth and provide instruction on preventive maintenance.

Most dentists are general practitioners, but some do specialize. The largest group of specialists are *orthodontists*, who straighten teeth. There are also *oral surgeons*, who operate on mouth and jaws; *pedodontists*, who specialize in dentistry for children; *periodontists*, who treat gums; *prosthodontists*, who make artificial teeth or dentures; *endodontists*, who do root canal therapy; and *oral pathologists*, who specialize in diseases of the mouth.

Most dentists are in private practice. About 5 percent teach in dental schools, do research, or administer dental health programs on a full-time basis. Many in private practice do this part-time.

Most dental offices are open five days a week, and some dentists have evening hours. Dentists usually work forty hours a week, although many work more than fifty. Because they are self-employed, they can adjust their schedules when necessary, and many maintain a part-time practice well past retirement age.

Earnings and Opportunities

Over 126,000 people practice dentistry, and employment is expected to grow by 24 percent in the next ten years. Earnings: $50,000 to over $100,000.

Training and Qualifications

Imagine how hard it must be to do delicate work within the confines of someone's mouth, and you'll realize what qualities a dentist needs: a high degree of manual dexterity, good visual memory, excellent judgment of space and shape, and a high level of diagnostic ability, to mention a few. The ability to put people at ease and to inspire confidence will also make time spent with patients easier. Good business sense and self-discipline will come in handy when setting up a practice.

Competition is keen for admission to dental schools. In selecting students, schools give considerable weight to college grades and also evaluate scores on a nationwide admission test administered to potential dental students.

Dental school generally lasts four academic years. The degree of doctor of dental surgery (D.D.S.) or an equivalent degree, doctor of dental medicine (D.M.D.), is conferred.

For Further Details

American Association of Dental Schools, 1625 Massachusetts Ave., N.W., Washington, DC 20036. American Dental Association, Council on Dental Education, 211 E. Chicago Ave., Chicago, IL 60611.

OPTOMETRISTS

Duties and Responsibilities

Our eyes are one of the most important parts of our bodies, and if our vision isn't what it should be, an optometrist is likely to be the medical professional we visit.

Optometrists examine people's eyes to detect vision problems, diseases, and other abnormalities. They also test for proper depth and color perception and a patient's ability to focus and coordinate the eyes. If necessary, they prescribe lenses and treatment. In cases of disease, the optometrist refers the patient to the appropriate health care professional. Most optometrists supply the prescribed eyeglasses and fit and adjust contact lenses. Optometrists also prescribe vision therapy or other treatment which does not require surgery. In some states, optometrists are licensed to use diagnostic drugs, and in several states they may also use drugs to treat eye diseases.

Optometrists should not be confused with ophthalmologists, who are physicians specializing in medical eye care, eye diseases, and injuries. Ophthalmologists also perform eye surgery and prescribe drugs, lenses, and other eye treatments. Optometrists are also sometimes confused with dispensing opticians, who fit and adjust eyeglasses but only according to prescriptions written by ophthalmologists or optometrists. Opticians are not licensed to examine eyes or prescribe treatment.

Although most optometrists are generalists, some specialize. For example, they may work with the elderly, with children, or with partially sighted people who can benefit from special lenses. Others work mainly with contact lenses or with patients who can benefit from vision therapy.

Most optometrists are in solo practices, but a growing number of young practitioners are forming partnerships or group practices because of the high cost of setting up an office.

Optometrists work in pleasant environments. Their work requires patience and great attention to detail. Most work over forty hours a week. Some have Saturday or evening hours for the convenience of their patients.

Earnings and Opportunities

Over 27,000 people are employed as optometrists, and the employment outlook is excellent, with a projected increase of 25 percent by 1995. Earnings range from $22,000 to $62,000, with some in excess of $100,000.

Training and Qualifications

Since most parts of an eye examination require use of finely tuned machinery, candidates should have good manual dexterity and feel comfortable working with delicate instruments. Sensitivity to a patient's needs is also important.

The doctor of optometry degree requires graduation from a four-year professional degree program. Most optometry students enter this program with a bachelor's degree.

Competition for admission is keen at the sixteen optometric schools.

Those wishing to obtain recognition as a specialist may study for a master's or Ph.D. degree in a specific area of concentration. One-year graduate clinical residency programs are available in the optometric specialties of family practice optometry, pediatric optometry, low vision rehabilitation, contact lenses, neuro-optometry, and hospital optometry.

For Further Details

American Optometric Association, 243 N. Lindbergh Blvd., St. Louis, MO 63141. Association of Schools and Colleges of Optometry, Suite 410, 600 Maryland Ave., S.W., Washington, DC 20024.

OSTEOPATHIC PHYSICIANS

Duties and Responsibilities

Osteopathic physicians combine the practice of medicine with the theory that recovery from disease can be aided by the manipulation of parts of the body. In their practice, they use surgery, drugs, and all other accepted methods of medical care as well as manual manipulation similar to that done by chiropractors. The manipulation focuses on the musculo-skeletal system of the body—bones, muscles, ligaments, and nerves.

Most osteopathic physicians are family doctors who engage in general practice. However, in recent years specialization has increased. In 1980, about 13 percent of all osteopathic physicians were practicing in specialties, including internal medicine, neurology and psychiatry, ophthalmology, anesthesiology, physical medicine and rehabilitation, dermatology, pathology, proctology, radiology, and surgery.

Almost 85 percent are in private practice. Osteopathic physicians are chiefly located in states that have osteopathic hospital facilities (though they can practice at other types of public and private hospitals as well). Three-fifths are located in Florida, Michigan, Pennsylvania, New Jersey, Ohio, Texas, and Missouri. More than half of all general practitioners are located in towns and cities having fewer than 50,000 people. Specialists practice mainly in larger cities.

Most osteopathic physicians work more than fifty or sixty hours a week. Those in general practice usually work longer and more irregular hours than specialists. As with any physician, the work requires dedication and a sincere devotion to one's patients.

Earnings and Opportunities

Over 19,000 people work as osteopathic physicians. Earnings compare favorably with those of other medical specialties.

Training and Qualifications

As with anyone who plans to study medicine, those who wish to become osteopathic physicians should be prepared for a great deal of hard study, as well as ongoing study in later years to keep abreast of the latest advances. Candidates should be emotionally stable and self-confident.

Almost all candidates enter osteopathic colleges after obtaining a bachelor's degree. They then must complete three to four years of professional study for the degree of doctor of osteopathy (D.O.). Schools admit students on the basis of their college grades, scores on the required New Medical College Admissions Test, and recommendations. An applicant's desire to become an osteopathic physician rather than a doctor trained in another field of medicine is an important qualification. A personal recommendation by an osteopathic physician may also help you gain admission.

During the first half of professional training, emphasis is placed on the basic sciences and the principles of osteopathy; the remainder of the time is devoted largely to experience with patients in hospitals and clinics.

After graduation, nearly all serve a one-year rotating internship that includes experience in surgery, pediatrics, internal medicine, and other specialties. Those who wish to specialize must have two to five years of additional training.

For Further Details

American Osteopathic Association, Department of Public Relations, 212 E. Ohio St., Chicago, IL 60611. American Association of Colleges of Osteopathic Medicine, 4720 Montgomery Lane, Bethesda, MD 20814.

PHARMACISTS

Duties and Responsibilities

Who hasn't been grateful to the neighborhood pharmacist for recommending an effective over-the-counter decongestant to help relieve a cold or giving advice on the best ointment for a slight rash? Good pharmacists not only dispense drugs and medicines prescribed by doctors and dentists, but they are knowledgeable enough to advise us on the use of nonprescription medicines as well.

At one time, pharmacists were responsible for actually mixing (called compounding) medicinal ingredients, but today most medicines are produced by manufacturers. Nonetheless, pharmacists must be experts on drug use, composition, and effects.

Pharmacists who work in community pharmacies may also buy and sell non-pharmaceutical merchandise, hire and supervise personnel, and oversee the general operation of the pharmacy.

Pharmacists in hospitals and clinics dispense inpatient and outpatient prescriptions and advise the medical staff on the selection and effects of drugs; they also make sterile solutions, buy medical supplies, and perform administrative duties.

About two-thirds of all pharmacists work in community pharmacies, and of these, one-fourth own their own. Most of the remaining pharmacists work for hospitals, pharmaceutical manufacturers, wholesalers, and government and educational institutions.

An increasing number of women are entering the profession. Currently only 19 percent are women, but this is expected to increase, since 51 percent of all pharmacy students are female, up from 28 percent in 1973–74.

Pharmacists work in areas resembling small laboratories. They spend a lot of time on their feet. Pharmacies are often open evenings and weekends, and pharmacists put in an average of forty-four hours a week. Those who also consult may work another fifteen hours.

Pharmacists at chain drugstores may advance to a management position. Hospital pharmacists may advance to director of pharmacy service or other administrative positions. Some go to work in related fields such as medical sales representatives for drug manufacturers. Some teach in colleges of pharmacy, supervise the manufacture of pharmaceuticals, or are involved in research and development of new medicines. Some add legal training to their credits and become patent lawyers or consultants on pharmaceutical and drug laws.

Earnings and Opportunities

Over 141,000 people are employed as pharmacists, and in the next decade this number should increase by 27 percent. Earnings range from $19,800 to $38,000 and more for the self-employed and those who do consulting.

Training and Qualifications

Five years of study beyond high school are required to get a bachelor of science (B.S.) or a bachelor of pharmacy (B.Pharm.) degree. Some colleges admit students directly from high school. However, most require entrants to have completed one or two years of pre-pharmacy education elsewhere. An increasing number are obtaining doctor of pharmacy (Pharm.D.) degrees (which require six to seven years of education) in order to do administrative work or college teaching.

Throughout the United States, licensing is required to practice pharmacy.

For Further Details

American Association of Colleges of Pharmacy, Office of Student Affairs, 4630 Montgomery Ave., Suite 201, Bethesda, MD 20014. American Council on Pharmaceutical Education, 1 E. Wacker Dr., Chicago, IL 60601. American Pharmaceutical Association, 2215 Constitution Ave., N.W., Washington, DC 20037.

PHYSICIANS

Duties and Responsibilities

Whether helping one get over the flu, setting a broken leg, or treating a cancer patient, physicians are the professionals we ultimately turn to when something goes wrong with our bodies. In their work, physicians perform medical examinations, diagnose illnesses, and treat people who are suffering from injury or disease. They also advise patients on how to keep fit through proper diet and exercise.

About three out of every ten physicians who provide patient care are generalists. However, recent years have seen a decline in the number of GP's (general practitioners). Now almost all medical school graduates obtain advanced specialty training in a residency program. Among the thirty-eight specialties for which there is postgraduate training are internal medicine, general surgery, obstetrics and gynecology, psychiatry, pediatrics, radiology, anesthesiology, ophthalmology, pathology, and orthopedic surgery.

More than 60 percent of the active physicians in the United States have office practices. About 25 percent work as residents or full-time staff members in hospitals. The remaining physicians teach or perform administrative or research duties.

Many physicians work long and irregular hours, but exact conditions depend greatly upon the specialty. A pathologist who oversees work done in a laboratory may work relatively normal business hours. An anesthesiologist may spend the majority of his or her hours meeting with patients in the hospital and then working with other doctors in the operating room. Dermatologists spend more time seeing patients in the office, while obstetricians or pediatricians usually make hospital rounds in the morning, see patients during office hours later in the day, and are on call many nights and weekends.

The majority of newly qualified physicians open their own offices or join associate or group practices.

Earnings and Opportunities

Over 405,000 people currently work as physicians, and the outlook for employment is very favorable, with a 34 percent increase projected over the next ten years. Physicians have among the highest earnings of any occupational group, ranging from $56,000 to $200,000 and up.

Training and Qualifications

Emotional stability, the ability to make decisions in emergencies, a willingness to study both in school and later on to keep up with medical advances, and a desire to help others are helpful qualities for future physicians.

Competition for getting into medical school is stiff. Academic records, scores on the New Medical College Admissions Test, as well as personal characteristics are all taken into consideration. Most medical students take four years to complete the curriculum for the M.D. degree, and after graduation, almost all M.D.'s serve a residency of at least three years in their specialty.

About 95 percent of all graduates expect to seek specialty board certification. Some who want to teach or do research take graduate work leading to a master's or Ph.D. degree in a field such as biochemistry or microbiology.

For Further Details

Council on Medical Education, American Medical Association, 535 N. Dearborn St., Chicago, IL 60610. Association of American Medical Colleges, Suite 200, 1 Dupont Circle, N.W., Washington, DC 20036.

PODIATRISTS

Duties and Responsibilities

No one likes it when his feet hurt, whether it's from squeezing a reluctant foot into the latest fashion in shoes, playing a fast-moving game of tennis, or just a plain old bunion. That's why a growing number of people are turning to podiatrists for help.

Podiatrists are doctors who diagnose and treat diseases and deformities of the foot. They perform surgery; fit corrective devices; and prescribe drugs, physical therapy, and proper shoes. They take X rays and perform or prescribe blood and other pathological tests to help in diagnoses.

In addition, podiatrists treat a variety of foot conditions, including corns, bunions, calluses, ingrown toenails, skin and nail diseases, deformed toes, and arch disabilities.

If symptoms of a medical disorder such as arthritis, diabetes, or heart disease are present, a podiatrist would refer the patient to another type of physician while continuing to treat the foot problem.

More than four out of every five podiatrists are generalists who provide all types of foot care. However, there are those who specialize in foot surgery, orthopedics (bone, muscle, and joint disorders), podopediatrics (foot ailments of children), or podogeriatrics (foot problems of the elderly). Sports medicine is rapidly becoming a growing specialty because of the increasing popularity of jogging, tennis, and racquetball and other fast-moving sports that tend to aggravate foot problems.

Most podiatrists work forty-hour weeks in comfortable surroundings. Those who are self-employed must work hard to establish their practices, but they enjoy the benefits of setting their own schedules and determining their own retirement age.

Earnings and Opportunities

Over 12,000 people work as podiatrists, and employment prospects are excellent, with a 52 percent increase in this number expected in the coming decade. Earnings: $50,000 and up.

Training and Qualifications

For those who want to become podiatrists, scientific aptitude, manual dexterity, and the willingness to study hard to complete the training are important assets. Business sense and the ability to put patients at ease are also helpful.

There are five colleges of podiatric medicine, and competition for admission is keen. Most applicants have at least a bachelor's degree with an overall grade point average of B or better. Good scores on the required New Medical College Admissions Test and recommendations are important factors in gaining admission.

The professional training itself is a four-year program. The first two years are spent in classroom instruction and laboratory work. In the final two years, students gain clinical experience while continuing their classroom studies. Graduates receive the degree of doctor of podiatric medicine (D.P.M.). For those who wish to specialize, additional education and experience are generally necessary.

For Further Details

American Association of Colleges of Podiatric Medicine, 20 Chevy Chase Circle, N.W., Washington, DC 20015. American Podiatry Association, same address as above. For information on licensing, contact the state board in the area where you wish to live.

PSYCHIATRISTS

Duties and Responsibilities

These medical doctors play a serious and crucial role in helping solve patients' mental and emotional disorders. Any given day may find a psychiatrist coping with anything from a patient threatening suicide to one involved in drug abuse.

Approximately 11 percent of all medical doctors specialize in the field of psychiatry. The field is often confused with that of psychologists, and many of the disorders they treat are similar. Both also use counseling and/or psychoanalytic techniques in treatment. However, psychologists gain the title of doctor through earning a Ph.D. and do not actually practice medicine. Psychiatrists have an M.D., which permits them to prescribe medicines and drugs as part of any therapy.

Most psychiatrists specialize. Some work solely with the elderly, focusing on the problems of aging, depression, senility, and separation from the family. Others work with children on difficulties such as stuttering, withdrawal, and aggression. When working with adolescents, psychiatrists often deal with suicidal tendencies, depression, alcoholism, and drug abuse. These issues may also come up in treatment of adults. In addition, psychiatrists may do marriage and family counseling, including treating sexual dysfunction or the psychological problems stemming from divorce and separation. And an increasing number of psychiatrists are now working on the recently recognized need of helping people cope with stress and anxiety in the workplace.

Most psychiatrists have their own practices, although some may also work on staff at a hospital or a mental health organization. Hours may be long and irregular. If a patient is contemplating suicide, this is obviously an emergency that cannot wait.

Advancement in the field comes about through building the size of one's own practice or increasing one's expertise, which may lead to a growing reputation in the field.

Earnings and Opportunities

Over 50,000 people are employed as psychiatrists, and the outlook for employment is favorable. Earnings range from $40,000 to over $200,000.

Training and Qualifications

Emotional stability, sensitivity, and the ability to counsel others are important qualities for psychiatrists.

For educational requirements, see "Physicians."

Careers in the Physical Sciences

It has been said that "the mind is where the heart is," and this is particularly true of people who choose careers in the physical sciences. It takes a special interest, love, and inclination to become an astronomer, chemist, geologist, geophysicist, meteorologist, oceanographer, or physicist. However, those who take on the challenges of these fields find them enormously rewarding.

The basic work of physical scientists is to investigate the structure, composition, and interaction of the earth and the gases that surround it and the universe. Some scientists work primarily in research to increase knowledge; others employ the results of research to solve practical problems in developing new products, locating new natural resources, or forecasting the weather, for example.

While some areas of the physical sciences can be entered with a bachelor's degree, most positions require candidates to have a master's and many to have a doctorate.

Opportunities in this field used to depend primarily on employment as professors at colleges and universities or they were tied to the availability of government funds. However, expanding scientific horizons and the financial rewards that accompany new discoveries are bringing increasing interest from private enterprise. This, in turn, means greater job opportunities than ever before.

ASTRONOMERS

Duties and Responsibilities

While stargazers' techniques have changed since the 1500s when Copernicus observed the skies, the role of the astronomer remains the same: to explore the heavens to discover and understand the nature of the universe. Astronomers are scientists who study the stars, the planets, and all other heavenly bodies, determining their composition, size, motion, and other properties, in order to ultimately unlock the secrets of the origin of matter and the evolution of the universe.

Today's astronomers and astrophysicists rarely look through regular telescopes. Advances in technology have made electronic and photographic equipment much more effective than the human eye. Astronomers now use extremely high powered and computer-enhanced telescopes, satellite observation, and radio telescopic equipment that can detect electromagnetic radiation. Spectroscopes provide information about the chemical composition of stars through analysis of the light they emit. As in most sciences today, computers are used to process a wealth of information, including solving the complex mathematical equations that relate to theories about the universe and the planets, providing data for navigation of spacecraft and calculating the orbits of planets, asteroids, and comets.

Over half of all astronomers work in colleges or universities. Most of the others work in observatories, and some are employed by the government in the space program or the Department of Defense. A few work for aerospace firms or in museums or planetariums.

Astronomers spend only a few weeks a year making observations, with the bulk of their time devoted to analyzing data. Almost all astronomers do research or teach, and thus spend much of their time in offices or classrooms. They write and publish reports, formulate theories, and research findings for others.

Astronomers advance professionally either by distinguishing themselves in scientific or academic circles at colleges and universities, or by taking more responsible and higher-paying research positions with government or private industry.

Earnings and Opportunities

Astronomy is a small field, and only about 3,000 people are employed in it. Employment is expected to grow slowly through the 1980s, and competition will be keen for the available openings. This is mostly the result of tight government funding for research projects. Earnings: $18,200 to over $50,000.

Training and Qualifications

An inquisitive and analytical mind, the ability to concentrate on detail, and a firm understanding of and interest in advanced mathematics and science are key requirements for those planning careers in astronomy. Many tests and research theories lead to dead ends, while others might provide small but significant breakthroughs, so perseverance is also important.

The general educational requirement is a Ph.D degree in astronomy, which includes work in astronomy, physics, and mathematics.

For Further Details

For a pamphlet containing information on careers in astronomy and on schools offering training, send twenty-five cents to Education Office, American Astronomical Society, University of Delaware, Newark, DE, 19711.

CHEMISTS

Duties and Responsibilities

Remember high school chemistry class—bubbling beakers, litmus paper, and test tubes full of chemicals? Well, chemists make a career out of what we only began to study.

Over half of all chemists work in research and development (R and D), where they investigate the properties, composition, and structure of matter and the laws that govern the combinations of elements and reactions of substances. In theoretical R and D, they look for ways to unlock the secrets of the elements without worrying about practical uses or considerations. In applied R and D they create new products or improve existing ones, everything from discovering new synthetic fabrics to testing ways to solve problems like energy shortages and air pollution.

Some chemists work in production, detailing the processes for using and making chemicals and substances. Others work in sales and marketing of chemical products; still others teach in colleges and universities or are consultants to government or business.

Chemists often specialize. *Analytical chemists* analyze substances. Analyzing the moon rocks is one example of their work. *Organic chemists* study the chemistry of carbon compounds. Many of our modern commercial products have come out of these studies. *Inorganic chemists* study compounds other than carbon. For example, they may develop materials to use in solid-state electronic components. *Physical chemists* study the physical characteristics of atoms and molecules and investigate how chemical reactions work. Their efforts may result in new and better energy sources.

Chemists usually work in offices, classrooms, or laboratories. While some may be exposed to health or safety hazards, there is little risk if the proper precautions are followed.

Many chemists begin their careers by testing products, working in technical sales, or as assistants to senior chemists. As they gain experience and competence, they may advance to more responsible positions. An advanced degree also helps to speed career advancement.

Earnings and Opportunities

Over 113,000 people are employed as chemists, and employment opportunities are expected to increase 22 percent by the mid-1990s. The majority of opportunities should be in private industry, particularly in the area of new product development. Those with a bachelor's degree earn between $17,200 and $32,000; those with a master's make 20 percent more; and Ph.D.'s make 50 percent more. Experienced chemists earn between $40,000 and $60,000 and up.

Training and Qualifications

Besides being interested in the formal course work, including mathematics and science, chemists should be curious and imaginative. They should like performing experiments, and need to have patience and concentration for checking and double-checking their research.

While graduate training is required for most research jobs, a bachelor's degree in chemistry or a related field is sufficient for many beginning jobs. A Ph.D. is generally required for all advanced positions, including teaching.

For Further Details

American Chemical Society, 1155 16th St., N.W., Washington, DC 20036.

GEOLOGISTS

Duties and Responsibilities

Through their studies of rocks, the structure and development of the earth's crust and its interior, geologists have a hand in everything from piecing together the earth's history and locating oil and gas deposits, to determining the worthiness of construction sites and utilizing geothermal energy.

Geologists may work on site using tools such as hammers, chisels, gravity meters, and seismographs. They also examine chemical and physical properties of specimens in laboratories using complex instruments to determine

the structure of minerals or to study the formation of rocks. They sometimes use computers to record and analyze their various findings.

Geologists specialize, and some of the fields include the following: *Marine geologists*, who study the ocean floor, exploring its makeup and its potential for providing energy sources. *Petroleum geologists* help on specific drilling projects or provide maps and other information to help locate the best deposits; *economic geologists* locate earth materials such as minerals and solid fuels. *Engineering geologists* assist the construction industry by providing recommendations for the suitability of sites for buildings, roads, tunnels, dams, and other structures.

Volcanologists study volcanoes to try to predict their eruption and minimize damage. *Mineralogists* classify minerals and precious stones, and *geochemists* study the composition and changes in minerals and rocks to understand the distribution and migration of elements in the earth's crust. *Geomorphologists* study landforms and forces such as erosion and glaciation that cause them to change.

Geologists who specialize in earth history include *paleontologists*, who study plant and animal fossils to trace the evolution and development of past life; *geochronologists*, who determine the age of rocks and landforms by the decay of their elements; and *stratigraphers*, who study the distribution of sedimentary rock layers.

Relatively new fields include *astrogeologists*, who study geological conditions on other planets, and *geological oceanographers*, who study the rock on the ocean floor and continental shelf.

Most geologists work for private industry, primarily petroleum and mining related businesses. Some are employed by construction firms; others work for the government, usually in the Department of the Interior. Geologists also work for colleges and universities and at museums.

Work locations vary from mine shafts, building sites, archaeological digs, and volcanoes to laboratories, offices, and classrooms.

Geologists usually begin their careers in field exploration or as research assistants in laboratories. With experience, they can be promoted to project leaders, program managers, or other management and research positions.

Earnings and Opportunities

Over 34,000 people are employed as geologists, and employment opportunities are quite good. The number of geologists is expected to increase 24 percent in the next ten years. Salaries range from $22,500 to $48,000.

Training and Qualifications

Being analytical and curious, having the physical stamina needed for fieldwork, and possessing the ability to work as part of a team are important qualities for geologists.

A bachelor's degree in geology or a related field is required for most positions, and an advanced degree is important for promotion and for many college and research positions.

For Further Details

American Geological Institute, 4220 King St., Alexandria, VA 22302. Geological Society of America, Membership Dept., P.O. Box 9140, Boulder, CO 80301.

GEOPHYSICISTS

Duties and Responsibilities

When an expert is interviewed on a news broadcast about the size, force, and possible cause of a recent earthquake, that person is likely to be a geophysicist. Their work is to explore the physical properties and processes of the earth—including its electric, magnetic, and gravitational fields—and that study has important applications in mining, construction, and energy exploration.

Geophysicists usually specialize in one of three areas—solid earth, fluid earth, or upper atmosphere. Utilizing their knowledge of the physical aspects of the earth, solid earth geophysicists search for oil and mineral deposits, map the earth's surface, and study earthquakes. *Exploration geophysicists* search for oil and mineral deposits using seismic equipment with which sound waves are bounced off underground rock layers to determine the probability of locating oil. *Seismologists* study seismic data to locate earthquakes and faults; they study the effects of underground nuclear explosions; they assist in the planning for construction of bridges, dams, and buildings by evaluating the underground nature of proposed sites. Sometimes they use explosives or other methods to create sound waves that reflect off the bedrock. *Geodesists* study the size, shape, and gravitational field of the earth and other planets. Their principal task is to make the precise measurements necessary for accurate mapping of the earth's surface.

Hydrologists study the distribution, circulation, and physical properties of underground and surface waters. Some are concerned with water supply, irrigation, flood control, and soil erosion.

Geophysicists also study the atmosphere and investigate the complex nature of the earth's magnetic and electric fields. *Planetologists* study the composition and atmosphere of the moon, planets, and other bodies in the solar system.

Geophysicists' studies often involve the use of complex instruments. They use satellites to conduct tests from outer space, and computers to collect and analyze data.

Most work for oil, gas, or mining companies, either as consultants or in the areas of exploration, research, and education. Most divide their time between office responsibilities, laboratory time, and fieldwork, which may involve extended travel and research in remote areas.

With experience and usually some advanced education, geophysicists can advance to jobs such as project leader or program manager or other management and research jobs.

Earnings and Opportunities

Over 12,000 people are employed as geophysicists, and job prospects are excellent. The developing use of solar radiation and geothermal power to generate electricity, along with the search for oil, will contribute to the growth of employment. Earnings: $18,500 to $34,000 and up.

Training and Qualifications

Being analytical, curious, and having the ability to communicate well and work as part of a team are assets for geophysicists.

For most beginning jobs, a bachelor's degree in geophysics or a related specialty field is sufficient. Graduate training is important for those who want to advance or pursue careers in research or education.

For Further Details

American Geophysical Union, 2000 Florida Ave., N.W., Washington, DC 20009. Society of Exploration Geophysicists, P.O. Box 3098, Tulsa, OK 74101.

METEOROLOGISTS

Duties and Responsibilities

Weather affects what we wear, how a farmer plans his work, what route a plane flies, and even how our economy is doing in any given quarter. Meteorologists study the earth's atmosphere, and the best-known application of this science is to better understand and forecast the weather. It is vital and fascinating work.

In studying the atmosphere, scientists try to understand the physical characteristics, motion, and processes of the atmosphere and determine the way it affects our environment.

Meteorologists are also involved in related areas of air pollution control, fire prevention, agriculture, air and sea transportation, and they study the trends in the earth's overall climate.

Meteorologists who specialize in studying the weather are known as *operational meteorologists* and are the largest group of specialists. Using weather satellites and worldwide observers, they study current weather information such as air pressure, temperature, humidity, and wind velocity in order to make short- and long-range predictions. Although a few forecasters continue to prepare and analyze weather maps, most of the information today is analyzed by computer.

Physical meteorologists study the chemical and electrical properties of the atmosphere. They research the effect of the atmosphere on transmission of light, sound, and radio waves, as well as studying the factors that affect the formation of clouds, rain, snow, and other weather phenomena.

Climatologists study trends in climate and analyze past records on wind, rainfall, sunshine, and temperature to determine the general weather patterns that make up a region's climate. These studies are used to plan heating and cooling systems, design buildings, and aid in effective land utilization.

Thousands of members of the armed forces do forecasting and other meteorological work, and the largest employer of civilian meteorologists is the National Oceanic and Atmospheric Administration (NOAA), whose workers are stationed in all parts of the United States and in foreign countries. Commercial airlines also employ meteorologists to forecast weather along flight routes and to brief pilots on atmospheric conditions. Others work for private weather consulting firms; companies that design and manufacture meteorological instruments; and firms in aerospace, engineering, utilities, radio, television, and other areas.

(Your local TV weather person is probably a meteorologist.)

Weather stations are open around the clock, seven days a week, so the work of meteorologists frequently involves night work and rotating shifts.

Earnings and Opportunities

About 4,000 people work as meteorologists, and the employment outlook is fair, with a 14 percent increase in the number of jobs expected in the next decade. Earnings range from $13,800 to $90,000.

Training and Qualifications

An interest in science, the ability to concentrate on detail, and an inquisitive mind are good qualities for meteorologists.

The preferred educational requirement for entry-level jobs in weather forecasting is generally a bachelor's degree with a major in meteorology.

For Further Details

American Meteorological Society, 45 Beacon St., Boston, MA 02108. National Weather Service, Manpower Utilization Staff, Gramax Bldg., 8060 13th St., Silver Spring, MD 20910.

OCEANOGRAPHERS

Duties and Responsibilities

The earth's oceans are the province of the oceanographer, whose domain is a vast one— two-thirds of the earth's surface.

Oceanographers explore the ocean's potential as a source of food, fuel, and minerals, and gather information about the very nature of the earth itself. In addition to their work in the laboratory, these scientists work at sea and under it, on ships, in submersible vessels, and even as divers themselves.

Much of their time is spent analyzing information and examining and classifying different types of plant and animal life and

minerals. The oceanographer's tools include sonar equipment, microscopes, specialized mapmaking devices, computers, and computer-assisted equipment.

Most have a specialty. *Biological oceanographers* study plant and animal life in the ocean, which is helpful to the fishing industry. *Physical oceanographers* study the waves, tides, and currents and the relationship between the sea and the atmosphere in order to develop more accurate ways of predicting the weather. *Geological oceanographers* study the underwater mountain ranges, rocks, and sediments; and sometimes their knowledge contributes to finding valuable minerals, oil, and gas beneath the ocean floor. *Chemical ocean-ographers* study the chemical composition of ocean water and sediments as well as chemical reactions in the sea. *Oceanographic engineers* design and build instruments for oceanographic research and operations. They also lay cables and supervise underwater construction.

Many oceanographers work in colleges or universities; others are employed by the government (generally the Navy and the National Oceanic and Atmospheric Administration); some work in private industry, mainly in fishing, mining, or petroleum exploration.

Beginning oceanographers with a bachelor's degree usually start as research or laboratory assistants doing routine collection, computation, or analysis. As they gain experience, they may direct surveys and research programs or advance to administrative or supervisory jobs in research laboratories.

Earnings and Opportunities

Over 2,800 people work as oceanographers, and employment is expected to grow. Ocean research will be important to the mining and energy industries as they look for more ways to find and recover natural resources from the ocean floor. Salaries can range from $14,500 to $48,000, and some earn $50,000 and higher.

Training and Qualifications

Curiosity, analytical ability, the ability to work as part of a team, and the physical stamina to do fieldwork on ships are key qualities in this job.

A bachelor's degree in oceanography or a related field (biology, physical science) is a minimum requirement for entry into the field. Because competition is likely to be stiff in the coming years, those who have Ph.D.'s will have the best opportunities for employment and advancement.

For Further Details

American Society of Limnology and Oceanography, I.S.T. Bldg., Great Lakes Research Division, University of Michigan, Ann Arbor, MI 48109. International Oceanographic Foundation, 3979 Rickenbacker Causeway, Miami, FL 33149.

PHYSICISTS

Duties and Responsibilities

The physicist's job is to study and describe in mathematical terms the properties and interactions of matter and energy, from subatomic particles to the structure of the universe. They do this through systematic observation and experimentation. They explore the basic laws governing such principles as gravity, electromagnetism, and nuclear interactions; and their work has led to discoveries and innovations. For example, the flight of astronauts could never have been accomplished without the work done by physicists. Their knowledge of nuclear radiation has led to the use of irradiation therapy in medicine whereby harmful growths are destroyed while healthy tissues are preserved. In recent years, physicists have made great contributions to scientific progress in the areas of nuclear energy, electronics, communications, aerospace, and medical instrumentation.

The equipment they develop and use has also had practical application in other areas. For example, lasers, once found only in the physics lab, are now used in surgery, and microwave devices are now commonly found in ovens. Sophisticated measurement techniques developed by physicists are now also used to detect and measure the kinds and number of cells in blood or the amount of mercury or lead in foods.

Most physicists work in research and development. Some do theoretical research such as investigating the structure of the atom or the nature of gravity. Some physicists do applied research and help develop new products. For instance, advancements in solid-state physics led to the development of transistors and then to the integrated circuits used in calculators and computers.

Most physicists specialize in one or more branches of the science, and growing numbers are going into fields that combine physics and a related science, such as astrophysics, biophysics, chemical physics, and geophysics.

One-half of all physicists work for companies that manufacture electrical equipment, aircraft, missiles, or scientific instruments. Others teach and/or do research in colleges and universities; still others work for hospitals, commercial laboratories, and independent research organizations.

As they advance, they may become project leaders or research directors. Some rise to top management jobs. Those who develop new products or processes sometimes form their own companies.

Earnings and Opportunities

Over 37,000 people are employed as physicists, and the outlook for those with graduate degrees is very good during the coming years. Employment of physicists should increase 37 percent by 1995. Earnings range from $25,600 to $50,000 and more for those in management.

Training and Qualifications

Mathematical ability, an inquisitive mind, and a good imagination are necessary qualities for physicists. Graduate training in physics or a closely related field is almost essential for the majority of entry-level jobs and for advancement. Those with masters' degrees may qualify for some research jobs, and many teach and assist in research while studying for a Ph.D. The doctorate is usually required for full faculty status and for industrial or governmental jobs heading up research and development programs.

For Further Details

American Institute of Physics, 335 E. 45th St., New York, NY 10017.

Careers in Retailing

Retailing is where the final sales are made, where people get together, deals are struck, and money changes hands. After all the planning, designing, manufacturing, and shipping, someone must render the final service—selling the product.

There are giant nationwide firms and tens of thousands of entrepreneurs involved in this multibillion-dollar market. Career opportunities are bountiful, appealing to almost every type of personality and offering almost limitless growth.

Retailing allows for great job flexibility and plenty of opportunity for career mobility through on-the-job training and/or management development. One can rise within a store or organization (sales-clerk-to-store-manager stories are not unheard of), or move on to start one's own business based on the skills learned in another job. Another excellent career path for retailers has only recently started to open up. While apparel manufacturers traditionally have trained their own management, today they are looking to top retail managers to fill manufacturing management slots because of the retailers' knowledge of the customer.

Hard work—including some nights, weekends, and holidays—and a competitive spirit are vital, and for those with drive the possibilities are limited only by the imagination.

BUYERS

Duties and Responsibilities

When one thinks of a buyer one may well think of a store representative who is sent to Paris for the latest showing of the most famous designers, spending thousands, perhaps millions of dollars on goods to be brought back to the United States for resale.

While some buyers do travel to Europe and deal only in high fashion, there are many other types who are equally excited about their work. Think of it: Every department in large stores and discount chains has a buyer who selects the stock. If you're crazy about gardening tools or gadgets, china or children's wear, being a buyer may be a good career for you! If your interests are varied, no problem. Small stores are generally represented by only one or two buyers who may buy everything from flatware to clocks.

Good buyers have to develop a feel for what people want. They study market research reports, sales records, and constantly monitor consumer likes and dislikes. They read magazines and trade journals, observe competitors, and watch the economy in order to anticipate buying trends. Buyers must select merchandise that will sell quickly at well above the original cost, so they must also learn to accurately assess the resale value of goods.

To keep informed on existing products and the development of new ones, buyers attend trade shows and visit manufacturers' showrooms. Goods are usually ordered during these buying trips or when sales representatives call.

Understanding a budget is very important. Basic department needs must be planned for, and every buyer wants cash on hand for the latest hot item. Buyers have busy schedules, and their work is heavily people-oriented. In addition to working with manufacturers' representatives, they are in contact with store executives, assistant buyers, sales workers, and customers.

No job in retailing is likely to be nine to five, Monday through Friday, and being a buyer is no different. Special sales, conferences, and travel may mean more than a forty-hour week, and working Saturdays is not uncommon. The amount of travel varies with the type of merchandise, but most buyers spend at least four or five days a month on the road. Jobs are located throughout the U.S., though the majority of buying positions are found in metropolitan areas.

Most trainees begin as assistant buyers, selling merchandise, supervising salespeople, checking materials received, and keeping account of stock on hand. An experienced buyer may advance to merchandise manager, who oversees all buying and selling activities. Some later move up to executive jobs, such as general merchandise manager for a store or chain. Others use the job as a stepping-stone to having their own retail establishment.

Earnings and Opportunities

Over 150,000 people are employed as buyers, and the outlook for employment is very good, with a 30 percent increase projected in the next decade. Salaries range from $19,000 to $28,000, with some workers earning between $60,000 and $100,000.

Training and Qualifications

Buyers must be risk takers who have self-confidence, planning ability, and good judgment. Management skills must be acquired in order to supervise the sales staff, assistant buyers, and others. Retailing is a highly competitive business, and a buyer should like a fast-paced work life and do well under pressure.

An increasing number of employers prefer applicants who have a college degree. Many stores have training programs that combine classroom instruction with on-the-job experience.

For Further Details

National Retail Merchants Association, 100 W. 31st St., New York, NY 10001.

FASHION DESIGNERS

Duties and Responsibilities

The world of fashion design is an exciting, ever-changing one where creativity thrives; and while it may seem that one needs to be internationally famous in order to survive, that is actually not the case. There are plenty of jobs with clothing and accessory manufacturers and design houses, where many fashion designers are employed.

The responsibility of the fashion designer is to develop ideas for clothing production. They may be inspired by an old movie, a visit to a foreign country, or the idea may simply come about because of a combination of influences or because a specific need must be served, such as providing suitable business wear for the pregnant woman.

Designers record their ideas by sketching, draping, or sometimes by making patterns for them. Next, they select fabrics and trimmings that will allow a company to produce clothing within a certain price range and for the current market. Decisions vary depending on the prospective customer. For example, a famous designer might work with one type of design and fabric for his haute couture clients and then create different designs and choose less expensive fabrics when selling to the mid-range market. In many cases, designers oversee and supervise all stages of the production of the first garment and are completely responsible for finished work.

Some designers are self-employed and sell their ideas to various companies. Others design and oversee their own production. Design operations range from the men's wear designer who contracts to have his suits made in Hong Kong to the designer of children's sweaters who must supervise knitters who work in their own homes.

Design assistants work under the supervision of a designer and are generally responsible for transposing the sketches of the designer onto a model form using muslin. Next the assistant may work with the designer to select the fabric and special trimming.

With experience, assistants may eventually be responsible for working out the details of the designs and the sketches used by the production department.

Fashion adapters are the people who help make affordable designs that are similar to those of the trend-setting designers. They then work with the production department to select materials and production methods that enable the garment to be produced within the intended price range.

Earnings and Opportunities

Opportunities for employment are good. Earnings: $18,500 to $100,000 and up. Adapters and assistants make between $9,500 and $14,500.

Training and Qualifications

While creative talent and good ideas are by far the most important requirements for being hired, most who wish to enter the field have attended a two-year program in fashion design where they have gained an understanding of textiles, a knowledge of pattern-making and production techniques, as well as a background in clothing construction methods. Others have graduated from college with a major in fashion design.

IMAGE CONSULTANTS AND PERSONAL SHOPPERS

Duties and Responsibilities

Considering the needs of the client is the key ingredient to being a successful image consultant or personal shopper, two professions that are growing owing to the increasingly hectic pace of most business people's lives.

Personal shoppers may be self-employed or they may be on staff at better department stores, and their job is to see to the needs of people who want shopping assistance. For example, some department stores offer executive shopping services for business people (generally women); and customers, who have usually paid a membership fee, may phone in and

ask to see a selection of a certain type of clothing in a particular size. The personal shopper then prepares for the upcoming appointment with the client by gathering possible items from throughout the store. Generally, a selection of matching accessories will be brought in as well. The shopper then meets with the client in a private dressing room where the shopper facilitates the visit by switching sizes when necessary or combing the store's other departments for that perfect additional accessory. The shopper may also write up the order and see to having clothing tailored and/or mailed out if necessary.

At other times, personal shoppers are supplied by the store to help customers ranging from visiting foreign dignitaries to wealthy individuals who want to accomplish a lot of shopping on one trip. Functioning as a personal salesperson, the shopper shows the customer from department to department, handles packaging, sees to the sending of items, and generally does what he or she can to make the customer's visit a pleasant one.

Don't have time to shop for your mother's birthday present? Looking for the perfect sugar and creamer to go with your new dishes? A growing number of people have started businesses where they serve as personal shoppers for people who are too busy to shop for themselves. Sometimes charging by the hour, other times charging a percentage of the items purchased, these personal shoppers take care of any and all needs of their clients. Some set up a reminder system whereby they notify clients of birthdays and anniversaries. They consult with the client as to appropriate gifts and then take care of the shopping and wrapping.

Women have long had a reputation for having fine taste in what to wear, but with the increasing number of working women, more and more have realized that they really don't have any intuitive ability in selecting the right outfit for every occasion. What's more, they don't have the time. What they do have, though, is the money to pay someone to help them out, and this is the work of *image consultants*, a new breed of entrepreneur. Most consultants begin by doing an on-site analysis of the client's wardrobe, helping to select what items to keep. Next, an evaluation is given of what colors and styles are becoming to the client, and usually a shopping trip with the client follows in order to select the new items. Some consultants go so far as to provide a client with a chart to show what blouses go with what suits. Image consultants may charge per hour or per day, and some charge a percentage of the price of items purchased. Still others provide ongoing services for an annual fee. While some consultants do work with men, the growth in the field has been in serving the needs of businesswomen.

Earnings and Opportunities

Outlook for employment is good. Earnings: $14,500 to $24,000.

Training and Qualifications

The ability to understand the needs of others and a good eye for the aesthetically pleasing are helpful qualities for these workers.

While no particular training is required, most who do this type of work have at least some college education; and work experience in the retail field is helpful. Otherwise, drawing upon one's personal shopping skills is a very important part of succeeding.

IMPORT/EXPORT AGENTS

Duties and Responsibilities

Do you like foreign travel? Are you a good shopper? Do you have an eye for selecting bargains and/or choosing something that appeals to others? If so, you may be interested in becoming an importer (someone who brings goods into the U.S.) or an exporter (someone who finds foreign markets for American-made goods)—professions that can be both exciting and profitable. Imports and exports total in the hundreds of billions.

The kinds of goods traded between countries range from automobiles to children's shoes, from cameras to silk pajamas. The good agent diligently researches the market before selecting the merchandise. Are these items already available in the country where they would be sold, and if so, at what price? Import/export agents must also consider the cooperativeness of the governments involved, any rules and restrictions, customs duties to be paid, packing and shipping rules, and customs regulations, as well as how the items will be transported.

Once these details have been worked out,

outlets for selling must be found. Most agents prefer to sell the merchandise wholesale to department or specialty stores. Making the initial sales and establishing relationships can require a lot of time and legwork.

The amount of travel varies. Some agents prefer to spend a great deal of time traveling, seeking out new markets. Others make do with two or three buying trips a year and spend the remainder of the time at their home bases.

Though many people working in the import/export business are self-employed, some have become import traffic managers; others work for trade associations; and still others study to become customs attorneys or work as customs brokers who know how to get items through customs with as few problems as possible.

Earnings and Opportunities

Opportunities are good. Earnings: $25,600 to $200,000 and up.

Training and Qualifications

While there are no special educational requirements, many who enter the field have a college degree and/or work experience in some aspect of marketing or retailing. Knowledge of the language of the country with which one plans to work is also a help.

For Further Details

American Association of Exporters and Importers, 11 W. 42nd St., New York, NY 10036. World Trade Institute, 1 World Trade Center, New York, NY 10048.

MERCHANDISERS

Duties and Responsibilities

How many times have you stopped to look at an attractive display in a store window, then decided to go in and just "look around," and ended up buying something? Eye-catching store windows are one of the responsibilities of merchandisers, who advertise their stores' goods through the promotional display of merchandise. They design and install displays of clothing, accessories, furniture, food, electronics, and hundreds of other items in store windows, showcases, and on the sales floor.

Merchandisers use imagination and creativity as well as an understanding of color, composition, and design when creating an overall setting. They may choose a tennis-match theme, for example, to advertise sports equipment, clothes, and gear. Every seven to fourteen days they dismantle old displays and replace them with new ones.

In stores that employ a large staff of display workers, each one may specialize in an activity such as design, carpentry, painting, making signs, or setting up the displays. A display director usually supervises the activities of all

departments and confers with the store, merchandising, and sales manager to select merchandise for promotion and approve displays.

In smaller stores, merchandisers may construct some of the props themselves, using hammers, saws, and other tools. They may be assisted by carpenters or painters.

Most merchandisers are employed by department and clothing stores, but they are also employed by variety, drug, shoe, book, and gift shops. Some work on a freelance basis, and others work for manufacturers, either designing prepacked displays or working in the field to help clients properly display their merchandise.

Creating a design and then making it a reality can be very rewarding for the merchandiser. Normal hours are thirty-five to forty a week, though during busy seasons such as Christmas and Easter they may work nights and weekends to prepare special displays. Part-time help to model or demonstrate products may also be used.

A successful merchandiser might advance to become display director in a large store, and then progress to sales promotion director or head of store planning. Freelance work is another avenue for advancement. Those working for manufacturers usually end up with careers in sales and marketing.

Earnings and Opportunities

Over 26,000 people are employed as display workers, and job prospects are excellent. Earnings: $8,500 to $35,000.

Training and Qualifications

An eye for design, creative ability, imagination, manual dexterity, and mechanical aptitude are important qualifications for this job.

A high school diploma is the minimum requirement for most starting jobs. While many merchandisers learn their trade through informal on-the-job training, additional education is important for advancement. Display-related courses are offered at community and junior colleges, fashion and merchandising schools, and art schools. Some employers, especially manufacturers, seek applicants who have completed college courses in art, interior decorating, fashion design, advertising, marketing, or related subjects.

MODELS

Duties and Responsibilities

"More than just a pretty face" might well be said about the women and men who choose the modeling profession, for in addition to being attractive, models are performers—performers who must sell what they wear or the product they have been hired to demonstrate.

At the top of the profession are *photographic models,* who work mainly on a freelance basis for advertising agencies, magazines, and photographers. Theirs are the faces you see on magazine covers, billboards, and in advertisements of all kinds.

Fashion models generally work for clothing manufacturers, designers, department stores, or dress salons. They may model in formal runway fashion shows where their movements are carefully choreographed, usually against a backdrop of special lighting and music. They may also work in private showings, in stores, restaurants, or on the sales floor.

Showroom or *fitting models* are employed by clothing manufacturers to model for the buyers who visit the showroom. Models are also used to demonstrate new products and services at exhibits, trade shows, and sales meetings, or to appear at conventions, benefits, and political rallies. Some pose for painters, sculptors, photographers, or art students.

Television producers sometimes employ models in commercials or demonstrations of cosmetics, shampoos, and the like. Models with acting experience may be preferred.

Life as a model can mean trips to exotic locations, but it is also very physically demanding. Hours may be long and conditions may not always be ideal. A model often has to work under hot lights in the studio, but might also be expected to pose in a bathing suit on a cold beach in midwinter.

While full-time work is available, most models freelance through modeling agencies. During slow periods or while a model is building a reputation, assignments may be infrequent. Many models work at other jobs to support themselves.

Some models start their careers as children or teenagers and are able to move up in the profession as they gain exposure and experience. Many students, housewives, and actors use part-time modeling as a source of income. Most have to make it while they're young, since that is the look in greatest demand.

Modeling can be a stepping-stone to other jobs in the fashion field, such as consultant for a cosmetic firm or fashion coordinator for a department store. Some models become buyers or sales representatives, and a few go on to become actors or actresses.

Earnings and Opportunities

Over 60,000 people are employed as models, and job opportunities are good. Earnings: $15,000 to $50,000 and up.

Training and Qualifications

Models should enjoy working with people and should exhibit poise and self-confidence under pressure. Physical stamina is also important.

Most models have at least a high school education, while some have attended modeling school and others have been to college. A good portfolio of photographs is important in finding work, and being accepted by a modeling agency can be an enormous career boost.

For Further Details

World Modeling Association, P.O. Box 100, Croton-on-Hudson, NY 10520.

RETAIL SALESPEOPLE

Duties and Responsibilities

"May I help you?" These words spoken by a courteous, efficient salesperson can often make the difference between "sale" and "no sale" in a retail business.

A salesperson's primary job is to interest customers in merchandise, whether it's automobiles, refrigerators, video cassettes, or socks. This may entail reassuring a customer that a garment is becoming, checking the fit of a child's shoe, or explaining and demonstrating the various benefits of different models of dishwashers. In some jobs, such as selling books or computers, specialized knowledge is required. Most salespeople write out sales slips, receive cash payments, process charges, and give change and receipts. They handle returns and exchanges of merchandise, and also keep their area of the store neat. In small stores, they may help order merchandise, stock shelves, mark prices, take inventory, and prepare displays.

Salespeople are employed in stores of all kinds, from the small card shop employing one person to the giant department store with hundreds of workers.

Most salespeople work in comfortable environments, though car salespeople may have to be outdoors in bad weather.

Workweeks are usually forty hours. Because Saturday is a busy day in retailing, however, most employees work then and get a day off midweek. Evening work is common, and longer hours may be scheduled during Christmas and other peak sales periods. Part-time and temporary work is usually available.

One form of promotion for the salesperson is to graduate to selling "big ticket" (expensive) items such as large appliances, furniture, and rugs, on which commissions are usually paid.

Employers today tend to hire college graduates for management trainee positions. However, salespeople with less than a college diploma can still advance to administrative or supervisory positions. Retail experience can also be an asset in qualifying for sales work with wholesalers or manufacturers, where there are also good jobs to be had.

Earnings and Opportunities

Over 3 million people are employed in retail sales, and it is estimated that this number will increase about 25 percent in the next decade. While starting pay for salespeople is often minimum wage, those with experience or on commission can make between $12,000 and $48,000. Most employers allow salespeople to buy merchandise at a discount of 10 to 25 percent.

Training and Qualifications

Most employers expect applicants to have at least a high school education. Some have benefited from training received in high school distributive education programs (available in thousands of schools) where they worked part-time while taking courses in subjects such as merchandising and accounting. Adults can also benefit from these programs through adult and continuing education programs.

In small companies, new employees are likely to be trained by a more experienced worker; large stores usually have formal training programs.

For Further Details

U.S. Department of Education, Division of Vocational/Technical Education, Washington, DC 20202.

Careers in Sales

Whether we realize it or not, the business of selling affects each of us constantly. Virtually everything we possess and every service provided for us has been sold to someone by someone else, long before it was sold to us.

For example, someone persuaded the grocer to stock a certain type of tomato soup; someone else sold the drugstore chain on keeping your favorite shampoo in stock; still another salesperson sold you insurance on your car.

The sales field is made up of several levels of distribution, each one requiring its own brand of expertise, knowledge, and ability in order to meet the needs of its customers.

Direct sales are those made directly to the individual consumer and run the gamut from dinnerware sales made at home parties to the selling of insurance, real estate, stocks, bonds, or cosmetics. Most of these salespeople call on prospective customers by phone and in person.

Retail selling is what goes on in a store and covers items such as food, clothing, autos, appliances, and furniture, to name a few.

Wholesalers or *distributors* are the middlemen who buy from one party and sell to another, who then turns around and sells the product to a third. They take the risk of purchasing, warehousing, selling, and distributing products ranging from food to books. Wholesale salespeople may travel extensively, covering several states or even the entire nation.

Manufacturers or those who provide a service (such as insurance companies who sell financial protection) reach customers through a variety of means. Some do it through their own retail outlets; others work through wholesalers, distributors, or franchisees; still others utilize their own sales force to sell directly to retail outlets, other companies or individuals. Salespeople who are part of a manufacturer's sales force may have territories ranging from a large geographical area to a single city block.

Millions of men and women earn their living by selling, and because sales is such a vast field, there are great job opportunities. You can sell almost anything you'd like, depending on your interests and talent. What's more, sales positions are very rewarding, both personally and financially.

Salespeople are paid in many different ways, but usually it all boils down to how well each individual sells. In order to encourage maximum production, companies usually build a high degree of incentive into the earnings packages of salespeople; and salary, bonuses, commissions, and profit sharing may depend on performance. Salaries often range up to $100,000 or more.

Educational requirements vary. Some salespeople are high school or vo-tech grads, others have Ph.D.'s. Some companies prefer to train their own salespeople, and they look for bright, trainable individuals. Others prefer to hire people who already have applicable sales experience. Some companies seek out special expertise. To sell springs or variable drive motors, for example, you really need to be a mechanical engineer. Those in certain medical sales areas can benefit from a degree in biology or pre-med.

New employees generally start out as sales trainees, though they may have titles such as client development specialist or new accounts specialist. Once a salesperson has moved into management, advancement usually takes the form of a natural progression from a position such as sales manager to area manager, then marketing manager, regional manager, national sales manager, and vice president of sales. A career in sales can also lead to top management. Many presidents of Fortune 500 companies come from sales. In addition, many salespeople start their own businesses.

ADVERTISING SALES REPRESENTATIVES

Duties and Responsibilities

Advertising is very much a part of our society. We are constantly bombarded with messages from every side: on radio and television; in newspapers, magazines, and the yellow pages; as well as via billboards, direct mail, and through promotional items like giveaway calendars bearing company slogans.

When we think about the people behind the ads, most of us probably think of the creative team who conceived, wrote, filmed, drew, or photographed the piece. However, the person who assures that the ad is seen, not only by hundreds, thousands, or millions of people but by people likely to respond to the ad, is the advertising salesperson. (Titles range from account executive to media or space salesperson.)

As a representative of a particular advertising medium, the salesperson's job is to convince potential advertisers that their product or service will be more successful if it is advertised in his medium. Like any salesperson, he or she first must identify who is most likely to be interested in reaching his or her market. For example, one radio station might appeal to the teenage market, while another is geared to people who have retired. Newspapers, magazines, and TV programs all have specific audiences. The media go to great lengths to document their demographics and show what this means to the prospective buyer of advertising space or time. A salesperson must discuss with potential customers what it costs to reach each reader, viewer, or listener, and provide a comparison of this with the competition.

While the advertising salesperson does not usually write the finished ad, he or she (or a department within the company) may make creative suggestions to help a company visualize how its product or service could be sold.

A sale may take countless calls by phone or in person. It's not unusual to spend a year or more cultivating a relationship with a potential customer before the customer is ready to buy.

Once the sale is made, salespeople encourage the advertiser to monitor the response. The salesperson then uses those results to convince the company to continue or increase its advertising.

Earnings and Opportunities

There is always room for one more good salesperson on a staff. Earnings run from $14,800 to $22,000 for beginning sales reps, and from there to $60,000 and up for experienced reps.

Training and Qualifications

A congenial personality, the ability to manage one's own time, perseverance, and a goal-oriented approach are excellent qualities for advertising salespeople.

Background and educational requirements vary depending on the type of advertising being sold. Usually a degree in either marketing, advertising, business administration, or liberal arts is acceptable, although some technical publications may look for those with an engineering or scientific degree in the appropriate field.

Some companies take people from within the company who have no prior experience and develop them into salespeople; others hire only sales representatives with a background in their field and/or applicable sales experience.

For Further Details

Sales and Marketing Executives International, 6151 Wilson Mills Road, Suite 200, Cleveland, OH 44143.

AUCTIONEERS

Duties and Responsibilities

"Ten, twenty, twenty-five, thirty. Do I hear forty from the gentleman in the back of the room? Who'll give me fifty? Do I hear fifty?" Who hasn't heard and admired the remarkable pace and patter of the auctioneer?

What they sell ranges from paintings and jewelry to automobiles and household items as well as farms, farm equipment, livestock, real estate, and government surplus items. Depending on their specialty, they may auction fine art at outstanding auction houses in New York City or San Francisco, or they may preside on site at estate and bankruptcy sales or sell livestock at county fairs.

Though they are certainly at their most visible when actually conducting an auction, auctioneers actually have many responsibilities in order to prepare for the event. They must be very knowledgeable in their fields, since their duties begin with the appraisal of the items to be sold. Next, a decision must be reached as to whether to sell items separately or in lots. Then items must be listed, tagged, and put on display. The auctioneer may also be responsible for advertising the auction and preparing the catalog.

Once the auction begins, the auctioneer is responsible for keeping things moving, and a strong ability to sell is paramount. In many ways, the auctioneer may demonstrate hard sell at its finest. The item must be clearly described, and all benefits or special features pointed out. Once the bidding begins, the auctioneer must be aware of all interested parties and keep careful track of where the bidding is at all times. Keeping the crowd interested is also a challenging part of the work.

Most auctioneers are self-employed, and their ability to get work obviously depends strongly on their reputations. They are usually paid on a commission basis, typically 6 percent for real estate auctions and 20 percent or more for household items, so there is great pressure to perform well.

The work is very fast-paced, and many auctioneers primarily do their work outdoors. They may often travel in order to take certain jobs within their specialty. Night and weekend work is common, and some specialties are seasonal.

Earnings and Opportunities

Opportunities for auctioneers are good, and the field itself is growing. Earnings for a successful auctioneer can be as high as $40,000 to $50,000.

Training and Qualifications

Sales ability, good business sense, a talent for holding the attention of a crowd, and extensive knowledge in one's field are important qualities for auctioneers.

Auctioneers come from a variety of backgrounds, and there is no specific educational requirement. Some auctioneers learn their trade by working with established auctioneers; others attend special schools of auctioneering.

For Further Details

National Auctioneers Association, 135 Lakewood Dr., Lincoln, NE 68510. American Society of Auctioneers, 4209 Lindell Blvd., Suite 408, St. Louis, MO 63108.

AUTO AND CAR PARTS SALES REPRESENTATIVES

Duties and Responsibilities

Americans love their cars, and whether it's buying a brand new automobile or picking up a part for their current one, they want to be dealing with knowledgeable and responsible salespeople.

In making a sale, a *car salesperson* must first identify the customer's needs. Is he looking for a fancy sports car or a family car that gets good mileage? The salesperson then helps the customer select the type of car that meets those needs and tells him about such aspects of performance as mileage, ride, and handling. Car prices are negotiable, so the salesperson must be good at getting the best price possible and closing the sale.

Once the sale is made, sales workers fill out the necessary forms for license plates and registration and may arrange for financing and insurance as well.

Car salespeople are usually assigned showroom hours (frequently evenings or weekends) when they help walk-in customers. However, successful salespeople also develop and follow up leads in order to meet their sales quotas.

Salespeople with managerial ability may advance to assistant sales manager, sales manager, or general manager. Others open their own dealerships or may become partners in one.

Car parts salespeople generally work for wholesale and retail automobile parts stores selling to repair shops, service stations, mechanics, and do-it-yourselfers. Sales reps frequently sell a wide variety of parts for many makes and models of vehicles, so they must be able to quickly identify and locate any of the parts requested. When a part is unavailable, the salesperson may look for an interchangeable part or place a special order.

In addition to writing up orders and collecting payments, salespeople also keep parts catalogs and price lists up to date, replenish stock, and unpack incoming shipments. In some firms, they may also repair parts.

Parts salespeople generally work a forty-hour week, which may include some work on Saturday and Sunday, when some shops are open.

Those with ability may become department managers or store managers. Some become outside sales representatives for parts wholesalers and distributors selling parts to repair shops, service stations, trucking companies, and other businesses. Some open their own shops.

Earnings and Opportunities

Over 157,000 people work as car salespeople, and about 105,000 are employed as car parts salespeople. Car salespeople are paid by commission on sales, and earnings run from $12,000 to $85,000. Parts salespeople earn $10,000 to $28,000.

Training and Qualifications

A high school diploma is generally the minimum educational requirement for car sales. Previous sales experience or other work requiring contact with the public is also helpful.

Most learn the business on the job. In large

dealerships, on-the-job training may be preceded by classroom training on how to follow up leads, make sales presentations, and close sales.

Parts salespeople also learn on the job, usually starting as parts deliverers or trainees.

For Further Details

National Automobile Dealers Association, 8400 Westpark Dr., McLean, VA 22102. Automotive Service Industry Association, 444 N. Michigan Ave., Chicago, IL 60611.

COMPUTER SALES REPRESENTATIVES

Duties and Responsibilities

The computer field is booming, and sales opportunities in data processing are both diverse and plentiful. Salespeople may find themselves selling any one of a variety of products, including mainframes (large computers like those used by the airlines to keep track of reservations), minicomputers (small computers used by businesses to do things like payroll, inventory, billing, and accounting), and microcomputers (machines such as word processors, personal computers, and the automatic cash registers found in fast food restaurants). Salespeople must also be knowledgeable enough to sell software (the programs that tell the computers what to do, such as computing taxes, updating inventory, analyzing marketing statistics, and literally thousands of other functions) and peripheral equipment (printers, drafting equipment, and machine tools).

The salesperson begins by calling on prospective clients and exploring their needs. He or she then recommends the data processing equipment that will enable the client to save money and produce more work faster and better. (The service the computer can provide is what's important to the client—not the hardware itself—and this is always the sales rep's selling point.) Some sales are relatively simple and may be accomplished in a short time. Others are highly complex and may take six months, a year, or longer to complete.

Even after installation of a new system, the salesperson keeps in close touch with the client to make sure that everything goes according to plan, and the client usually turns to the original salesperson when problems arise.

As the new computers are brought on line, the salesperson also looks for opportunities to sell related products such as paper for the printer or additional terminals. Salespeople spend much of their time out of the office. They also handle correspondence and keep up-to-date on their company's latest products as well as those of the competition.

Earnings and Opportunities

In the next decade there will be tremendous growth in the computer field, and much of this will be in the areas of sales and service. Opportunities to move into management will increase. Earnings range from about $16,800 to $24,500 to start, and from there to $58,000 and above for management positions.

Training and Qualifications

A college degree is preferable in this field and is a requirement for those who aspire to move into management. Because the clientele is so diverse (including a great many engineers, scientists, accountants, marketing experts, and business people) degrees and experience in accounting, business, or engineering are advised.

Most companies have their own training programs. However, any additional courses in sales, marketing, management, and data processing will be beneficial. Those who want to get ahead should keep on the cutting edge of innovation, both as learners and teachers, reading extensively and writing for publication as well.

For Further Details

Sales and Marketing Executives International, 6151 Wilson Mills Road, Suite 200, Cleveland, OH 44143.

DIRECT SALES REPRESENTATIVES

Duties and Responsibilities

Companies such as Mary Kay, Amway, Tupperware, and Avon have grown into multimillion-dollar success stories because of direct sales representatives who work from their homes. Personal flexibility and the possibility of very substantial incomes are the benefits to the salespeople who select this line of work.

The basic responsibilities of the direct salespeople are to solicit orders, collect payments, and then deliver the merchandise. Keeping inventory and accurately recording transactions are important parts of the job.

Salespeople sell everything from kitchenware and household products to jewelry, cosmetics, and clothing. They become the representatives of the companies whose products interest them, and generally learn the trade by attending several company-sponsored training sessions. The company then supplies a sales kit that includes instructions, samples, catalogs, price sheets, and other sales support information. Some companies require salespeople to sell from stock they have purchased, which means that an initial outlay of cash is required, and representatives must take the chance that they will be able to sell what they've bought.

Some companies encourage one-on-one selling; others advocate sales parties and build in incentives in the form of free gifts for friends or neighbors who will sponsor selling parties for the representatives—the higher the sales volume for the party, often the better the gift! The aim of most salespeople is to build a steady clientele who will buy from them regularly.

Representatives attend regularly scheduled sales meetings that are designed to keep enthusiasm high. Incentives are important.

Earnings are on commission, and the representative's percentages are sometimes increased after certain sales levels are reached. Some companies also pay representatives a percentage on any sales of representatives whom they have recruited for the company. And of course, Mary Kay is known for the pink Cadillacs she presents to representatives who produce a high volume of sales for the year.

Earnings and Opportunities

Over 3 million people are employed in direct sales, and opportunities are excellent. Earnings range from $100 per week for those who work part-time to $35,000 a year and up.

Training and Qualifications

Direct selling offers excellent opportunities for all types of people, and a desire to sell is the main qualification for entering the field. While it may attract anyone who wants to be self-employed, it may be especially appealing to those who need additional flexibility, such as moonlighters, mothers of small children, students, and retirees. It combines the benefits of setting one's own hours with the possibility of establishing a successful, lucrative career in sales.

For Further Details

For *Who's Who in the Direct Selling Industry* (a list of potential companies to represent), send a stamped, self-addressed envelope to the Direct Selling Association, 1730 M St., N.W., Washington, DC 20036, or write: The Council on Opportunities in Selling, Inc., 630 Third Ave., New York, NY 10017.

FOOD SALES REPRESENTATIVES

Duties and Responsibilities

The Coke on the supermarket shelf, the steak you ate at a restaurant the other night, and the jar of imported mustard at the specialty shop down the street all share at least one thing in common: a food sales representative helped bring each to the marketplace. What's more, a recent survey of the food industry shows that sales representatives are currently in great demand.

Food salespeople are usually assigned to cover a certain territory, within which they are responsible for cultivating all potential customers. Representatives set priorities for sales calls according to whom they think will buy and/or consume the greatest quantity of their products. They then make appointments to see purchasing agents, and in person they provide information about their products, usually emphasizing strengths like quality, price, delivery, planned ad campaigns, and public acceptance.

Once an order is placed, salespeople complete all paperwork and tell the company how much merchandise should be shipped. In some cases, they also check customer credit, although this is more frequently done by another department of the company.

Salespeople also provide feedback from the field. They listen carefully to the needs of their clients and report back to the company's marketing departments, which can then evaluate the information in terms of design, packaging, and marketing of future products.

Some food salespeople represent manufacturers and sell food by the carload to wholesalers and large food and drug chains; others sell directly to specialty stores; some work as local merchandisers helping store managers set up special displays to boost sales. Others represent either manufacturers or wholesalers and sell directly to the end user or retailer, such as restaurants, schools, hospitals, bakeries, or other food manufacturers.

Food sales representatives suffer the same ups and downs, successes and disappointments, as all salespeople. They spend a lot of time driving and/or waiting to talk to purchasing agents. They also spend their days planning their schedules, making appointments, and studying literature about the company's products. In some cases, representatives are away from home for extended periods of time.

Advancement opportunities are excellent. Those who demonstrate talent and ability can move into management and may become area, district, regional, or divisional managers.

Earnings and Opportunities

There will always be a need for food sales representatives, and the job outlook is excellent for the coming years. Earnings range from $15,000 to start to $26,000 and higher for specialty sales and management positions.

Training and Qualifications

Optimism, warmth, a desire to meet new people and expand one's horizons are all good qualities for those who would like to try sales as a career. A desire for recognition and a willingness to try new ideas will also prove helpful.

Some food sales organizations will accept applicants with a high school diploma, but most require some college education. Although exceptional sales and managerial talent will always be recognized, promotion possibilities will be enhanced by a college degree in business or marketing. In some circumstances, a degree in hotel management can be very helpful.

For Further Details

Sales and Marketing Executives International, 6151 Wilson Mills Road, Suite 200, Cleveland, OH 44143.

MANUFACTURERS' SALES REPRESENTATIVES

Duties and Responsibilities

In any manufacturing company, the sales force is vitally important. Its success is crucial to the company's bottom line. And because they are so visible, talented sales representatives can use that opportunity to shine. Thus, it is not unusual for top executives to have risen from the ranks of salespeople.

A sales representative visits prospective buyers to analyze their needs, to tell them about his company's products, and suggest how these products can meet the buyers' needs. Prospective buyers may be factories, banks, schools, hospitals, wholesale or retail firms, to name a few. If the buyer is convinced, a sale will be made. Sometimes representatives promote their products at trade shows and conferences.

Technical salespersons, also called industrial salespersons, sell products such as electronic equipment or major machinery, which can be quite expensive. For that reason they do more than extol the virtues of their product. For example, they may recommend new manufacturing techniques and supply the buyer with additional technical data or estimates of cost savings through the use of their product. They present this information to company officials, all in an effort to negotiate a sale. The process may take many months. Sometimes they work with engineers in their own companies adapting products to customers' special needs. In addition, technical salespeople sometimes train customers' employees to operate and maintain new equipment, and they make frequent visits to make certain that it is functioning properly.

Manufacturers' sales representatives spend most of their time visiting prospective customers. They also prepare reports on sales prospects, plan their work schedules, draw up lists of prospects, make appointments, handle correspondence, and study literature about their products.

Large numbers of salespeople are employed by the printing and publishing, chemical, fabricated metal products, electrical, and other machinery industries, as well as the transportation industry. Some work out of a company's home office, often located at a manufacturing plant. The majority, however, work out of branch offices. In addition, there are many independent sales representatives who freelance as manufacturers' representatives.

Earnings and Opportunities

Over 440,000 people are employed as manufacturers' sales reps, and the outlook for employment is quite good. Most companies pay salespeople a combination of salary and commission, salary and bonus, or salary, commission, and bonus. Earnings range from around $17,000 to $23,600 at the entry level, up to $100,000 and higher.

Training and Qualifications

An interest in selling, the ability to manage one's own time, and a pleasant personality and appearance are helpful qualities for sales representatives.

A college degree is becoming increasingly desirable. Manufacturers of nontechnical products usually seek graduates with degrees in liberal arts or business administration, while manufacturers of technical products prefer those with degrees in science or engineering.

Many companies, especially those that manufacture technical products, have formal training programs for beginning sales reps that last two years or longer.

For Further Details

Manufacturers' Agents National Association, P.O. Box 16878, Irvine, CA 92713.

SALES ADMINISTRATORS

Duties and Responsibilities

Making the sale may be the name of the game in business, but no one knows better than the sales administrator how important it is to watch what it costs to produce that sale.

Unlike the sales manager who goes out into the field to hire, train, supervise, and motivate salespeople, the sales administrator stays in the home office and picks up the loose ends. This vital and important function frees the sales manager to do his or her job while at the same time providing the sales force with all of the necessary backup and data that they require in order to perform their jobs more effectively and efficiently.

As part of the sales and marketing team, sales administrators participate in decision making, forecasting and preparation of annual sales and marketing budgets, and they prepare related reports. They also analyze monthly sales reports and compare those figures with the cost of sales to determine whether or not the department is meeting or exceeding its profit margins. In so doing, they investigate areas where sales were too costly and make recommendations to upper management as to how sales could be increased or expenses reduced in order to improve profitability.

In some cases, sales administrators are responsible for handling consumer complaints and distributor claims. They may also work with the legal department to see that all product labeling and documentation are in full compliance with state and federal licensing statutes.

Administrators are deeply involved in the preparation of price schedules and keep on top of competitive pricing analysis, new product development, and price changes. They also oversee the commission rates and expenses of the sales staff, making sure that they meet company policies and procedures.

Earnings and Opportunities

There are excellent opportunities in this fast-paced field, since the economic belt-tightening of the 1980s has led an increasing number of companies to expect more production from their sales staffs. Earnings range from $15,000 for assistant administrators to over $50,000 for senior administrators with departmental authority.

Training and Qualifications

Attention to detail, working well as part of a team, and having the ability to direct the efforts of tough, hard-driving salespeople are important qualifications for this job.

While a few individuals start work in secretarial or clerical positions and work their way up to be sales administrators, most people in these jobs are college graduates. Though the field of specialty varies, courses in accounting, statistics, and marketing are an asset; and certainly those with degrees in business administration increase their opportunities to advance in the field.

For Further Details

Sales and Marketing Executives International, 6151 Wilson Mills Road, Suite 200, Cleveland, OH 44143.

SALES MANAGERS

Duties and Responsibilities

For a fascinating, challenging, ever-changing career, it's hard to beat working in sales, and those who move into sales management will find that being in charge of this important aspect of business is exciting as well as personally and financially rewarding.

Sales management comes under many different titles, often dictated by the area that the job controls. Branch manager; area manager; zone, district, regional, or national manager; as well as international manager all describe jobs involving sales management.

One of the major functions of the position is to recruit, hire, train, and organize a staff of salespeople. Setting territories, assigning accounts, and seeing that new salespeople are properly trained and that existing staff are kept up to date on the latest product information and sales techniques are all part of the job. Both classroom and field instruction methods are used, and sometimes sales managers accompany staff members on sales calls, either to introduce new workers to existing accounts or to observe a salesperson in action.

Sales managers also run sales meetings, set up motivational contests, and plan for and organize regional or national sales meetings. Attendance at trade shows and association meetings and writing for trade magazines are also important. Managers may also write or oversee the preparation of sales training materials and sales manuals as well as bulletins and newsletters.

Sales managers usually work very closely with the marketing department to develop and implement a comprehensive marketing plan and to aid in market research and new business development in order to have the necessary advertising and promotional support needed by their field staffs. Some companies even connect the two departments by having them report to one person, who usually holds the title of vice president of sales and marketing.

Sales managers usually set their own budgets and have full profit and loss responsibility for their operations. They are responsible for sales department customer relations and are often involved in developing proposals and making bids and negotiating sales agreements on deals made with both industry and government.

If a company sells through other outlets, the sales manager may work with the dealers, distributors, or franchisees in order to help train their sales forces in product knowledge and sales techniques. They also help these groups develop and implement their own marketing plans.

Sometimes sales managers work with the engineering and production departments to improve the company product and/or their service. Because of the information salespeople bring in from the field, they can keep the design department apprised of any innovations by the competition and can provide direct feedback from customers.

In some businesses, sales managers must be familiar with federal and state regulations on sales activities, especially when they are involved with multilevel sales departments, franchising operations, independent contractors, or manufacturers' representatives.

Top sales managers frequently have the opportunity to move into corporate management; a good number rise to head major companies, since selling provides an excellent background for running a corporation.

Earnings and Opportunities

There are probably more opportunities in sales than in any other field today, so the outlook for employment is excellent. Earnings range from $22,000 a year to $100,000 and above, with some in top management making more than $250,000 annually.

Training and Qualifications

A talent for motivating others and the ability to sell are important qualifications for sales managers.

As in all sales fields, these workers come from different walks of life and various educational backgrounds. A college education is not always required, but most large firms look first for those who have a college degree. Those with an M.B.A. or who further their education by taking courses in marketing and sales, advertising, contract negotiations, employee recruitment, training retention, or motivation stand a better chance of reaching corporate headquarters. In the final analysis, however, it is the ability to sell and to develop that skill in others that ultimately counts in this job.

For Further Details

Sales and Marketing Executives International, 6151 Wilson Mills Road, Suite 200, Cleveland, OH 44143.

WHOLESALE TRADE SALES REPRESENTATIVES

Duties and Responsibilities

Have you ever wondered how the corner pharmacy or the neighborhood hardware store obtains the merchandise it sells? Each probably bought it from a wholesale trade salesperson whose job is to visit local retailers and industrial and commercial firms and sell them goods at wholesale. As representatives of wholesale distributors, they offer the buyer the convenience of not having to deal with a multitude of manufacturers' representatives.

Wholesale trade sales representatives visit buyers for retail, industrial, and commercial firms, as well as institutions such as schools and hospitals. They show samples, pictures, or catalogs that list the products they carry. A sales representative for a wholesale stationery distributor, for example, may visit buyers at local stores several times a year to show notepaper, greeting cards, or envelopes made by several different manufacturers. Wholesale salespeople provide retailers with a great many services. They may check the store's stock and order items that will be needed before the next visit. They help retailers improve or update ordering and inventory systems and advise them about advertising, pricing, and window and counter displays. Sales representatives keep records of sales, forward orders to their wholesale houses, prepare reports and expense accounts, plan work schedules, draw up lists of prospects, and make appointments.

The largest employers of wholesale reps are firms that sell machinery to industrial and business users. Other major employers are companies that sell food products, motor vehicles and parts, hardware, plumbing, and electrical goods.

Most sales reps operate out of offices in wholesale houses, although they spend most of their time out of the office. Depending on the product sold, the size of their territory might range from a small section of a city to several states.

Sales reps often work long, irregular hours. Although they call on customers during business hours, they may travel at night or on weekends to meet their schedules. They may spend evenings writing reports and orders.

Experienced workers with leadership and sales ability may advance to supervisor, sales manager, or other executive positions.

Earnings and Opportunities

Over 1.1 million people work as wholesale salespeople, and employment is expected to rise 27 percent in the next ten years. Workers are sometimes paid a commission in addition to a salary. Earnings range from $15,000 to $90,000 and up.

Training and Qualifications

A willingness to work hard, the ability to manage one's own time, and a neat and friendly appearance are helpful qualities for future wholesale representatives.

Background requirements depend on the product line and market. Certain products require technical backgrounds. For example, drug wholesalers look for people with a college degree in chemistry, biology, or pharmacy.

Some employers hire high school graduates as sales trainees. They may work in several non-selling jobs before actually working with experienced salespeople.

For Further Details

Sales and Marketing Executives International, 6151 Wilson Mills Road, Suite 200, Cleveland, OH 44143.

ENTERTAINMENT AND LITERARY AGENTS

Duties and Responsibilities

Contrary to popular belief, Americans are not totally committed to the idea of "do it yourself." Just as often, American ingenuity means that when we need something done, we seek out someone who can do the job for us and do it better.

All kinds of people use agents: actors, athletes, writers, entertainers, models, job seekers, employers, home buyers and sellers and renters. And for good reason. Our society has become much more complicated, and most of us cannot begin to cope single-handedly with its complexities. Our choices of jobs, where we live, salaries, and so forth have become so broad that we need someone to help us.

Talent agents represent actors, athletes, concert artists, and models. They book engagements for their clients and negotiate the terms of their contracts. They stipulate services to be performed, hours, remuneration, including wages, share of gate, bonuses, residuals, fringe benefits, expenses, and the promotion that will be done on behalf of the client. In this capacity, agents are essentially salesmen and, like any salesman, must be realistic about the strengths and weaknesses of their "product," and they must know the market.

In addition, many agents advise and counsel clients on investments, tax shelters, and other financial matters. Agents or their assistants may also make travel and hotel arrangements, and in general smooth the way for each engagement.

Agents' backgrounds vary. Some come from the business management, consulting, accounting, or legal profession; others are themselves former actors, athletes, or entertainers.

They are normally paid a percentage of each contract they arrange. Most are self-employed, but as their lists of clients grow most add other agents and support people to their staffs.

Literary agents represent writers. They know the ins and outs of the publishing industry, and keep up with the book market. Many literary agents were formerly editors for publishing houses before starting their own agencies or joining existing ones. A few have editors on their staffs to review materials submitted by authors, and in some cases help the author fine-tune a piece. When an agent finds a property he likes and thinks is marketable, he submits it to one or more publishers. Once the sale is agreed upon, the agent then negotiates the advance, the rate of royalties to be paid on book sales and TV, movie, paperback, and foreign rights. Agents are paid a percentage of the authors' advances and royalties.

Agents in every industry experience the thrill of launching real talent, but they also know the frustration of not being able to find the right "home" for a person or property in which they strongly believe. In the beginning of their careers especially, agents must be prepared to face both lean and plentiful times.

Earnings and Opportunities

Opportunities in the field will continue to grow. Earnings range from $8,000 for part-time involvement to more than $100,000.

Training and Qualifications

Business sense, negotiating skills, confidence, and a willingness to take risks are good qualities for agents.

There is no one specific educational requirement for becoming an agent, although the majority are college educated.

Agents have always tended to be business-oriented entrepreneurs, but more and more agents today are college graduates who enter the profession to make a living using their knowledge and love of music, theater, movies, or books. Those with training in accounting, law, or financial management have an advantage, and can offer clients additional services based on that background.

For Further Details

Independent Literary Agents Association, Box 5257, FDR Station, New York, NY 10150; Society of Authors' Representatives, Box 650, Old Chelsea Station, New York, NY 10113.

INSURANCE AGENTS AND BROKERS

Duties and Responsibilities

Insurance agents and brokers are in the business of selling protection. They ensure that we have the financial resources we need in the event of loss of life, health, or property. The best insurance salespeople are experts at matching a customer's needs with the right kind of coverage for the best price.

Insurance agents and brokers do basically the same kind of work. An agent, however, works for a specific insurance company, while a broker is an independent business person who represents a number of different companies and places policies directly with the particular company that best suits a client's needs.

Agents and brokers sell three basic types of insurance: life, property-liability (casualty), and health. Life insurance agents, sometimes called life underwriters, offer policies that pay out when a policyholder dies. Depending on the situation, a life policy can also be designed to provide retirement income, funds for children's education, or other benefits desired by a family.

Casualty insurance agents sell policies that protect individuals and businesses from financial losses resulting from car accidents, fire, theft, or other misfortunes. In industrial or commercial policies, casualty insurers cover such items as workers' compensation, product liability, and medical malpractice.

Many life and casualty agents also sell health insurance policies that cover the costs of hospital and medical care or loss of income due to illness or injury. Some agents also advise clients about securities, such as mutual fund shares or variable annuities.

The insurance industry is very much affected by social change. More women in the work force, for example, means an increasing need for women to buy life and disability insurance. Rising incomes stimulate a need for annuities and other investment products. In addition, product liability, legal, kidnapping, and pollution insurance are all areas where sales are likely to expand.

Agents and brokers may work evenings or weekends to suit the convenience of customers, and some work part-time.

Advancement may mean moving up to become sales manager in a local office; some become company vice presidents. One out of four establish their own agencies or brokerage firms.

Earnings and Opportunities

More than 325,000 people are employed as insurance agents or brokers, and the outlook for employment is quite good, with a 25 percent increase in this number projected over the next decade. After the initial training period, starting salaries range from $16,300 to $19,600. Many work on a commission basis, and earnings for experienced agents and brokers range from $20,000 to over $100,000.

Training and Qualifications

While employers prefer college graduates, many high school graduates with potential are hired for this line of work. Agents and brokers must be licensed.

For Further Details

The National Association of Life Underwriters, 1922 F St., N.W., Washington, DC 20006. Insurance Information Institute, 110 William St., New York, NY 10038. Independent Insurance Agents of America, 100 Church St., New York, NY 10007.

REAL ESTATE AGENTS AND BROKERS

Duties and Responsibilities

Selling real estate can be a very lucrative way of making a living for the go-getter who enjoys helping a family or business owner find the right property to buy.

Most real estate agents and brokers deal in residential property. To answer the questions of potential buyers, they must know the local housing market and the location of schools, churches, synagogues, shopping facilities, and public transportation. They must also be thoroughly familiar with tax rates and local zoning laws, and know where to obtain financing for a purchase.

Others, usually agents in larger firms, specialize in commercial, industrial, or other types of real estate. The agent or broker who sells or leases business property must understand leasing practices, business trends, and location needs. Those who sell or lease industrial properties must also know about transportation, utilities, and labor supply.

Agents spend a great deal of time meeting with potential buyers to assess what they want and can afford, and they may have to show many homes before getting a favorable response. Agents also obtain listings, which are owner agreements to sell their properties through the agent's firm. Much time is spent on the phone following up on leads gathered from advertisements and personal contacts.

Brokers are independent business people who not only sell real estate but also rent and manage properties, make appraisals, and develop new building projects. They manage their own offices, advertise properties, and handle other business matters.

Most real estate firms are relatively small; some brokers operate a one-person business. Large firms may have several hundred real estate agents operating out of many branch offices. A growing number of brokers, currently about 30 percent, have entered into franchise agreements with national or regional real estate organizations. With a franchise, the broker pays a fee in exchange for the privilege of using the more widely known name of the parent organization.

Most of the agent's time is spent outside the office, showing properties and meeting with prospective clients. They usually work long hours—often more than fifty a week. Evening and weekend work is common in order to suit the convenience of clients.

Earnings and Opportunities

Over 580,000 people sell real estate as their primary occupation, and many others sell on a part-time basis. The outlook for employment is excellent. The number of jobs is expected to increase 33 percent in the next ten years. Earnings are based on commissions and range from $15,000 to over $100,000.

Training and Qualifications

Maturity, honesty, a neat appearance, and enthusiasm are important qualities for real estate agents. Like all salesmen, they must be able to sense the needs of customers and motivate them to buy.

All agents and brokers must be licensed throughout the United States. All states require prospective agents to be high school graduates who are at least eighteen years old, and candidates must pass a written test.

Training is available at colleges and schools or through large real estate firms.

For Further Details

National Association of Realtors, 430 N. Michigan Ave., Chicago, IL 60611.

Careers in Service Occupations

Far from the whir of giant industry there are scores of jobs in businesses that are vital to each of us because they provide important services that meet many of our day-to-day needs. We hardly think of them on a regular basis, but without them we'd be lost.

Consider the individual skills and contributions of the barber, the floral designer, jeweler, funeral director, furniture upholsterer, to name just a few. Some of these jobs require creative and technical skills, with talents passed down through generations of specialists. Others are relatively new, designed to meet the ever-changing needs of our rapidly growing society. But whatever their particular route of development, these numerous service occupations offer rewarding careers. Many provide the advantages of self-employment, and for those who enjoy the challenge of running a business, these jobs are hard to beat.

ANTIQUES DEALERS

Duties and Responsibilities

Is the chair Chippendale or Hepplewhite? What's the market right now for a Queen Anne chest? Is the Tiffany lamp authentic? These are the questions antiques dealers must consider as they evaluate whether or not to acquire certain items for resale.

Recent economic changes have brought a new focus to the work of antiques dealers as more and more people turn to these collectibles as a hedge against inflation. To the dealer, this means an increase in possible customers as well as added competition on the market.

The basic job of the antiques dealer is to buy available goods at the lowest price possible in order to resell them at a profit. They shop at estate sales, secondhand shops, garage sales, private homes, and at auctions. Part of the challenge of the job is being able to identify the period and authenticity of many items ranging from clocks and cradles to the finest in glassware. Shopping for goods may require travel, often to remote areas, in order to find the best buys. Trips abroad are frequent for dealers who specialize in certain period items. Some antiques dealers develop a specialty and shop only for antique jewelry, toys, paintings, prints, or certain types of furniture. Others specialize in English or French furniture and accessories, in Oriental specialties, Eskimo art, music boxes, or stained-glass windows.

Often an item must be restored in order to sell it for maximum value, so the good dealer knows where to go for expert help in woodworking, refinishing, and upholstering.

Utilizing their expertise, many appraise antiques for insurance and estate purposes. They also act as auctioneers for estates and sometimes operate regular auctions for their own goods and for clients who wish to dispose of rare antiques.

Most antiques dealers are self-employed, and start-up capital is needed in order to have the funds to make one's first purchases. Some dealers choose to open retail outlets or galleries, which may mean employing staff members to help with buying goods and/or running the store. Other dealers sell privately to wealthy clients or to decorators.

Risk is inherent to the business. Often a dealer will invest in an item without knowing that there is a definite market for it, or if there is one, what people will pay. Experience and a keen eye are one's only protection against these mistakes. However, those who acquire the knack of successful dealing are destined to do well as the popularity of collectibles continues.

Earnings and Opportunities

Opportunities for employment are good, and earnings range from $14,500 to $48,000 and up.

Training and Qualifications

Business sense, knowledge of antiques, the ability to spot value, and sales ability are important qualities to bring to this field.

No particular education is required, but most who enter the field have a high school diploma and more than likely a college degree.

APARTMENT MANAGERS

Duties and Responsibilities

From showing apartments to hiring and supervising handymen, apartment managers are responsible for the broad range of duties involved in the day-to-day operations of an apartment building or complex.

These managers handle all the normal business operations necessary, including taking care of the payroll, providing repair and maintenance services, and responding to particular tenant requests. In locations where there are grounds, tennis courts, swimming pools, and other amenities, the manager must also see to their maintenance and upkeep. Finding tenants through advertising and other means is a prime responsibility. Having leases signed, collecting deposits, and in some cases collecting the monthly rents also call for diligence, perseverance, and sales ability. In addition, managers enforce the building's rules, settle disputes, and represent the owners in all matters of policy and operation. Their chief role is to run the building as efficiently as possible, providing the necessary services, and administering the budget.

Some managers are provided with rent-free apartments at the site they manage. Others may have only an office on site. Still others may work for a larger building management company and make daily visits to their properties.

Managers generally work a normal five-day workweek, but they may be called upon to work nights or weekends in an emergency. Also, to keep their units fully rented, they may have to show apartments evenings and on weekends.

Some complexes cater to retirees, others to young singles, and still others to families. Each of these situations presents its own set of challenges and tasks.

Earnings and Opportunities

Prospects for employment continue to look bright, mainly because of the growing number of apartment buildings and complexes being developed across the country, particularly in the Sun Belt.

Earnings range from $19,500 to $35,000 and up. In those situations where the employer requires a manager to live on the premises, such a rent-free apartment can provide an excellent tax-free supplement to the salary.

Training and Qualifications

Good communications skills, some knowledge of business, and the ability to work well with all types of people are important qualities for this field. Larger complexes look for the same skills and training as required in hotel and motel management. Real estate background is also helpful.

Some come to this job later in life after jobs as managers in other fields, or after military or civil service. While there are no specific educational requirements, a high school diploma is advised. The job is one of great responsibility, and work experience that provided an understanding of basic management techniques and a knowledge of personnel and budget administration would be helpful.

CHILD CARE WORKERS

Duties and Responsibilities

About half of all American women with children under six are working, and that number is expected to continue to increase throughout the 1980s. Who's minding the children? In many cases the answer is a new breed of child care worker who takes his or her job very seriously and may even be specially trained for the task.

The work of a care giver is active, demanding, and often extremely rewarding, because in few other jobs can one be so totally loved by those with whom one works. The duties of the job vary from reading a story, giving a hug, or tucking a child in for a nap to supervising rough-and-tumble outdoor play or helping a child master a new skill. All workers must be disciplinarians at times, and those who care for more than one child must be adept at mediating disputes.

Workers must also be prepared to cope with emergencies. How do you bring down a high fever? What should you do to stop excessive bleeding? How can you help a baby who is choking? These are just a few of the problems that may occur when taking care of small children.

Those who perform their duties in the home inevitably find other details to attend to when both parents are working. Errands must be run and the house kept in good order. Some of these workers receive room and board in lieu of extra salary and may be asked to work at any time of the day or night. Others may live elsewhere, but their hours can be long, since the working parents put in a full day.

Some people establish day care for children in their own homes. Usually those who are caring for three or more children are considered a family child care center and must be licensed.

Day care assistants are non-professionals who aid in the care of children at day care centers. Depending upon the center, workers may be responsible for such tasks as setting up projects, helping prepare meals, and taking care of clean-up afterwards. At other places, they may work more directly with the children, supervising playground activities, helping with clothing exchange, or putting children down for naps.

Earnings and Opportunities

Opportunities for employment are excellent, and salaries range from $7,200 to $16,500.

Training and Qualifications

Love of children, patience, stamina, and flexibility are excellent qualities for child care workers.

While no formalized instruction is required, education can still be important, since many parents are looking for care givers who can provide stimulation as well as nurturing. A course in first aid is also a plus. In addition, "nanny" schools are springing up across the nation in order to train people who would like to care for children in the family home. Graduates of these programs have their pick of jobs and can command top salaries in the field.

FLORAL DESIGNERS

Duties and Responsibilities

Few things are lovelier than a fragrant arrangement of fresh flowers. Floral designers are professionals who bring a combination of creativity and expertise to the natural beauty of flowers and plants, to produce floral decorations, gifts, and tributes.

Designers must know the names, care, and handling techniques of flowers and flowering plants. Seasonal availability and price are also important. Designers may receive orders for flowering plants, bouquets, corsages, centerpieces, funeral flowers, and artificial or dried-flower arrangements. Arrangements for weddings and parties offer additional opportunities to be creative.

Designers are very important to the success of flower shops, because beautifully designed arrangements invite customers to browse and buy.

Designers usually work from a written order that includes price, date, and time and place of delivery. Sometimes the customer specifies color and type of flower, but often those decisions are left to the designer. He or she must take into account the price of the order when determining the number and variety of flowers used. Flowers are chosen to provide contrasting form, color, harmony, and depth; and leafy branches may be used to provide background. Some orders may take fifteen minutes or more to prepare.

Designers may also help customers make selections, and during quiet times they may arrange store planters and terrariums, help with window displays, or take inventory.

Many designers own their own flower shops and must combine artistic ability with business management and sales ability. They must know flowers, how to buy wisely, how to use past records for future orders, and how to care for flowers and plants to avoid loss.

Most designers work in retail flower shops. The work environment is generally pleasant and the workweek forty hours, though long hours are required around holiday times.

Floral designers with supervisory ability may advance to manager or design supervisor in large flower shops.

Earnings and Opportunities

About 56,000 people are employed as floral designers, and there will always be openings because of job turnover. Experienced designers usually earn between $9,500 and $21,000. Earnings for self-employed florists do vary greatly depending on the location and successful management of the business.

Training and Qualifications

An eye for artistic design, good color sense, and manual dexterity are strengths in this job. Candidates should preferably have a high school diploma and be able to do the arithmetic necessary to write up bills. Experience gained by working part-time in a flower shop while still in school is also helpful.

Though many designers learn their craft on the job, more and more are taking courses in floral design offered in adult education programs, junior colleges, and commercial floral design schools. Longer programs, some offering a college degree in floriculture and floristry, can provide training in flower growing, marketing, and shop management.

For Further Details

Society of American Florists, 901 N. Washington St., Alexandria, VA 22314.

FUNERAL DIRECTORS AND EMBALMERS

Duties and Responsibilities

When a loved one dies, arrangements must be made—sometimes quite unexpectedly and almost always under very difficult circumstances. A funeral director who can guide the bereaved family with compassion in the organizing of the service and interment can be one of the most valuable people in their lives at that time.

Funeral directors provide much-needed expertise in many areas. They are consulted as the family decides whether to have a burial or cremation; whether there should be a viewing, a funeral service, and if so, what kind. Directors also provide information about Social Security forms to be completed, how to submit notices for the newspaper, and many other details that we normally never think about.

When it comes to actually organizing the funeral, directors see that the deceased is picked up from home or hospital and kept until the funeral services are over. They supply or arrange for everything—hearses, chapels, flags, flowers, caskets, announcements, ministers, ushers—as well as a shoulder to cry on when necessary.

Some supervise large staffs including secretaries, bookkeepers, salespeople, hostesses, ushers, drivers, and embalmers. In addition, those associated with mausoleums or cemeteries have staffs to care for the buildings and grounds.

Embalmers are responsible for preparing the body for interment in a vault or for burial. This includes draining the vital fluids and replacing them with a special preservative solution. They may also do cosmetic reconstruction of faces and hands on accident victims using paraffin, plastics, polymers, eyelashes, hair, and makeup.

For those in managerial jobs, the hours can be long and irregular and the pace hectic, especially if there are several funerals on the same day. The work is hard, and those who choose this profession must have a sincere desire to help people and give of themselves.

Embalmers and funeral directors can move to more responsible positions in larger establishments, purchase an existing funeral home, or start their own.

Earnings and Opportunities

There will be a continuing need for workers in this field, so the outlook for employment is good. More women are entering the profession—up from 5 percent graduating from schools a decade ago to over 25 percent graduating today. Earnings range from $15,000 to $60,000 and more for the self-employed.

Training and Qualifications

A mature outlook, the ability to cope calmly with life and death, and a commitment to serving others are helpful qualities in this profession.

A high school diploma is necessary in order to enter embalming school, and there are both two- and four-year programs available, with a one-year internship required for licensing. Experience is gained in such schools by giving free service to indigents or through arrangements with funeral homes in the area.

HAIRDRESSERS

Duties and Responsibilities

How we look makes a big difference in how we feel about ourselves, and for that reason, most of us are very particular when it comes to choosing a barber or hairdresser.

Barbers have traditionally specialized in quick haircuts for men. Today, however, more and more are gaining reputations as "hairstylists," and many work in salons where they shampoo, cut, and style hair for both men and women. Some now also color, straighten, and perm hair, although in some states, barbers are required to have a cosmetologist's license in order to perm or color hair. Some still offer hair and scalp treatments, shaves, and facial massages. They also fit and care for hairpieces.

Hairdressers (known formally as cosmetologists and also called hairstylists, beauticians, or beauty operators) are more traditionally associated with women's beauty salons. They also shampoo, cut, trim, and style hair, and may be expert in giving permanent waves and straightening hair and in the many methods available to lighten or darken hair color. Cosmetologists may also give manicures, scalp and facial treatments, provide makeup analysis, and clean and style wigs and hairpieces.

Workers must keep scissors, combs, and other instruments sterilized and in good condition, and the work area must be kept clean as well. Those who own or manage a shop may also order supplies, keep records, and hire and supervise employees. Some shops also sell lotions, tonics, and cosmetics.

Barbers and hairdressers also work in department stores, hotels, hospitals, and prisons. Seventy-five percent of all barbers operate their own businesses, as do many cosmetologists. Some teach in cosmetology schools or become demonstrators of cosmetics in department stores. Others become sales representatives for cosmetic firms or open businesses as beauty or fashion consultants. Some work as examiners for state cosmetology boards.

Earnings and Opportunities

Over 112,000 people are employed as barbers, and more than 513,000 work as cosmetologists. The outlook for employment is quite good, with a 10 percent increase in jobs expected for barbers and 20 percent for cosmetologists in the next ten years. Barbers earn from $12,000 to $17,000, with some in excess of $26,000. Cosmetologists earn between $13,000 and $21,000.

Training and Qualifications

To obtain a barber's license, applicants must be graduates of a state-approved barber school, and be at least sixteen (eighteen in some states). Some states require a high school diploma.

For a cosmetology license, applicants must generally have graduated from a state-licensed cosmetology school, pass a physical examination, and be at least sixteen years old.

For Further Details

National Beauty/Barber Career Center, 3839 White Plains Rd., Bronx, NY 10467. Associated Master Barbers and Beauticians of America, 219 Greenwich Rd., P.O. Box 220782, Charlotte, NC 28222. National Hairdressers and Cosmetologists Association, 3510 Olive St., St. Louis, MO 63103. National Association of Barber Schools, Inc., 304 S. 11th St., Lincoln, NE 68508. National Association of Cosmetology Schools, 1990 M St., N.W., Suite 650, Washington, DC 20036.

JEWELERS

Duties and Responsibilities

Whether for investment or adornment, people have always loved jewelry—from the earliest civilizations to the present day—and it's likely they always will. For that reason alone, jewelers will continue to be in demand.

Jewelers work in jewelry stores and repair shops, where they offer many services to customers. Much of their time is spent repairing jewelry, which may involve enlarging or reducing rings, resetting stones, or replacing broken clasps and mountings. Some jewelers also make jewelry by hand, repair watches, and do hand engraving. A small number are qualified gemologists and appraise the quality and value of diamonds and other gemstones.

Administrative duties must be seen to by

those who manage stores or departments or own their own shops. They must hire employees, order and sell merchandise, and see to running the business.

Some jewelers work in factories, and most of these workers specialize in just one part of the jewelry manufacturing process. For example, some make molds to cast jewelry or dies to stamp it. Others do finishing work, such as setting stones and engraving. Following their own designs or those of jewelry designers, they shape the metal with pliers or other hand tools or cast it in molds. Individual parts are soldered to form the finished piece.

Those who work in or own retail shops have a great deal of customer contact and may work long hours during holiday seasons when business is especially good.

In manufacturing, jewelers sometimes advance to supervisory jobs. Jewelers who work in jewelry stores or repair shops may become salaried managers. After acquiring the necessary finances, over 40 percent open their own businesses. (Opening a jewelry store is costly because an inventory of expensive merchandise must be obtained.)

Earnings and Opportunities

Over 28,000 people are employed as jewelers, and opportunities in jewelry stores and repair shops are expected to increase by 13 percent in the next decade. Salaries range from $11,500 to $30,000, and those who are self-employed can earn much more.

Training and Qualifications

Repairing and making jewelry is precise, delicate work requiring finger and hand dexterity, good eye-hand coordination, patience, and concentration. Artistic ability is important for those who plan to design their own work, and sales ability is a must for those who want to own their own shops.

Candidates should have a high school education. Store and shop owners prefer graduates of technical training programs over people with no experience; technical training may last from six months to three years.

In jewelry factories, manufacturers provide on-the-job training in jewelry-making skills for their production workers. Training can last three to four years, depending on the difficulty of the specialty being taught.

For Further Details

Jewelers of America, Time-Life Building, Suite 650, 1271 Ave. of the Americas, New York, NY 10020.

PRIVATE INVESTIGATORS

Duties and Responsibilities

While private investigators may not live the glamorous lifestyles of TV's private eyes, their work can involve assignments that require imagination, physical ability, and nerves of steel, while providing a certain degree of danger. However, unlike their counterparts on TV and in films, real-life private eyes also undertake jobs that require painstakingly routine and repetitious sleuthing.

Private investigators—working either for a detective agency or on their own—are usually engaged by law firms, private businesses, or individuals. Depending upon the type of as-

signment, they often spend time on the telephone or in any number of government offices where they can track down official records. This work involves research and double-checking, along with extensive phone or personal interviewing. Some investigators perform fieldwork that involves surveillance, tailing, plus video and photographic evidence gathering. They file oral and written reports on their work, providing details of their investigations to the clients.

Investigators may be called upon to check into people's backgrounds for credit or insurance reports; to monitor their activities in connection with divorce, child custody, or other legal proceedings; to track down missing relatives, often in connection with inheritances; to look into reports of employee theft at business locations; to comb official records; to verify employment applications; to check out suspected insurance fraud; to detect computer fraud; to protect executives; or to advise on home or office security.

Some investigators are on staff at major companies where they check into backgrounds of people applying for jobs, credit, or insurance. Some check into the validity of suspicious customer complaints.

Work schedules can be erratic. While much of the job can be done during the normal business day, surveillance or interviewing may have to be done at other times, and travel can take one away from home for extended periods.

Earnings and Opportunities

Outlook for employment is good. The need for employment and insurance application checks will continue to grow, and there seems to be little slowdown in the rate of divorce cases and missing persons work provided by law firms and individuals. Earnings range from $15,000 to $75,000. Self-employed investigators work on a fee basis, usually a daily rate plus expenses.

Training and Qualifications

An inquisitive mind, knowledge of basic research techniques, a good telephone manner, and keen observational skills are helpful in this line of work.

There is no formal route to becoming an investigator, although many come from various police and law enforcement bodies. A high school diploma is advised at the very least. Many colleges and junior colleges offer courses in criminology, criminal law, and law enforcement, which would be helpful. From there, expertise must be gained through on-the-job experience with investigatory firms or in the investigation or security offices of large businesses.

Careers in the Social Sciences

Studying all aspects of human society, past and present, is the work of social scientists. From the archaeologist seeking the ruins of ancient cities and the anthropologist investigating the lifestyle of a primitive culture to the political scientist trying to determine why people vote the way they do, it is a broad and varied field.

From their work, we learn from the past, and educators, government officials, and business executives try to use that information to address broad social, economic, and political issues.

Educational requirements vary, but advanced degrees are generally a plus.

While opportunities in the field are somewhat limited, the person with drive and a sincere interest will almost surely find a place where his or her skills are needed.

ANTHROPOLOGISTS

Duties and Responsibilities

Our most common image of the anthropologist is that of the scientist who goes off to live in a remote land to study some primitive tribe—Margaret Mead undoubtedly comes to mind. While this kind of study is still important, today's anthropologist has entered the realm of modern society and is almost as likely to be studying city teenagers, drug addicts, politicians, or corporate executives.

Anthropologists study people, their characteristics, and the cultures they create, and they generally specialize.

Cultural anthropology, sometimes called ethnology, is the study of the customs, culture, and the social life of groups. These scientists may spend many months or years living with a group to learn about its way of life, often focusing on just one aspect of group life, such as kinship, ecological adaptation, or economics. Though traditionally concerned with non-industrialized societies, more and more of their research is focusing on groups in modern societies.

Linguistic anthropologists study the role of language in various cultures and the way it relates to people's behavior and thought patterns.

Physical anthropologists are concerned

with humans as biological organisms. They study the evolution of the human race and look for the earliest evidence of human life. They also study the effects of heredity and environment on different populations. Their knowledge of the human body enables them to work as consultants on projects as diverse as the design of military equipment and the sizing of clothing. *Anthropometrists* specialize in the measurement of the body or skeleton.

A growing number of scientists are specializing in *applied anthropology,* where they are concerned with the practical application of research findings. *Medical anthropologists,* for example, may study cultural attitudes toward medicine to help formulate a health program for a particular group. *Urban anthropologists* examine the influence of city life upon people and their institutions. About four out of five anthropologists work in colleges and universities. Some work for museums, the government, consulting firms, or do freelance work.

ARCHAEOLOGISTS

Duties and Responsibilities

While not all archaeologists have the chance to face the adventure of opening King Tut's tomb, all do share the same zeal for exploring the mysteries of the past. In looking for, finding, and analyzing the remains of ancient cultures, they provide us with tangible links to and additional knowledge about the civilizations that came before us. Their work can range from careful study in laboratories and libraries to exploratory digs in deserts, forests, or cities.

Archaeologists often perform time-consuming rigorous exploration of possible sites where remnants of ancient man can be found. These digs, as they are called, can be painstaking, monotonous, and frustrating. But when finds are made and artifacts located, the process of recovery and analysis can yield exciting results. Working partly from history and geography and partly with science and technology, the archaeologist can study pieces

Earnings and Opportunities

Over 8,000 people work as anthropologists, and the outlook for employment is fair. Earnings range from $21,000 to $42,000.

Training and Qualifications

Intellectual curiosity, communication skills, perseverance, and the ability to be objective and systematic in doing research are important qualities for anthropologists. Physical stamina is also important for those involved in fieldwork.

A master's degree is sufficient for many beginning positions, although top positions and academic appointments are generally reserved for individuals who have a Ph.D.

For Further Details

The American Anthropological Association, 1703 New Hampshire Ave., N.W., Washington, DC 20009.

from the past and provide glimpses into a culture through identification of an item and analysis of its age. With luck, the item will match other known remnants from a particular region or era and thus provide us with more knowledge of how a certain culture lived, worked, and thought.

Most archaeologists specialize by location or period. Some study the lives of ancient Greeks, while others are uncovering clues about early South American culture. Recent digs have even taken place around the site of Custer's Last Stand in order to gain a better understanding of exactly what happened and why.

Most archaeological work is performed in connection with a museum, university, or scientific institution. Many archaeologists work for colleges or universities, and a good number have administrative jobs at museums. Still others are employed by governments who fund archaeology programs designed to help better understand the country's past.

While study of items recovered during a dig can take place in a laboratory or an office, the actual digs require long periods of time away from home, and the schedule can be quite rigorous.

Increasingly, archaeologists are finding themselves in a battle, facing advances in growth and technology while trying to hold on to the past. As cities expand and more highways are built, more and more of the areas of ancient study are being affected.

Earnings and Opportunities

Outlook for employment is fair. Earnings range from $16,500 to $48,000.

Training and Qualifications

Analytical ability, intellectual curiosity, perseverance, and stamina are important qualities for archaeologists.

A master's degree is sufficient for many beginning positions, but promotion to top positions and the better academic appointments are generally reserved for individuals who have a doctorate.

Museums and scientific institutions who fund digs usually provide for students to go along, since it is the best way for future archaeologists to learn.

For Further Details

The Society for American Archaeology, 1703 New Hampshire Ave., N.W., Washington, DC 20009. The Archaeological Institute of America, Box 1901, Kenmore Station, Boston, MA 02215.

GEOGRAPHERS

Duties and Responsibilities

Most of us think of geography as one of those subjects we are required to take in school, but which has almost no connection to the "real" world—certainly not an area with career possibilities. But in fact, geographers research a wide range of essential social, economic, and environmental issues. They study the distribution and location of natural characteristics of the earth's surface, such as landforms, climate, soils, vegetation, water, and mineral resources. They study the earth's division into continents and countries, and their inhabitants and industries. Such information helps explain why people live where they do and how they earn their livings.

Usually geographers specialize. *Economic geographers* study the geographic distribution of an area's economic activities such as manufacturing, forestry, agriculture, or communications. Frequently they work for private firms helping to evaluate the best locations for industrial sites.

Political geographers study the relationship of geography to politics. They define and describe the political boundaries of cities, counties, and administrative subdivisions as well as offshore areas.

Physical geographers study the physical characteristics of the earth, such as the vegetation patterns, wildlife distribution, and climates. Frequently there are specialists within this specialty, such as geomorphologists, who study landforms, or hydrologists, who study water. Climatologists, for example, study overall climate conditions in order to determine the significance of climatic conditions for defense, conservation, agriculture, health, transportation, marketing, and other activities.

Cartographers compile and interpret data and design and construct maps and charts using drafting equipment. Increasingly, computers are becoming important in this work.

Medical geographers study the effect of the environment on health and take into account such factors as climate, vegetation, mineral traces in water, and atmospheric pollution.

There are also urban geographers, regional geographers, and many subspecialties within the specialties.

Research techniques vary. Geographers analyze maps, aerial photographs, and data transmitted by satellites. They make use of advanced statistical techniques and mathematical models, and routinely use computers to analyze or map the data they have obtained.

About 40 percent of all geographers work for private industry, including such firms as publishing houses, real estate development corporations, and transportation firms. Colleges and universities employ about 35 percent. Some work for scientific foundations and research organizations or run their own consulting services.

Earnings and Opportunities

Over 15,000 people are employed as geographers, and outlook for employment is fair. Salaries range from $22,500 to $36,000.

Training and Qualifications

Creative and intellectual curiosity and an objective and systematic approach to research are important to geographers.

A bachelor's degree with a major in geography is the minimum educational requirement for beginning positions in government or industry or to teach in secondary schools. However, a master's degree is becoming increasingly important. It is the minimum requirement for junior college teaching positions and is important for advancement in business and government. A Ph.D. is required for professorships at major colleges and universities.

For Further Details

Association of American Geographers, 1710 16th St., N.W., Washington, DC 20009. American Congress on Surveying and Mapping, 210 Little Falls St., Falls Church, VA 22046.

HISTORIANS

Duties and Responsibilities

For the history buff or the avid student, there is probably no more ideal job than that of historian.

The basic work of historians is to study and analyze past events, institutions, ideas, and people. Historians do not accept information at face value but take each document, record, or spoken account and attempt to establish its validity. Part of the job is to try to determine the significance of their findings, sometimes developing theories that help explain the past or the present.

Historians almost always specialize. Some focus on a particular country or region, others study a certain period of time. Others specialize in the history of a field like art, economics, religion, or medicine.

About 70 percent of all historians teach in colleges or universities. Like other faculty members, they may also lecture, write, and do consulting work.

An increasing number of historians are doing other things besides teaching. *Archivists* and *curators* work for museums, libraries, or historical societies, where they identify, classify, and preserve historical documents, artifacts, or other material. They may prepare special exhibitions or publications for the public or may assist scholars in their research. They also do extensive research and writing.

Biographers study the lives of individuals, using as sources diaries, news accounts, personal correspondence, and interviews with friends, relatives, and associates. Biographers are typically also writers whose aim is publication in books or journals.

Ever since Alex Haley's *Roots* there has been an increasing interest in family history, and *genealogists* earn their living tracing family histories. They use birth, death, and marriage certificates, court and military records, wills, records of real estate transactions, and other personal and historical documents in their work.

Public historians help policymakers address increasingly complex social and economic problems. Such historians might be asked to assist in the preparation of an environmental impact statement or to provide information for a community development plan.

Much of the historian's work is done independently, reading and writing research reports. Many experience the pressures of deadlines and tight schedules. Travel is sometimes necessary to collect information or attend meetings.

Earnings and Opportunities

About 20,000 people are employed as historians, and employment possibilities are poor. Earnings: $18,200 to $42,500 and up for executive positions.

Training and Qualifications

Intellectual curiosity, creativity, patience, persistence, and the ability to evaluate information objectively and systematically are excellent skills for historians.

Graduate education is usually necessary. A master's degree in history is the minimum requirement for the position of college instructor, but a Ph.D. is required at many institutions.

Most historians in the federal government and in nonprofit organizations now have Ph.D. degrees or their equivalent in training and experience.

For Further Details

Organization of American Historians, Indiana University, 112 N. Bryan St., Bloomington, IN 47401. American Historical Association, 400 A St., S.E., Washington, DC 20003. Office of Museum Programs, Arts and Industries Bldg., Room 2235, Smithsonian Institution, Washington, DC 20560. American Association of Museums, 1055 Thomas Jefferson St., N.W., Washington, DC 20007.

POLITICAL SCIENTISTS

Duties and Responsibilities

If you've always been fascinated by politics but aren't interested in running for office, then a career in political science may be just right for you.

Political scientists study political and administrative behavior in order to understand how government works and how it might be improved. They aid government and community leaders who develop the policies and plan programs that meet our society's needs. They analyze the organizations and operation of governments at all levels in the United States and abroad. They explore such subjects as public opinion, political parties, elections, special interest groups, and intergovernmental relations. They also study the roles and relationships between federal, state, and local governments, including the Presidency, Congress, state legislatures, and the judicial system. Public administration and public policymaking are also of interest to political scientists.

In the course of their work, political scientists collect a great deal of information. Depending on the subject under scrutiny, they might conduct a public opinion survey, analyze election results, or compare various tax proposals. Some research is highly quantitative and involves the use of sophisticated simulation and modeling techniques.

About three-fourths of all political scientists work in colleges and universities, where they may divide their time between teaching, research, and consulting.

Some political scientists work as researchers or consultants for nonacademic organizations that provide information to public officials, political parties, government administrators, legislative staff and committees, citizens' groups, legislative reference bureaus, taxpayers' associations, and business firms. For these clients, they may study subjects such as the ramifications of government reorganization or ways to mobilize support for a particular issue.

Political scientists also hold government jobs both here and abroad. They deal with legislative or administrative matters in areas such as foreign affairs, international relations, intelligence, housing, economic development, transportation, environmental protection, social welfare, and health.

Some also work as lobbyists or consultants to business firms, trade associations, public interest groups, and other organizations. Some work for large banks and corporations, analyzing political conditions in foreign countries to help these organizations formulate investment plans abroad. Other political scientists work as journalists and as advisers to candidates for political office.

On a day-to-day basis, political scientists study and interpret data, prepare reports, and meet with government officials, business executives, and others.

Earnings and Opportunities

About 15,000 people are employed as political scientists, and job opportunities are fair. Earnings: $17,500 to $55,000.

Training and Qualifications

An interest in the political process, intellectual curiosity, an analytical mind, and the ability to communicate skillfully are important qualities for political scientists.

While a bachelor's degree may be sufficient to qualify as a trainee in government, business, or industry, graduate training is generally preferred. Students with a master's degree can qualify for teaching positions in junior colleges and for administrative and research positions in government, industry, and research or civic organizations.

A Ph.D. is required for appointment to academic positions in some colleges and universities, and is becoming increasingly important for nonacademic jobs because of stiff competition in the field.

For Further Details

Board of Examiners, Foreign Service, Box 9317, Rosslyn Station, Arlington, VA 22209.

SOCIOLOGISTS

Duties and Responsibilities

How and why people form groups are the questions that fascinate sociologists. It is their job to study the origin, behavior, and interaction of the wide variety of groups, including families, tribes, communities, and governments, as well as groups that have formed for social, religious, or political reasons. In doing so, they aid educators, lawmakers, administrators, and others involved in social problems and social policy.

There are many areas of specialization, including social organization, social psychology, rural and urban sociology, racial and ethnic relations, industrial sociology, and criminology and penology. In addition, *medical sociologists* study social factors that affect mental and public health; *demographers* study the size, characteristics, and movements of populations; *gerontologists* study the problems of the aging; and *social ecologists* study the effect of the physical environment and technology on people.

To develop their theories, sociologists must collect information, test its validity, and then analyze the results. They frequently use controlled conditions, surveys, or case studies; and the use of statistical and computer techniques in sociological research is increasing. Sociologists work closely with other professionals, including psychologists, physicians, economists, political scientists, anthropologists, and social workers.

Over two-thirds of all sociologists are employed by colleges and universities, where, in addition to teaching, they may consult and do research work. Some sociologists work primarily as administrators. They may administer social service programs in the areas of law enforcement, family counseling, or health services, and may work for government, community, youth, or religious organizations. A number of sociologists are employed as consultants, and they may advise on solutions to social problems, such as halfway houses and counseling for ex-offenders, or they may direct market research for advertisers and manufacturers. A few work for government agencies. Those in the federal government work primarily for the Departments of Defense, Health and Human Services, Interior, and Agriculture. Some demographers work for international organizations such as the United Nations, the International Bank for Reconstruction and Development, or the World Health Organization.

Some sociologists also hold managerial, research, and planning positions in corporations, research firms, professional and trade associations, and consulting firms.

Earnings and Opportunities

About 21,000 people are employed as sociologists, and employment opportunities are poor. Salaries range from $24,000 to $38,000.

Training and Qualifications

Intellectual curiosity, analytical ability, and the capability to work independently and communicate well orally and in writing are important qualifications for sociologists.

The Ph.D. is required for permanent research and teaching positions in colleges and universities and is essential for senior level jobs in many nonacademic environments.

Those with masters' degrees can qualify for administrative and research positions in public agencies and private businesses. Graduates with bachelors' degrees may get jobs as interviewers or as administrative or research assistants. Many work as social workers, counselors, or recreation workers in public and private welfare agencies.

For Further Details

American Sociological Association, Career and Research Division, 1722 N St., N.W., Washington, DC 20036.

Index

Index